D0953487

Smart
Growth

Smart Growth

Building an Enduring Business by
Managing the Risks of Growth

....

Edward D. Hess

Columbia Business School
Publishing

Columbia University Press
Publishers Since 1893
New York   Chichester, West Sussex
Copyright © 2010 Columbia University Press
All rights reserved

Library of Congress Cataloging-in-Publication Data

Hess, Edward D.
   Smart growth : building an enduring business by managing the risks of growth /
Edward D. Hess.
      p.   cm.
   Includes bibliographical references and index.
   ISBN 978-0-231-15050-7 (cloth : alk. paper)—ISBN 978-0-231-52175-8 (ebook)
   1. Corporations—Growth.   2. Small business—Growth.   3. Business planning.
   4. Management.   I. Title.
   HD2746.H47 2010
   658.4'06–dc22

                                                              2009048025

∞

Columbia University Press books are printed on permanent and durable acid-free paper.
This book is printed on paper with recycled content.
Printed in the United States of America

          c   10   9   8   7   6   5   4   3

References to Internet Web sites (URLs) were accurate at the time of writing.
Neither the author nor Columbia University Press is responsible for URLs
that may have expired or changed since the manuscript was prepared.

To Katherine Leigh, whose sparkle for life is as joyous to share today as it was thirty years ago when we met.

And to the University of Virginia: its Law School for giving me the opportunity to be part of Wall Street and the Darden Graduate School of Business and its Faculty and Students for giving me the opportunity to be part of their Mission.

Contents

....
Acknowledgments

NO ONE WRITES a book alone. In my case this work is the result of a career of learning from teachers, clients, research companies, collaborators, students, mentors, and friends, too many to name. Although I am solely responsible for this work, it exists because of the generosity of many others.

I extend my gratitude to my teachers, mentors, and colleagues, with special thanks to Professors Sydney Jourard, Charlie Davison, Antonin Scalia, Lyle Bourne, Richard D'Aveni, Bill Fulmer, Robert Drazin, Robert Kazanjian, L. G. Thomas, Jag Sheth, Kim Cameron, Ed Freeman, S. Venkataraman, Alec Horniman, Bob Landel, Luann Lynch, Paul Simko, Jim Freeland, Mark Haskins, and Sherwood Frey, Jr.

I am also indebted to UPS, Sysco, Stryker Corporation, Best Buy, American Eagle Outfitters, Outback Steakhouses, Tiffany & Company, FEDEX Freight, and TSYS for allowing me inside their organizations to begin my research. Thanks also to the 54 private company CEOs who generated my interest in managing the risks of growth.

Thanks to Deans Al Hartgrave, Tom Robertson, Maryam Alavi, and Greg Waymire for giving me the opportunity to join academia and supporting my work while at Goizueta Business School. Thank you to David Newkirk, CEO of Darden Executive Education, for the opportunity to teach and learn from so many executive education clients.

Thanks to my research assistants Dr. Shizuka Modica, Cassy Eriksson, and Rick Green for their work in making this a reality. To Mike Lenox, Elizabeth O'Halloran, and Sean Carr of the Batten Institute at the Darden

Graduate School of Business, thank you for your support and friendship. Thanks to Darden Professors Ming-Jer Chen, Peter Debaere, Ryan Quinn, and Jared Harris for sharing their expertise.

To Myles Thompson, publisher and editor at Columbia Business School Publishing, for your belief in the importance of the ideas expressed in this book and for your encouragement and belief that together we could contribute something meaningful to the current debate in our country with regard to its financial system. Thank you to his team, Marina Petrova, Marisa Pagano, and Julia Kushnirsky, who were superb partners. Thank you also to the two anonymous reviewers for their thoughtful and helpful comments.

The writing of this book and some of its research were generously funded by both the Batten Institute and the Darden School Foundation at the Darden Graduate School of Business at the University of Virginia. Special thanks to Dean Bob Bruner for his support and friendship and for setting the highest standards for all of us in intellectual rigor and servant leadership and to my colleague, collaborator, and teaching teammate, Professor Jeanne Liedtka, who brings superior intellect, humility, energy, and constant improvement to our work.

To my wife, Kate Acuff, who not only has sustained me with her love and support on our life journey together but also has enabled me to be more than I could have been without her. Thank you for playing a special role in this book with your insightful editing, critique, and comments. It has been fun!

Smart Growth

....
Smart Growth

BUILDING AN ENDURING COMPANY
BY MANAGING THE RISKS OF GROWTH

O NE ONLY HAS to look at the recent financial crisis in the United States to
see that good companies can self-destruct or self-inflict serious wounds
by pursuing poor quality growth or by failing to manage the risks of growth.
Examples are Merrill Lynch, Citicorp, AIG, Washington Mutual, and Lehman
Brothers. Outside the financial services industry, one can also find good companies that have created serious problems for the same reasons.

In this book, I challenge some commonly held business beliefs about
growth. First, I challenge the commonly held business beliefs ("Growth Mental Model") that

1. businesses must continuously grow or they will die;
2. growth is always good;
3. public company growth should occur continuously and smoothly; and
4. quarterly earnings should be a primary measure of public company
   success.

These beliefs drive short-term business behaviors that in too many cases
defer or destroy long-term value creation, decrease competitiveness, and can
lead to premature corporate demise. Adherence to these beliefs can also
result in the creation and manufacture of earnings that have no business
purpose other than to help companies meet quarterly earnings estimates.
These earnings neither are evidence of a company's future earning power
nor provide meaningful information regarding a company's economic and
strategic health and competitiveness.

Unfortunately, the Growth Mental Model reigns and permeates the public markets as well as private businesses. Many privately owned businesses believe that they must grow or they will die and that all growth is good. In reality, for both public and private companies, growth can be good or growth can be bad. In many cases, it is just as likely that growth can harm a business as it is likely that growth can enhance its survivability.

For U.S. public companies, the Growth Mental Model has been operationalized by what I refer to as "Wall Street Rules" that measure compliance. The Wall Street Rules dictate that public companies should grow continuously and smoothly. Furthermore, according to the Wall Street Rules, the best way to measure growth and predict the future prospects of corporate health is the metric of quarterly earnings. This focus on quarterly earnings is not merely retrospective. Predictions of future earnings growth is a banner waved to all investors. To get such predictions, financial analysts, with the input of management, create and announce quarterly earnings estimates. Companies are generally rewarded with increased stock prices for meeting or exceeding those consensus estimates. So powerful are these estimates of future growth that even strong companies who can report growth but fail to meet the estimates can be penalized by declining stock prices.

Making sure Wall Street Rules are met has given rise to a large and profitable fee business involving accountants, investment bankers, and lawyers who are paid well to help companies legally produce earnings that comply with Wall Street Rules, which I shall call the "Earnings Game." Those earnings are qualitatively different from real, authentic earnings that arise from a company selling more products/services to more customers in arm's-length transactions or from operating more efficiently or productively ("Authentic Earnings"). The arsenal of methods companies can use to play the Earnings Game includes accounting elections, valuations, judgments, reserves, elections, channel stuffing, liberalizing credit policies, structured finance transactions, financial engineering, related party transactions, investment transactions, and serial acquisitions. These noncore, nonoperating earnings help companies meet Wall Street Rules, which supports stock prices for investors and, as importantly, the value of managements' stock options. The creation of earnings through accounting rules and the manufacture of earnings through nonoperating or non-arm's-length transactions are the Earnings Game.

The challenge for investors and others wanting to evaluate a company's underlying strength is that the Earnings Game is not clearly transparent, and studying a company's quarterly or annual reports may not suffice. As a result, in most cases investors cannot determine whether a company's earnings were the result of Authentic Earnings or the Earnings Game. An un-fortunate outcome of the Wall Street Rules is that the Earnings Game can mask or hide business sickness. Another unfortunate outcome is that corporate decisions are often made solely to meet the current quarter's earnings estimate.

The primacy of the Growth Mental Model has been accepted for decades. As far back as 1954, *Time* magazine, in an article, stated "Grow or Die Is the Chief Axiom of US Business." Although pervasive, there has been remarkably little systemic evaluation of the viability of the Growth Mental Model as a robust and useful approach to guiding business behavior or assessing business strength. As Chapter 1 shows, the origins and the basis of the Growth Mental Model are mysteriously hard to find. It appears that it has reached axiom status without rigor or empirical data as its foundation. Furthermore, it has permeated MBA programs, Wall Street, the business press, strategy and management consulting, and the investment community, resulting in a nearly maniacal focus on the Wall Street Rules and short-term earnings results.

The Growth Mental Model assumes that all growth is good and makes growth the key objective of a business. This results in people just assuming or accepting the assumption that every business must grow or it will die. This focus on growth fuels an insatiable drive for more—more stores, more markets, and more growth—often without adequate focus on the risks of such growth.

Smart Growth

Smart Growth as a concept rejects the Growth Mental Model because it is not based on science and does not represent reality. There is no justification in business, economics, or other disciplines for its dominance. Smart Growth rejects Wall Street's edicts that growth must be continuous and smooth, occurring each quarter, because there is no scientific or business basis for those rules. In fact, the research contradicts the likelihood of achieving that outcome. Smart Growth rejects the Earnings Game and believes business health should be measured solely by Authentic Earnings, which can include strategic acquisitions.

Smart Growth rejects the assumption that every business must grow or it will die. Smart Growth's objective is to create enduring businesses, which continue to meet the needs of their customers, employees, owners, and the communities in which they operate. Smart Growth is not antigrowth. Smart Growth believes that improvement is more important than growth. And if a company continuously improves in ways that meet customers' needs faster, better, or cheaper than the competition, then growth may occur if the business makes the decision to grow. Smart Growth believes that growth should be a rigorous conscious decision rather than an assumption. And Smart Growth rejects the belief that all growth is good.

Smart Growth believes that growth creates business risks that need to be managed and that being better is more important than being bigger. If not properly managed, growth can stress a company's culture, its customer value proposition, its people, its execution processes, and its quality and financial controls. Growth is change. Growth changes businesses and people. Growth is a complex dynamic process that rarely happens smoothly or predictably without mistakes, bumps in the road, or detours.

Displacing the Growth Mental Model is not an easy task. However, supplanting the Growth Mental Model with a concept that is more realistic and is a better gauge of corporate health is a goal worth pursuing. Using research on growth theory from the fields of economics, strategy, organizational design, biology, and systems theory, I concurrently challenge the Growth Mental Model and ground Smart Growth in both science and business reality.

In addition, based on my research, I present case stories illuminating the key concepts of Smart Growth: building an enduring company by constant improvement that utilizes an internal growth system that includes an experimental growth/innovation model, a rigorous growth decision process, a growth risks audit, and a growth risks management process, which results in authentic growth.

At a very basic level, it is important to acknowledge that growth can be good or growth can bad for a company depending on the circumstances. Growth is a complex change process that changes an organization, the people in it, and the myriad relationships both within a company and in its business environment. Growth should never be an assumed goal. Growth should be a conscious and rigorous management decision made only after weighing its pros and cons and developing both a growth strategy and a plan to manage the risks created by growth.

Organizational managers and leaders need to understand the circumstances in which growth can be bad:

- Growth can outstrip the capabilities and competencies of a company and its management team.

- Growth can stress quality and financial controls and destroy or dilute one's culture.
- Growth can dilute one's customer value proposition, weakening one's competitive position.
- Growth can take management's focus off of operational excellence, weakening existing business.
- Growth can put a business in a different competitive space, facing tougher, bigger, well-capitalized competitors.

When faced with the decision about whether or when to grow a company, I submit that business leaders and managers should continuously ask themselves the following questions:

1. Why should we grow?
2. How much should we grow?
3. Are we ready to grow?
4. What are the best ways for us to grow?
5. What are the risks of growth?
6. How can we manage those risks?

This book is written for business leaders and managers, strategy and management consultants, policy makers, accountants, investment bankers, and business students to provide an alternative way to think about and manage growth, which would replace the Growth Mental Model. Smart Growth is based on the notion that it is not only possible but also often desirable to limit or manage the rate of growth in order to be a successful company. Determining whether to grow, when to grow, and how to grow require important and complex decisions that need to be made objectively and not by blindly following the Growth Mental Model that equates success with growth.

Organization of the Book

Chapter 1: Defining the Growth Mental Model sets forth the pervasiveness of the Growth Mental Model and the lack of specificity of not only its origins but also its basis or justifications. Chapter 1 concludes with a case story about Tiffany & Co. that for years has espoused its strategy as "Growth Without Compromise" in an attempt to grow smartly. Tiffany has been a

Smart Growth company. The case questions whether public market pressures are now challenging its strategy.

Chapter 2: Smooth and Continuous Company Growth—The Exception Not the Rule challenges the belief that growth should be continuous and smooth by examining six research studies that show how difficult it is for public companies to grow continuously and smoothly for periods of time. Continuous growth is revealed to be the exception not the rule. In academic terms, the Growth Mental Model is severely flawed; in practitioner terms, it is unrealistic. Chapter 2 concludes with the Sysco story that illuminates how Sysco has built an internal self-reinforcing growth system that has made it a growth leader for years—one of the exceptions. Sysco is a Smart Growth company that understands that growth is more than a strategy. Sysco is a constant improvement execution champion.

Chapter 3: Economics—Theories of Growth looks at the works of leading economists in the Neoclassical, New Growth, Industrial, Behavioral, and Complexity schools of economics to test the Growth Mental Model along with the work of Edith Penrose and Joseph Schumpeter. The only support for continuous smooth growth in the field of economics is the theoretical ability to create a linear production mathematical formula that a leading economist describes as not what we see in reality. A scientific model that does not reliably reflect or predict real-world behavior is generally discarded. So should be the Growth Mental Model. Economics states that corporate growth rates are hard to predict and are nearly random. Chapter 3 concludes with McDonald's growth story that illustrates the fact that growth is not continuous in good companies and discusses McDonald's strategic focus on being better, not bigger. McDonald's is another example of a Smart Growth company.

Chapter 4: Organizational Design and Strategy—Theories of Growth examines research dealing with corporate half-truths, sustainable competitive advantage, hypercompetition, and growth progression, all of which challenge the validity of the Growth Mental Model. This research is the basis for many of the assumptions underlying Smart Growth. In addition, I introduce the Darden Growth/Innovation Model and the concept of an Enabling Internal Growth System. Chapter 4 concludes with a discussion of another Smart Growth company, Best Buy, and examines how it executed a major change in its business model by creating a new internal growth system.

Chapter 5: Biology—Theories of Growth ventures into the field of biology to look for support or challenge to the Growth Mental Model. This chapter cites work on nonlinear growth, how fast growth and size increases predator risk, and findings in complex adaptive systems, all of which challenge the Growth Mental Model. This chapter concludes with two stories: the Procter & Gamble Company's (P&G) twenty-plus-year story of growth spurts, CEO changes, restructurings, product management reorganizations, and alternating top-line and bottom-line focuses, and private company Defender Direct's story of personal and business model evolution.

Chapter 6: Smart Growth—Authentic Growth exhorts the need for the investment community, boards of directors, and business leaders to reward the production of Authentic Earnings as contrasted with earnings created by the Earnings Game. The Earnings Game may enable the creation of inferior quality earnings that are legal, but they are qualitatively different from earnings created by Authentic Growth. Unfortunately, no one has studied the magnitude of this issue despite significant consensus that it exists. My concern is that the Earnings Game may create an earnings bubble supporting unsupportable stock valuations, which challenges the financial integrity of our financial markets. This chapter concludes with the Coca-Cola case, which looks at the various ways Coca-Cola has historically created its earnings.

Chapter 7: Managing the Risks of Growth—Public Companies looks at how growth can stress an organization's culture, people, customer value proposition, execution and quality control processes, and financial controls. I discuss Starbucks, Harley-Davidson, and JetBlue and introduce two more growth tools: the Growth Decision Process and the Growth Risks Audit. This chapter also discusses the Home Depot story and examines how its growth strategy diluted its culture and customer value proposition.

Chapter 8: Managing the Risks of Growth—Private Companies looks at the findings of my recent research dealing with the challenges of managing growth in fifty-four high-growth private companies located in twenty-three different states and in different industries. This research illuminates the complexity of growth, the human dynamics of growth, and the need to manage the pace of growth so as not to outstrip capabilities or lose the essence of the business. This chapter concludes with the story of Room & Board, a successful private Smart Growth company that rejected the Growth Mental Model.

Chapter 9: It Is Time for Smart Growth advocates changing the unrealistic, myopic view of corporate growth contained in the Growth Mental Model and replacing it with the Smart Growth concept. Smart Growth rejects the Growth Mental Model, the Wall Street Rules, and the Earnings Game as well as the assumptions that all growth is good and that bigger is better. To do this requires systemic change.

I suggest that we should replace "grow or die" as the gold standard of success with a different objective: being a high-quality, enduring company that continues to deliver compelling customer value propositions while creating value for shareholders, employees, and communities. As a country, we need less premature economic destruction, dislocation, job insecurity, and community instability. It is time for the business world to take back control of business from Wall Street and those who earn their living from volatility and transactions.

Chapter 9 discusses two more stories of Smart Growth companies: Costco and UPS. Costco has resisted Wall Street pressure to change its employee wage policy and its mark-up policy to protect its business model, and UPS has built an internal people-centric high-accountability growth system.

My research and consulting have exposed me to many cases where business leaders who blindly followed the Growth Mental Model ultimately destroyed good businesses and jobs and hurt many families and communities. I began my corporate growth research in 2002 having worked professionally in investment banking, private equity, and strategy consulting. In those careers, I had accepted the Growth Mental Model without critically thinking about its biases and limitations. I made my living helping finance and create growth companies. When I launched my research on corporate growth, I had no intention of challenging the Growth Mental Model, which had served me so well. Rather, I wanted to gain a better understanding of why so few companies were able to grow successfully over long periods of time. What I discovered surprised me and led to further research, which led me to develop this alternative model. The results of my research, consulting, and teaching are found in this book.

This book is not anti-growth; this book is about the reality of growth. Growth is a complex process, and this process does not fit into a deterministic, linear, mechanistic equilibrium world as mathematically modeled by neoclassical economics. My research and real-world experience have taught me that business growth is the result of a complex interrelationship of business and its environment, and it depends upon many human beings, with their cognitive limitations, being able to perceive and process information and communicate with each other in a manner that results in learning and adaptation to constantly evolving situations. This dependence of business growth on human behavior makes smoothness, prediction, and continuity difficult. The one-size-fits-all approach of the Growth Mental Model should not continue to dominate business thinking and behavior. The research and analysis presented here in support of the Smart Growth concept demonstrates it is a better concept for understanding and guiding business growth.

Growth can be good and growth can be bad. It depends. Growth should not be assumed; rather growth should be a conscious decision made only after evaluating the risks of not growing versus the risks of growth and devising ways to mitigate the risks of the chosen path.

CHAPTER 1

....

Defining the Growth Mental Model

What Is a Mental Model?

A mental model consists of beliefs or assumptions that are firmly held even without regard to whether those beliefs are true.[1] These beliefs drive behaviors and become part of a person's cognitive makeup. If believed by enough members of a community, those beliefs can become a group's mental model, an industry's mental model, or even a society's mental model.[2] Everyone creates and uses mental models. How we define ourselves or the goals of business provides the contours of how we process information. Information challenging our mental models, which are not easily subject to dislodgment, is often rejected.[3] One of my colleagues calls this result "cognitive blindness," because we do not even process information that disagrees with our models of how we view the world.

Think about how companies define their business. Is Mars Foods a candy company or chocolate company? The answer to that question defines their business alternatives. Defined as a candy company, it would not consider selling chocolate covered vitamin C tablets for children. But defined as a chocolate company, it may consider doing so because it broadens its market to vitamins and chocolate covered medicines.

Another example, Coca Cola, used to define itself as a carbonated beverage company. What would the company Coca Cola look like today if it had earlier redefined itself as a beverage company? Perhaps Coca Cola would have bought Starbucks. It could have changed the scope of its potential market significantly earlier in its history. UPS did try to expand its market space in 1998 when it changed its definition of itself from a package delivery company to a synchronized commerce solutions provider. The difficulty

UPS encountered in doing so reflects how entrenched the previous mental model of the company as a package delivery company, and the structures and processes in place to support it, had become.

Peter Senge, in his book *The Fifth Discipline,* defines mental models as "deeply engrained assumptions, generalizations, or even pictures that influence how we understand the world and how we take action."[4] Mental models, once formed, are hard to topple, often becoming axiomatic and accepted by new members of a group or industry without fresh critical inquiry of their rightness or validation.

What Is the Growth Mental Model?

The pervasive mental model about growth that guides the business activities of most business leaders and managers is: "grow or die." This mental model permeates entrepreneurship, private company, and public company thinking. Googling "businesses, grow or die" yields over 4 million hits. Early evidence of the pervasiveness of "grow or die" comes from the opening line of a June 28, 1954, *Time* magazine article entitled: "The New Magic Word in Industry."

Likewise, in the book, *Mergers and Acquisitions from A To Z,* authors Andrew Sherman and Milledge Hart state in their introduction: "In business there is one simple rule: grow or die."[5] In 1973, Random House published a book by Dr. George Land entitled *Grow or Die: The Unifying Principle of Business Transformation,* which Random House nominated for the Pulitzer Prize and National Book Award.

The renowned management consultant Ram Charan also talked about grow or die in one of his books.[6] Other business authors Robert Tomasko and Bo Burlingham acknowledge and question the universal applicability of the grow or die axiom.[7]

Even newspapers and magazines publish articles about grow or die. Paul Brown wrote in the *New York Times* on November 13, 2007: "If you Google 'grow or die' you get more than 11 million hits. So, clearly, there is something to the idea that if a business is not expanding, it is withering away."[8] Likewise, Jerry Useem, wrote an article appearing in *Fortune* magazine on April 30, 2007, entitled "The Big . . . Get Bigger" and stated, "But that's what 'grow or die' really means: You'd better grow, and also, you'd better grow the size of that growth."[9] James Surowiecki, in a *New Yorker* magazine article (June 9, 2008) entitled "All Together Now?" wrote, "CEOs of public companies often feel what you might call the 'grow or die' imperative."[10]

The acceptance of this mental model is not limited to a few articles. *Fast Company* magazine held two workshops in October and November 2007 called "Grow or Die." Bill Breen, writing in *Fast Company* (December 19, 2007) in an article entitled "Living in Dell Time," stated that "Michael Dell is fond of saying that in the high-tech business, you either grow or die."[11]

By no means exhaustive, these are examples of the broad acceptance of the chief axiom of business—grow or die. Under this axiom there are only these black or white choices. Surprisingly, I found no author or researcher who explained either the origin or the empirical justification for the axiom. People have accepted it seemingly without questioning its basis. Likewise, I found no studies testing the validity of the assumption that a business must grow or die or stating the scientific basis of the axiom.

Smooth and Continuous Growth—Wall Street Rules

While the belief that a business is either growing or it is dying permeates the business environment, if you are a leader or manager of a public company, your Growth Mental Model likely includes the following:

1. Public companies should continuously grow.
2. The growth of public companies should be smooth and linear.
3. Such growth should occur predictably every quarter.

These beliefs have been enshrined into "Wall Street Rules" that effectively reward or punish businesses for how well they adhere to the Growth Mental Model's mandates. The Wall Street Rules create significant pressure for public companies to meet or beat quarterly earnings estimates and to continuously grow from year to year as well as quarter to quarter. Quarterly earnings estimates are supposed to be not only higher than the same quarter's previous year's earnings but also higher than the previous quarter's earnings. Company managers correctly believe that if quarterly or year-to-year estimates are consistently met, they will be awarded with higher stock market valuations because investors value the predictability of earnings. The penalty for failing to meet quarterly earnings estimates often is a material stock price decline.[12]

What is interesting is that these Wall Street Rules have been accepted without any formal adoption by any regulatory body or industry standards body. The high stakes of quarterly earnings estimates have resulted in a serious, perhaps unintended, consequence—the creation of the "Earnings Game": the manufacture or creation of nonoperating or noncore earnings by companies solely to meet quarterly earnings estimates.

There are at least four ways public companies can produce earnings: (1) the authentic way, which entails either selling more goods or services to more customers in arm's-length transactions or by operating more efficiently or productively ("Authentic Earnings"); (2) creating earnings through legal accounting elections, valuations, reserves, and judgments, or changing credit policies; (3) managing the timing of earnings by deferring expenses, accelerating income, channel stuffing, or deferring investments; and (4) manufacturing nonoperating earnings by either selling assets or engaging in nonoperating financial transactions. For meeting quarterly earnings estimates all four types of earnings count the same. And, as Chapter 2 describes, six research studies conclude that it is very difficult for a company to consistently grow relying on only Authentic Earnings.

As a result, to satisfy Wall Street Rules, most companies have to resort to playing the Earnings Game: creating earnings using the three nonauthentic ways, each of which results in a lucrative fee business for accounting, legal, and investment banking firms that help companies create or manufacture earnings to erase the deficit between Authentic Earnings and estimated earnings. The fact that many firms reap substantial profits from helping companies comply with the Wall Street Rules entrenches the rules and the Growth Mental Model more deeply into the psyche of public markets, irrespective of their validity as a measure of a company's strength.

A leading mutual fund innovator and business leader, John Bogle describes the Earnings Game this way:

> Another example of the real-world consequences: Our financial system has, in substance, challenged our corporations to produce earnings growth that is, in truth, unsustainable. When corporations fail to meet their numeric targets the hard way—over the long term by raising productivity; by improving old products and creating new ones; by providing services on a more friendly, more timely, and more efficient basis; and by challenging the people of the organiza-

tion to work more effective together . . . —they are compelled to do it in other ways that often subtract value from you, from me, and from society.[13]

In his 2003 Shareholder Letter, Berkshire Hathaway CEO Warren Buffett described the Earnings Game this way: "Over the years, Charlie [Munger] and I have observed many instances in which CEOs engaged in uneconomic maneuvers so that they could meet earnings targets they had announced. Worse still, after exhausting all that operating acrobatics would do, they sometimes played a wide variety of accounting games 'to make the numbers.'"[14] The pressure on management to play the Earnings Game is immense because in reality growth does not occur predictably, smoothly, and continuously, as Chapter 2 shows. Consequently, in teaching hundreds of corporate middle managers a year in executive education programs, I am struck by their consistent talk about how everything they do is evaluated by its short-term quarterly earnings impact and how many decisions are made solely on that basis irrespective of the company's mid- or long-term needs. The Growth Mental Model necessitates the Earnings Game, which distorts corporate earnings and can stifle needed long-term investments.

The dominance of the Wall Street Rules is documented by Professors John Graham, Campbell Harvey, and Shivaram Rajgopal in a leading survey of over 300 public company CFOs. The survey revealed that those executives believed that: (1) earnings per share is the most important financial metric to institutional investors and analysts; (2) meeting quarterly earnings estimates maintains or increases stock prices and failing to meet them decreases stock prices; (3) quarterly earnings estimates need to be higher than the same quarter in the previous year or the last reported quarter; (4) the majority of CFOs would defer creating value, if necessary, to meet quarterly earnings estimates; and (5) failing to meet quarterly earnings estimates would hurt their careers.[15]

To supplement the survey findings, the authors interviewed twenty-two CFOs about their views on quarterly earnings. One CFO summarized it this way: "You have to start with the premise that every company manages earnings."[16] The authors found compelling their finding that 80% of the CFOs surveyed would either decrease discretionary spending (R&D, advertising, or maintenance) to meet a quarterly earnings target and 55% would delay starting a value creation project to meet quarterly earnings estimates. CFOs further believe it is necessary to smooth earnings to avoid negative surprises because they believe investors value predictability.

Arthur Levitt, the former chairman of the Securities and Exchange Commission (SEC), talked about the Earnings Game in a speech he gave on September 28, 1998, at the NYU Center for Law and Business where he stated:

> Increasingly, I have become concerned that the motivation to meet Wall Street earnings expectations may be overriding common sense business practices. Too many corporate managers, auditors, and analysts are participants in a game of nod and winks. In the zeal to satisfy consensus earnings estimates and project a smooth earnings path, wishful thinking may be winning the day over faithful representation.
>
> As a result, I fear we are witnessing an erosion in the quality of earnings, and therefore, the quality of financial reporting. Managing may be giving way to manipulation; Integrity may be losing out to illusion.[17]

Unfortunately, even with the public uproar and legislation passed after the accounting and corporate shenanigans of Enron, WorldCom, and others, and ten years after Chairman Levitt's speech, the Earnings Game remains alive and well.

Earnings Game Example

Krispy Kreme's experience is a good example of how complying with the Wall Street Rules can overtake a good business. Krispy Kreme was a successful doughnut chain based in Winston-Salem, North Carolina, that had been in business for over fifty years when it went public in 2000. Krispy Kreme's initial public offering (IPO) was very successful and Krispy Kreme rode rapid store expansion until 2005 when it replaced its CEO and four other senior officers and appointed a Special Committee of Independent Directors to investigate its accounting policies, which resulted in Krispy Kreme having to restate some earnings. The Krispy Kreme press release, dated August 10, 2005, reported the findings of the Special Committee:

> The Krispy Kreme story is one of a newly public company, experiencing rapid growth, that failed to meet its accounting and reporting obligations to its shareholders and the public. While some may see the accounting errors discussed in our summary as relatively small in magnitude, they were critical in a corporate culture driven by a nar-

rowly focused goal of exceeding projected earnings by a penny each quarter.[18]

Such short-term focus on Wall Street Rules is reinforced somewhat by two other systemic facts: (1) the average tenure of a public company CEO today is about six years[19] and (2) the average stock holding period of most large institutional investors is about one year.[20] All of these factors lead to short-term mutuality of interests. Concurring, Professor Alfred Rappaport, in 2005, described the quarterly earnings game: "Financial analysts fixate on quarterly earnings at the expense of fundamental research. Corporate executives, in turn, point to the behavior of the investment community to rationalize their own obsession with earnings."[21]

Although widely complied with, not everyone agrees with the imprimatur of the Wall Street Rules. Its focus on short-term earnings and its underlying assumptions have been criticized by leading finance professors and big business organizations such as the U.S. Chamber of Commerce and the CFA Centre for Financial Market Integrity and the Business Roundtable Institute for Corporate Ethics.[22]

In 2002, Professor Michael Jensen and Joseph Fuller, CEO of the strategy consulting firm The Monitor Group, expressed concern that management's short-term focus can lead to value-destroying behavior and hurt long-term performance and competitiveness. They exhorted corporate managers:

> They must not bow to analysts' demands for highly predictable earnings. The art of analysis includes the capacity to understand phenomena like seasonality, cyclicality, and random events. Companies do not grow in a constant fashion with each quarter's results better than the last. In the long run, conforming to pressures to satisfy the market's desire for impossible predictability and unwise growth leads to the destruction of corporate value, shortened careers, humiliation, and damaged companies.[23]

Thomas J. Donohue, president of the U.S. Chamber of Commerce, addressed the quarterly Earnings Game at the November 2005 Wall Street Analyst Forum:

> The rules have now been changed to favor a culture of immediate financial gratification without regard to long-term costs. We've created an environment where a company's long-term value and health are all too easily sacrificed at the altar of meaningless short-term performance. We

focus on a company's numbers and ignore its business—and that philosophy poses a significant threat to our future competitiveness.[24]

Criticizing the importance placed on meeting quarterly earnings estimates, Donohue stated: "Risks and rewards go together. Hurricanes and oil crises happen. If you want smooth, predictable returns, then buy a bond."[25]

Likewise, the *Harvard Business Review* in June 2001 illuminated the foundational beliefs underlying the dominating tyranny of meeting quarterly earnings estimates. In his article, Harris Collingwood observes that "meeting analysts' expectations of a smooth, steady rise in earnings has become, at many corporations, an imperative that overrides even the imperative to deliver the highest possible returns to shareholders."[26]

While not challenging the underlying assumptions made about corporate growth, the CFA Centre for Financial Market Integrity and the Business Roundtable Institute for Corporate Ethics issued a report in 2006 entitled "Breaking the Short-Term Cycle."[27] Two years later, the Aspen Institute issued its "Aspen Principles."[28] Both advocate the diminution of quarterly earnings guidance and a return to a focus on long-term value creation.

This chapter sets forth what has become accepted as the Growth Mental Model, the Wall Street Rules, and the resulting Earnings Game. The rest of this book challenges the validity of the Growth Mental Model and sets forth a more empirically and reality-based concept of business growth, which I call Smart Growth. I also challenge the grow or die axiom by discussing situations where growth has destroyed business value.

We have in this country created a culture of growth premised on the ideas that more is always better and bigger is always better. Why does every business have to grow?

Why Should Your Company Grow?

Recently, I was a strategy consultant for a four-year-old private company with fifteen employees that had achieved spectacular success, reaching revenues of $20 million in its fourth year with an enviable net margin of 35%. The senior executives were all receiving compensation in excess of $500,000. The company had a diversified customer base with long-term contracts and the business seemed to have a differentiating customer value proposition that could withstand competition. Even with this track record, however, most of the senior management team was frustrated because the company was not growing fast enough.

I began this assignment by interviewing each executive separately. The first question I asked was, "Why do you want the company to grow?" The common response was, "Well, if you are not growing, then you are dying." I then asked, "Why is that?" The answers varied from "Gee, no one ever asked me that" to "Because that is the way the game works" to "Well if we are not growing, we cannot create opportunity for younger employees." I followed up with my next "Why?" and then another "Why?"

Most of these executives had never drilled down to understand why they believed that a business either grows or dies. I suggest this is not uncommon. Why is it necessarily so that if you are not growing you are dying? Why is it not possible to prosper and endure without growing so long as you continue to meet customer needs and beat the competition by learning and improving?

The executive whose initial reason for wanting to grow was to create more opportunity for younger people finally admitted that if new people were to advance and the business did not grow, then his earnings would decline, and he did not want to reduce his income. Another executive got to the point when he said that the only reason the company had to grow was so that he could do new things and would not get bored. However, he could not explain why that required growth.

The second question I asked each executive was, "What are your risks of growing like you want?" Again, the response was surprise. "Isn't growth always good?" No, as I explain in Chapter 7, growth is not always good. Growth can be bad; too much growth or growth too fast has prematurely caused the demise of many a company. After discussing the company's growth options and views of growth, generally, I then led the executives to take a Growth Risk Audit, also discussed in Chapter 7. After evaluating some of the risks of growth and the tradeoffs required, the company is now working on mitigating critical infrastructure risks before taking on more growth.

In doing my research on the prevalence of consistent market-leading organic growth in public companies, I studied Tiffany & Co., which adopted the strategy "Growth Without Compromise," an approach that eschews a strict adherence to the Wall Street Rules. I thought that was an unusual strategy and was pleased that the Tiffany executives allowed me to research their company and write a business school case about them.[29] Tiffany provides a study of a company that has worked to grow smartly by managing its brand so as not to dilute it. As you read the Tiffany case, note that it is questionable whether or not Tiffany's recent activities support the Growth Without Compromise strategy.

Tiffany & Co. Case

Today, Tiffany is the leading U.S. luxury jewelry brand, generating more than $2.9 billion in revenue through 184 global retail outlets and from catalog and Internet sales. Tiffany's market cap is approximately $2.6 billion.

Historically, Tiffany's strategy has been to manage its growth so that growth would not dilute but rather enhance the Tiffany brand it had worked so hard to create. Tiffany wanted controlled, smart growth. For nearly 170 years, Tiffany managed its brand carefully. Tiffany had executed its Growth Without Compromise strategy by limiting its annual store openings, phasing rollouts of new products, limiting sales of its lower-priced products, and refusing to license the Tiffany name outside of its core competencies. Furthermore, it stressed the focus on brand and quality in the training and management of its workforce.

However, change was on the horizon. In February 2007, Trian Fund Management LP, a fund run by the billionaire investor Nelson Peltz, announced that it had purchased a 5.5% stake in Tiffany, becoming its largest shareholder. Trian believed that Tiffany was undervalued and it stated that it wanted to help Tiffany improve its earnings by focusing on operational and strategic issues. But before I question the impact of Trian's investment, some background about Tiffany is required.

History

On September 18, 1837, Charles Lewis Tiffany and John B. Young established Tiffany as a stationery and fancy-goods store in New York City with the policy of nonnegotiable prices, which provided it with an air of exclusivity. That same year, the famous Tiffany blue box was introduced. In 1845, Tiffany produced its first catalog, and by 2007, the company was distributing more than 22 million catalogs annually.

Tiffany has long been known for the quality of its products. In 1851, Tiffany became the first U.S. company to use the 925/1000 sterling standard, which was later adopted as the U.S. sterling standard. In 1853, Charles Lewis Tiffany acquired sole control of the company and changed its name to Tiffany & Co. The timelessness of Tiffany creations is illustrated by Audubon, its top-selling sterling flatware, introduced in 1871 and still in demand. In addition, in 1886, Tiffany revolutionized the diamond ring industry by redesigning and raising the diamond setting up off the ring's band to allow more light to enter and show more of the diamond's brilliance. This created the signature Tiffany jewelry setting: the six-pronged diamond solitaire engagement ring. Since then, diamonds became central to Tiffany's brand. Tiffany's standards of purity for the metals it used in its jewelry once again reigned supreme in 1926, when its standard for platinum jewelry was adopted in the United States.

In 1956, the Parisian master jeweler Jean Schlumberger opened his salon within Tiffany and was followed by the designers Elsa Peretti in 1974, Paloma Picasso in 1980, and architect Frank Gehry in 2006. Tiffany further secured its place in American culture by revising the Great Seal of the United States in 1885 and by creating both the Super Bowl trophy in 1967 and the NASCAR trophy in 2004.

Tiffany's business stature evolved to more than jewelry. Tiffany's business was creating and maintaining its brand.

Mission

Tiffany's stated mission is to "enrich the lives of its customers by creating enduring objects of extraordinary beauty that will be cherished for generations." In layman's terms, Tiffany creates timeless fine jewelry that becomes family heirlooms. The Tiffany values are quality, excellence, and trust. People rely on Tiffany's reputation and its credibility.

Channels of Distribution

Tiffany sells its products through three channels: Tiffany stores or licensed concessions, catalog sales, and, more recently, the Internet. It operates more than 184 stores and concessions in the United States, Canada, Central and South America, Japan, and other Asia-Pacific countries. The breakout and historical growth of the company are shown in Table 1.1.

TABLE 1.1 Growth of Tiffany Retail Stores, Concessions, and Boutiques

NUMBER OF STORES

YEAR	UNITED STATES	CANADA, CENTRAL AND SOUTH AMERICA	EUROPE	JAPAN	OTHER ASIA-PACIFIC COUNTRIES	TOTAL
2000	42	4	8	44	21	119
2001	44	5	10	47	20	126
2002	47	5	11	48	20	131
2003	51	7	11	50	22	141
2004	55	7	12	53	24	151
2005	59	7	13	50	25	154
2006	64	9	14	52	28	167
2007	70	10	17	53	34	184

You can see from this table that Tiffany opened thirty new stores combined in 2006 and 2007 as compared to opening twenty-eight stores the previous four years.

Tiffany's Internet and catalog mailing lists included more than 3.5 million customers. In fiscal year 2007, the company received more than 770,000 orders via mail, telephone, and the Internet, up from 744,000 in 2006 and 704,000 in 2005.

Geographical Expansion

For almost 130 years, Tiffany operated its flagship store in New York City without a drive to open more stores. This accomplished the goal of brand control as well as maintained the Tiffany brand of quality. Tiffany's geographical expansion in the United States began in 1963, with the opening of its store in San Francisco. It opened its first store in Japan in 1972, placing a boutique inside the Mitsukoshi department store, and expanded to Europe in 1986, with the opening of a Tiffany store in London. By 2007, Tiffany had four stores in London, three in Paris, and one each in Vienna, Frankfurt, Munich, Milan, Rome, and Zurich.

Tiffany has historically limited its new-store openings. In the United States, for example, even though Tiffany believed it could accommodate forty-five more stores, it limited new-store openings to four or five a year. Part of the reason for this policy was that the company preferred to staff a new store with 50% current Tiffany employees and 50% experienced local salespeople from fine jewelry stores in the new area.

Operating Results

TABLE 1.2 Selected Financial Data for Years Ended January 31

EARNINGS DATA	2007	2006	2005
Net sales (in thousands)	$2,648,321	$2,395,153	$2,204,831
Gross profit (in thousands)	$1,475,675	$1,342,340	$1,230,573
Selling, general, and administrative expenses (in thousands)	$1,060,240	$959,635	$936,044
Earnings from operations (in thousands)	$415,435	$382,705	$294,529
Net earnings	9.6%	10.6%	13.8%
Capital expenditures	6.9%	6.6%	6.5%
Return on average assets	9.0%	9.4%	12.0%
Return on average stockholders' equity	14.0%	14.4%	19.2%
Company-operated Tiffany & Co. stores/boutiques	167	154	151

Product Mix

Prior to 2007, Tiffany jewelry product lines could be grouped into diamonds, other gemstones, and non-gemstone jewelry. Tiffany introduced new products in silver, gold, and platinum jewelry annually. The company managed its product development and new-design rollouts on an eighteen-month rolling basis, in a process that Jon King, the senior vice president of Merchandising, called an "iterative process," explaining, "We constantly assess and reassess." King was responsible for product design, development, and all merchandising product decisions. In describing Tiffany's management, King showed intensity, discipline, and emotion that came from being part of Tiffany: "Here, managing the brand is an excruciating process—the microscopic focus on the details of execution."

Products containing one or more diamonds accounted for 46% of Tiffany sales, with products containing one or more diamonds of one carat or more accounting for 10% of those sales.

Vertical Integration

Historically, Tiffany, contrary to popular management theories of the importance of outsourcing to the bottom line, was a vertically integrated company. For example, Tiffany owned diamond mines, had exclusive sole-source diamond-supply contracts, and owned diamond-cutting and polishing facilities in Southeast Asia and South Africa, together with diamond testing, grading, and measurement facilities. The company manufactures 58% of the products it sells, excluding diamonds, in its Rhode Island and New York manufacturing facilities. Tiffany justified its strategy of vertical integration on two grounds: vertical integration allowed it to control the quality of its brand, and it created new profit centers for the company. Tiffany CEO Mike Kowalski in an interview in 2006 with me explained Tiffany's focus on quality and protecting its brand:

> You find a lot of humility here—this management team, although we have been here over 20 years together, we know we were dealt a good hand. It is not about us. And we have learned that there are a limited number of things we do well, and we have to be focused and disciplined to do those things. We are a products company—not a brand to be licensed or to be affixed to other products. We do not believe that we can sell anything or any luxury item—we know how to create, manufacture, and sell the highest-quality, natural gem jewelry in the world. Pure and simple.
>
> In this management team, there is a deep realization that we not tarnish the brand—a not-on-my-watch mentality. And while some think there are ultimate limits to our top line, we want to be the most efficient producers of the highest-quality product in the world.

Tiffany's vertical integration even extended to its flagship stores, as the company owned the real estate for the store located at 727 Fifth Avenue in New York City (124,000 sq. ft.); the London store (152,000 sq. ft.), for which it paid $43 million; and the Tokyo store (61,000 sq. ft.), for which it paid $140 million. However, this level of vertical integration changed after the Trian investment.

Although Tiffany had a history of not compromising its brand and growing slowly, it also was entrepreneurial and looked for opportunities to expand its market through acquisitions, expanding product lines through arrangements with designers and expanding the options available to its customers.

Acquisitions/New Concept

In 2002, Tiffany acquired the Little Switzerland chain of discount jewelry stores, comprising twenty-five stores on eleven Caribbean islands. In 2004, Tiffany introduced a new concept with the opening of a pearl jewelry chain named IRIDESSE. By 2008, there were sixteen IRIDESSE stores in the United States. Tiffany physically separated IRIDESSE from Tiffany, however, to allow the IRIDESSE management team to be entrepreneurial and free from the "Tiffany way." In March 2009, during the economic crisis, Tiffany announced it was closing down IRIDESSE.

Designer Licenses

Beginning in 1956 with the Parisian artist and jeweler Jean Schlumberger, Tiffany was the sole licensee for jewelry by certain designers, including Elsa Peretti (since 1974) and Paloma Picasso (since 1980). Peretti's designs accounted for 11% of the company's sales, and Picasso's designs accounted for 3%. In 2005, Tiffany became the licensee for jewelry designed by the famous architect Frank Gehry, whose products accounted for 2% of Tiffany sales in 2007.

More Reasons to Buy

Tiffany customers generally buy for such special occasions as weddings, anniversaries, births, birthdays, graduations, promotions, and so forth. In addition, Tiffany customers historically have bought for someone other than themselves. In response, Tiffany has tried to create more selling opportunities by asking its customers to celebrate the key events in their own lives—to reward themselves by buying a gift to "celebrate your special times with Tiffany."

People

Employees are a key resource for promoting the Tiffany brand. Tiffany has more than 8,000 employees, of whom 6,000 are based in the United States. Of its U.S. employees, 1,300 are in manufacturing. For a retail operation, Tiffany has had a very low turnover rate: less than 10%. Tiffany's employee-satisfaction averages are high, and the company generally promotes from within. Not surprisingly, more than 50% of Tiffany employees own stock in the company.

In addition, the company has become more focused on training line employees and rewarding brand-enhancing behavior. In keeping with its strong people side of the business, the Tiffany management team has an average tenure of eighteen years. The company's president, Jim Quinn, has described the Tiffany environment as follows:

> There is only one star in this company, and it is Tiffany. It is not about me or Mike or us, it is about the brand and balancing reverence for the brand's history with keeping the brand timeless and timely with new quality development and products. Success is our enemy—we have to constantly examine whether we are doing the right things, fast enough. Tiffany is a magical place. We have married the product into our culture—the pursuit of excellence through the quality, value, and integrity of the product without elitism, but with Tiffany being part of our people and part of our customers' lives.

Managing Growth

Management viewed Tiffany as a U.S. icon. For management, following its mantra of Growth Without Compromise meant that, at all costs, the Tiffany brand must be protected from dilution, poor quality, and anything that would hurt its reputation or credibility. Managing growth, in part, was accomplished by limiting annual store openings, refusing to license the Tiffany name, and setting goals of 15% ROE, 10% ROA, and single-digit sales growth.

An example of Tiffany's brand management was clearly demonstrated in 2005, when the company did something generally unheard of on Wall Street: it raised prices in order to slow down the growth of entry-level price points in silver jewelry. The company was concerned about traffic count, service, delivery, and brand dilution. Tiffany believed it was selling too much product to a particular market segment, which could hurt the brand in the long run.

What Makes Tiffany?

Part of the reason for Tiffany's longevity and success was its leadership, which exhibited an understated passion, respect, and reverence for what Tiffany stood for. "While striving for quality, Tiffany has never been elitist. We always have had democratic stores—no doorman, no locked doors, no determination of who should be allowed inside. We are part of this country's history, and we are an American brand, American made," CEO Mike Kowalski declared proudly.

Growth Without Compromise?

Tiffany's adherence to its mission of Growth Without Compromise was well known to capital markets and investors. In fact, historically, Tiffany clearly enunciated its policy and stated that its stock was not the right investment for everyone. However, adherence to its historic mission, and its longtime policies of strictly controlling its brand, limiting growth, vertical integration, and developing a loyal workforce arguably has been challenged since 2007, when Trian became its largest shareholder.

Since Trian's investment, Tiffany has done the following:

1. December 2006: The company licensed its name to Luxottica to design, manufacture, and sell worldwide Tiffany eyewear and sunglasses. Luxottica operates over 5,700 optical and retail stores including Lens-Crafters and Pearle Vision.
2. August 2007: Tiffany sold the real estate for its Tokyo store for $327.5 million and leased it back.
3. September 2007: Tiffany sold the Little Switzerland chain for $32.9 million.

4. October 2007: Tiffany sold the real estate for its London store for $149 million and leased it back.

5. October 2007: Tiffany announced the creation of Tiffany & Co. Collections, a new small-format store with plans for seventy stores in the United States.

6. December 2007: The company announced a strategic alliance with Swatch to make and sell Tiffany branded watches. Under the agreement, Swatch can open Tiffany watch stores in certain international markets and sell Tiffany watches to third-party distributors.

7. 2007 and in 2008: Tiffany opened six new stores in the United States.

8. Fall 2008: The company opened a new smaller-format Tiffany store of approximately 2,600 square feet in California.

9. November 2008: Tiffany offered voluntary retirement to 800 U.S. employees.

10. February 2009: Tiffany sold $250 million of debt to Berkshire Hathaway.

The decisions to open more Tiffany stores quickly, open small concept stores, license the Tiffany brand to Luxottica, and partner with Swatch to open Tiffany watch stores and sell Tiffany watches to third parties raises the fundamental question as to whether Tiffany, by its actions, changed its Growth Without Compromise strategy. If so, why did Tiffany change?

Has Tiffany acquiesced in the Wall Street drive for as much growth as fast as possible to maximize shareholder value as fast as possible without regard to the long-term consequences? Tiffany is interesting because it raises the question of whether a public company can operate under a strategy of managed controlled growth and withstand pressures to grow as fast as possible. In Tiffany's case, Growth Without Compromise worked well for years, and Tiffany created and managed an enduring brand in a stewardship manner. If being a public company means you have to grow as fast as possible even if it may dilute your brand in the long term, then it is questionable whether Tiffany should even be a public company. Perhaps, at least as long as Wall Street Rules prevail, Tiffany could protect its brand better as a private company earning good, solid, risk-adjusted returns each year.

Tiffany is an example of the challenge management faces managing a brand and also meeting the public market's insatiable hunger for growth. Similar challenges confronted by Starbucks, Harley-Davidson, and Costco are examined later in the book.

Notes

1. Phil Johnson-Laird and Ruth Byrne, "The Mental Model Theory of Thinking and Reasoning," Mental Models, May 2000, www.tcd.ie/psychology/other/ruth_byrne/mental_models/theory.html (accessed March 23, 2009).

2. Patricia H. Werhane, "Mental Models, Moral Imagination and System Thinking in the Age of Globalization," *Journal of Business Ethics* 78, 3 (2008): 463.

3. Jonathan St. B.T. Evans, "Theories of Human Reasoning: The Fragmented State of the Art," *Sage* 1, 1 (1991): 83.

4. Peter Senge, *The Fifth Discipline* (New York: Doubleday, 1990), 8.

5. Andrew J. Sherman and Milledge A. Hart, *Mergers and Acquisitions from A to Z* (New York: AMACOM, 2006), 1.

6. Ram Charan and Noel M. Tichy, *Every Business Is a Growth Business: How Your Company Can Prosper Year After Year* (New York: Three Rivers Press, 1998), 22.

7. Robert M. Tomasko, *Bigger Isn't Always Better* (New York: AMACOM, 2005), 11; Bo Burlingham, *Small Giants: Companies that Choose to Be Great Instead of Big* (New York: Penguin, 2005), xvi.

8. Paul B. Brown, "More than One Way to Help a Business Grow," *New York Times*, November 13, 2007.

9. Jerry Useem, "The Big . . . Get Bigger," *Fortune*, April 30, 2007, http://money.cnn.com/magazines/fortune/fortune_archieve/2007/04/30/8405390/index.htm.

10. James Surowiecki, "All Together Now?" *The New Yorker*, June 9, 2008, www.newyorker.com/talk/financial/2008/06/09/080609ta_talk_surowiecki?printable=true.

11. Bill Breen, "Living in Dell Time," *Fast Company*, December 19, 2007, 5.

12. Dr. Steven Krull, "Corporate Guidance and Earnings Announcements: Are Companies Gaming the System to Beat the Analyst Mean When Announcing Earnings," Hofstra University, www.hofstra.edu/pdf/biz_mlc_krull3.pdf.

13. John C. Bogle, *Enough: True Measures of Money, Business and Life* (Hoboken, NJ: John Wiley & Sons, 2009), 10.

14. Warren Buffett, 2003 Shareholder Letter, Berkshire Hathaway, February 27, 2004, www.berkshirehathaway.com/letters/2003ltr.pdf.

15. John R. Graham, Campbell R. Harvey, and Shivaram Rajgopal, "Value Destruction and Financial Reporting Decisions," *Financial Analysts Journal* 62, 6 (2006): 27–39.

16. Ibid., 30.

17. Arthur Levitt, "The Numbers Game" (Speech, NYU Center for Law and Business, New York, September 28, 1998), www.sec.gov/news/speech/speecharchive/1998/spch220.txt.

18. *Summary of Independent Investigation by the Special Committee of the Board of Directors of Krispy Kreme Doughnuts, Inc.*, August 10, 2005.

19. Steven N. Kaplan and Bernadette A. Minton, "How Has CEO Turnover Changed? Increasingly Performance Sensitive Boards and Increasingly Uneasy CEOs" (NBER Working Paper Series 12465, 2006): 2.

20. Bogle, *Enough*, 133, 145.

21. Alfred Rappaport, "The Economics of Short-Term Performance Obsession," *Financial Analysts Journal* 61, 3 (2005): 65.

22. Thomas J. Donohue, "Enhancing America's Long-Term Competitiveness: Ending Wall Street's Quarterly Earnings Game" (Wall Street Analyst Forum, New York, November 30, 2005); Dean Krehmeyer, Matthew Orsagh, CFA, and Kurt N. Schacht, CFA, "Breaking the Short-Term Cycle: Discussion and Recommendations on How Corporate Leaders, Asset Managers, Investors, and Analysts Can Refocus on Long-Term Value," CFA Centre for Financial Market Integrity, Business Roundtable Institute for Corporate Ethics, July 2006 (1–19).

23. Joseph Fuller and Michael C. Jensen, "Just Say No to Wall Street: Putting a Stop to the Earnings Game," *Journal of Applied Corporate Finance* 14, 4 (2002): 45. Emphasis added.

24. Donohue, "Enhancing America's Long-Term Competitiveness."

25. Ibid.

26. Harris Collingwood, "The Earnings Game: Everyone Plays, Nobody Wins," *Harvard Business Review* 79, 6 (2001): 67.

27. Krehmeyer, Orsagh, and Schacht, "Breaking the Short-Term Cycle."

28. Judith Samuelson, "The Aspen Principles: A Better Way Forward," *Directors & Boards* (Summer 2008).

29. Edward D. Hess, "Tiffany & Company" (Case Study UVA-S-0141, University of Virginia Darden School Foundation, Charlottesville, 2007). This case has been updated for material events. All quotes are directly from the case.

CHAPTER 2

....

Smooth and Continuous Company Growth

THE EXCEPTION NOT THE RULE

I F YOU OWN, lead, or manage a *private* company, it is likely you have heard that you must grow the business or it will die. If you control, lead, or manage a *public* company it is likely you also have been told to make your quarterly numbers and that they need to be better than last year's same quarters results and/or even the last quarter's results.

In this chapter, I challenge the validity and practicality of the Growth Mental Model by reviewing six research studies involving public companies and showing that smooth and continuous growth is the exception not the rule. These six studies were not designed to test the Growth Mental Model, but nonetheless their findings are consistent and illuminating. In academic terms, the Growth Mental Model is severely limited. In practical terms, it is an unrealistic and a rarely achievable goal.

In spite of these findings, and the various statements by academics, business leaders, and former SEC Chairman Arthur Levitt discussed in Chapter 1, the Growth Mental Model and business pressures to meet its demands are strong today. Why is this the case? Although the Growth Mental Model's expectation of smooth and continuous growth may be unrealistic, do not forget that many people (lawyers, accountants, and investment bankers) earn fees from advice or transactions designed to help companies comply with the Growth Mental Model. Even if these efforts fail to satisfy the growth called for in the Growth Mental Model, there is money to be made from the resultant mergers, sales, acquisitions, and liquidations of companies that fall out of favor because they do not grow continuously and smoothly. The bottom line is that there is a strong financial interest in maintaining the status quo of the Growth Mental Model whether or not it makes good business sense.

Before examining the six studies, it is important to understand that these studies are descriptive but not necessarily predictive of future performance, and, like all empirical studies, they have limitations. The studies differ in the subsets of public companies they researched as well as the sample sizes, which range from 102 companies to more than 6,700 companies. Nonetheless, the consistency of the findings is revealing. What unites these studies is that they each conclude that for public companies smooth and continuous growth is the exception rather than the rule.

These studies show that smooth and continuous growth is not even common, occurring only in a small minority of cases. That result is interesting for at least three reasons:

1. How has the Growth Mental Model persisted when it is so divorced from reality?
2. Five of the six studies utilized public company reported revenue and earnings that likely included the different types of earnings creation and manufacturing alternatives discussed in Chapter 1. Even with efforts to create or manufacture reportable earnings, most of the companies were unable to meet the Wall Street Rules—a surprising finding. One study tried to discriminate between the character of earnings, and its results were consistent with the other five studies; consistent growth is difficult and achievable on average in less than 10% of the cases.
3. Three of the studies found that many of the companies that were able to report smooth continuous growth over their study period did so primarily through serial or successive acquisitions, that is, they bought the growth Wall Street wanted.

McGrath Study

In *The Search for Organic Growth* (Hess and Kazanjian 2006), Professor Rita McGrath of Columbia University Business School examined the importance of middle management in delivering growth.[1] McGrath discussed a 2004 study of U.S. and non-U.S. public companies with market capitalizations of at least $1 billion that asked how many of those companies were able to grow their revenues/sales by at least 5% a year for either three, four, or five years. Note that McGrath was not looking for high growth, just nominal continuous growth.

She found that only 248 U.S. firms were able to grow their revenues/sales by 5% a year for five years. And only 179 non-U.S. firms were able to grow their revenues/sales by 5% a year over four years. Thus, only 427 companies were able to grow 5% a year over the four- or five-year time periods. McGrath then asked how many of those firms were able to achieve that modest growth rate *without* making acquisitions or engaging in merger or other change of control transactions. Her results were surprising.

Of the companies reporting growth of at least 5% a year, approximately 93% of them achieved their growth primarily by acquisitions or mergers. Less than 7% of the companies that achieved the 5% a year growth rate did so primarily by core or organic growth, which is nonacquisitive growth. McGrath's results are consistent with the other studies discussed in this chapter that conclude that even modest continuous growth is very difficult to achieve unless one resorts to buying growth via acquisitions or mergers.

McGrath states: "One interpretation [of this study] is that acquisition activity as a source of growth may be far more prevalent than popular mythology suggests—indeed, moving the pieces of companies around through ownership exchanges seemed to be far more popular than creating growing businesses within the firm."[2]

Lipton

The second study is cited in work done by Professor Mark Lipton at the New School University in New York City. Professor Lipton's work focuses on the impact of different types of company visions on long-term growth. In his book *Guiding Growth: How Vision Keeps Companies on Course*, in discussing the commonly held belief that public company growth should be smooth and continuous, Lipton states:

Forget the books showing smooth, linear line graphs that predict aggressive growth as an unbroken trajectory. . . . Organizational growth is far from a smooth process . . . research dating back to the 1960s shows clearly how extended periods of growth are characterized more by near-catastrophic turbulence than by universally smooth and predictable experience.[3]

Lipton then refers to a study of more than 3,700 U.S. and non-U.S. firms with revenues greater than $500 million that found that only 3.3% had consistent profitable growth in the top line and bottom line and shareholder returns during the period 1990–1997.[4] Of those 3,700-plus firms, only twenty-one (less than 1%) had sustained growth over a twenty-year period. Again, consistent growth is difficult to achieve, thus challenging the Growth Mental Model.

McKinsey Study

In an article entitled "The Do-or-Die Struggle for Growth," three McKinsey consultants studied the performance of the 102 largest U.S. public companies ranked by both revenue and market capitalization during the time period 1994–2003.[5] What did they find? Similarly to the McGrath study, they found that of those 102 companies fewer than ten were able to grow revenues by at least 10% a year and grow their total return to shareholders (TRS) more than the average TRS growth for the S&P 500 without resorting to extensive acquisitions.

Of the 102 companies studied, thirty-two were able to attain growth faster than nominal GDP growth (around 5%) and outperform the TRS for the S&P 500. Interestingly, 90% of the thirty-two companies were limited to four high-growth industries—financial services, health care, high tech, and retail—leading the authors to conclude that being in the right industry at the right time could be a necessity for continuous growth. This last point is interesting because the Growth Mental Model does not contain the qualification or caveat that the likelihood of continuous growth may be dependent on the industry.

Corporate Executive Board Study

The Corporate Executive Board (CEB) undertook a study of all the companies (503 in total) that made up the Fortune 100 during the years 1955–2006 to see how many experienced growth stalls, or what I call growth plateaus, defined as periods when growth either stops or declines. Such stalls or plateaus end a continuous growth spurt.[6] The CEB identified stall points by analyzing a company's revenue growth rates for the ten years preceding and succeeding each year and looking for meaningful downward trends.

They found that 87% of all companies in their study experienced a stall and only 13% of the companies were able to achieve long-term real revenue growth of 6% or more without experiencing a decline of 4% or more during the study period. For most companies, then, growth was neither smooth nor continuous.

Furthermore, the CEB found that most stalls occurred between the $1 billion to $10 billion revenue range and not at the mega-cap companies. Most of the companies that were able to continuously grow were companies in their initial growth stage or in high-growth industries, which is similar to the McKinsey findings discussed above. Of the sixty-seven continuous growers, seventeen were financial service companies, nine were telecom companies, and nine were retail companies. Interestingly, once companies experienced breaks in their continuous growth path, only about 15% of them were able to restart another continuous growth path.

As in prior studies, the CEB study did not discriminate between the character or quality of revenue of the companies in the study; that is, it did not distinguish whether revenue was bought, manufactured, created, or gained through Authentic Earnings. Nonetheless, the CEB study, like the others examined in this chapter, challenges the Growth Mental Model and illustrates the difficulty of long-term smooth and continuous growth.

Hess's Organic Growth Index Studies

In 2002, after the Enron debacle, I began working to create a financial model that would illuminate those U.S. public companies that (1) created substantial economic value; (2) outperformed their industry performance averages; and (3) did so primarily by internal or organic growth, without resorting to material serial acquisitions or mergers or resorting to material earnings creation or manufacture. The result was the development of an Organic Growth Index (OGI) that built upon work done by the S&P Core Earnings Test and Merrill Lynch's Quality of Earnings Study.[7] The OGI studies are the only studies cited in this chapter that do not accept published revenue numbers as conclusive evidence of growth.

In March 2008, the Batten Institute at the Darden Graduate School of Business released the results of ten years of OGI research from 1996–2006 that applied the six-step OGI screening process to over 1,300 public U.S. companies. Under the six-step screening process, companies are successively screened to eliminate companies that are creating material revenue by engaging in earnings creation, earnings manufacture, material serial acquisitions or mergers to create growth.

What the OGI attempts to do is illuminate "primarily pure plays"— companies that grow consistently and that do so by creating revenue by selling more goods or services to more customers and by operating more efficiently or productively. That is, they do not materially create or manufacture earnings to generate good growth numbers for Wall Street. As you can see, the OGI screening process that stripped away created earnings eliminated many public companies from the winners' circle.

Table 2.1 shows the OGI results for six different overlapping five-year periods.

TABLE 2.1 OGI Results 1996–2006

STUDY PERIOD	SAMPLE SIZE	NUMBER OF "WINNERS"	PERCENTAGE OF "WINNERS"
1996–2001	834	68	8%
1997–2002	862	47	5%
1998–2003	860	59	7%
1999–2004	801	77	10%
2000–2005	793	85	11%
2001–2006	799	85	11%

Source: Edward D. Hess, "Organic Growth Index 'OGI' 1996–2006," 2008. Funded in part by the Batten Institute, Darden Graduate School of Business Administration.

"Winners" in the OGI results are companies that survived the screening process for each study period; they created substantial economic value and outperformed their industry norms, and they did so primarily from authentic growth. The sample size for each year of the OGI study varied somewhat. The study sample was drawn from the top 1,000 companies in the EVA Dimensions Performance Rank EVA/MVA model. I then eliminated real estate investment trusts and insurance and financial service companies. The companies that remained for each study year were my initial sample, which I then trimmed through a series of screenings and ultimately determined the winners.

Within each initial sample, the size of the companies varied: 50% of the companies had market capitalizations less than $2 billion; 34% of the companies had market capitalizations between $2 billion and $10 billion; and 16% of the companies had market capitalizations greater than $10 billion. What the OGI results show is that it is extremely rare to grow over a long period of time organically without creating, manufacturing, or buying income. Over the entire ten-year study period, only ten out of 1,300 different companies came through all time periods as winners, representing less than 1% of the companies studied. Only seven companies were winners during five different time periods and ten companies were winners in four different time periods. That is, only twenty-seven companies out of 1,300, or around 2%, were winners in at least four out of the six time periods. My studies are consistent with the above studies: smooth and continuous public company growth is the exception not the rule.

Not only did the winners show consistent growth, but also they were handsomely rewarded for doing so by the stock market. The twenty-seven winners generated stock returns without dividends during the time period 1996–2006 of 1,368.82% as compared to the DJIA returns of 143.56%, the S&P 500 returns of 130.27%, and the NASDAQ 100 returns of 204.90% for the same period. The Appendix lists the twenty-seven winners.

Wiggins and Ruefli Study

In 2002, Professors Robert Wiggins and Timothy Ruefli reported the results of their extensive twenty-five-year (1972–1997) study of 6,772 public U.S. companies, in which they examined by industry how many firms achieved superior performance as compared to their industry competition.[8] Wiggins and Ruefli studied company performance over two time periods— twenty or more years and ten or more years—and used two different measures of superior performance: ROA and Tobin's q. ROA is a measure of net income divided by total assets and Tobin's q looks at the ratio of market value to the replacement cost of assets. Tobin's q is analogous to the ratio of market value to book value.

Their findings confirm that achieving superior performance for at least ten years is the exception for public companies. Over the twenty-year study period, only four out of the 6,772 firms studied achieved superior performance using Tobin's q as the test. Only thirty-two firms did so using the

ROA test. Even using ROA, less than 1% of the sample achieved superior performance over the twenty-year period. Of the thirty-two firms showing superior performance using the ROA measure, eleven were retail or restaurant companies, a finding similar to my OGI determination of winners.

For the ten-year time period, the results reported by Wiggins and Ruefli were a little better: 5.17% of the firms met the superior performance standard using the ROA test and 2.16% of the firms did so using Tobin's q. Wiggins and Ruefli conclude:

> The key finding of this research for management practice is that the demonstrated rarity of achieving sustained superior economic performance implies that it is very difficult to achieve.
>
> The results also indicate that there may even be a question as to whether sustained economic performance is even a reasonable goal to set for a firm.
>
> The findings here indicate that for some industries sustained superior performance may not be achievable, and for many other industries may be so rare as to be practically unachievable.[9]

Their conclusion that the rarity of consistent growth questions whether that goal is even reasonable challenges a key premise of the Growth Mental Model. In addition, like the results found by McKinsey's and my work, Wiggins and Ruefli's superior performance companies were more likely to be found in certain industries.

Conclusion—Six Studies

These six studies, although they did not set out to challenge the Growth Mental Model, show that smooth and continuous growth is rare over even modest periods of time. Furthermore, even with a range of tools and consultants available to management to "create" growth, sustained growth is extremely hard to achieve.

In McGrath's study, only about 7% of the companies growing 5% a year were able to do so without resorting to acquisitions. Lipton's study showed that only 3.3% of the companies studied were able to grow revenue earnings and stock value during 1990–1997. McKinsey showed that less than 10% of the companies studied were able to grow continuously without resorting to acquisitions. The CEB study showed that only 13% of its companies did not experience growth stalls. My OGI study showed that over a ten-year period less than 3% of over 1,300 companies were able to achieve high growth primarily through organic growth. Wiggins and Ruefli found that only 5.17% of the companies they studied were able to achieve superior performance over a ten-year period, and less than 1% of the 6,772 companies that were able to do so for twenty years. As Professor Larry Greiner states when talking about the stages of corporate growth: "Smooth evolution is not inevitable or indefinitely sustainable; it cannot be assumed that organizational growth is linear."[10]

These six studies demonstrate the difficulty of achieving smooth and continuous growth. Given the rarity of smooth and continuous growth, is it reasonable to have the exception become the general rule to which all are judged? If the probability of continuous growth is rare, why should this be the standard by which we evaluate the health of a company?

The studies in this chapter demonstrate that the Growth Mental Model fails to describe how businesses actually perform and certainly should not be used to predict growth or be routinely adopted as a strategic business goal. It is divorced from reality. In research science, when a model does not or cannot reliably predict behavior it is discarded. So should be the Growth Mental Model.

Before moving on to Chapter 3 and looking at economic theories of growth, I want to discuss one of the companies found to be a continuous grower in the CEB study and one of the ten winners in my OGI study for the entire ten-year study period (1996–2006): Sysco Corporation. In addition to including Sysco in my OGI study, I have studied the company and written a Darden case study that illuminates how Sysco has been able to achieve its envious growth history. Sysco is an exception not the rule.

Not only is Sysco an exception because it has produced growth consistently, but also Sysco illustrates some key concepts about how companies can create a self-reinforcing enabling growth system that produces authentic growth. As you read the case, please focus on how Sysco has aligned its strategy, structure, culture, HR policies, and execution processes, along with its measurement and reward policies, to drive desired behaviors. Some points to consider are: How has Sysco increased its top-line growth? How has Sysco achieved growth through cost efficiencies and productivity? How has Sysco used acquisitions to grow? How does technology enable Sysco's growth? What role do measurements play in managing growth? Why are Sysco's employees so loyal and productive? What is the relationship between Sysco's customer connectedness and constant improvement process?

Sysco Corporation Case

In 2008, Sysco was the leading wholesale distributor of food, food products, and related services to the restaurant and food service industry.[11] Sysco's annual sales exceeded $37 billion, and it controlled an estimated 16% market share. For the past twenty years, Sysco has achieved a sales compound annual growth rate (CAGR) of 11% and earnings before taxes CAGR of 14% in a low-margin industry, the wholesale distribution of food and food service products. Historically, Sysco's growth has come primarily from domestic geographical expansion, product expansion, new-customer segments, and operating efficiencies. Underlying its results has been a growing market for the number of meals eaten outside the home.

Sysco's growth story shows the power of a relentless focus on execution excellence and the power of high employee engagement, management continuity, and homegrown talent. Sysco evidences the type of internal growth system that can produce consistent high performance. This growth system links one's strategy, structure, culture, execution processes, people policies, leadership model, measurement, and reward systems in a consistent, seamless, linked, and self-reinforcing manner so as to drive the desired employee behaviors.

History

Formed in 1969, Sysco went public in March 1970, with the merger of nine separate family-owned entrepreneurial food service operations. In 1969, Americans were eating out frequently, and industry studies predicted that half of all meals would be eaten away from home by the year 2000, primarily because women who had entered the workforce during World War II were continuing to work. With less time to cook, working women wanted more prepared food. John F. Baugh, the entrepreneur who founded Zero Frozen Foods Distribution Company in Houston in 1946, envisioned a national food service distribution organization.

Active in industry organizations, Baugh shared his idea with friends with whom he had much in common, all across the country. All were self-made and held tight financial control over their operations. All treated their employees with respect, and all were family oriented. Baugh believed that each could maintain autonomy but, at the same time, gain strength by combining their companies into one new corporation and going public.

Investment analysts and industry peers, however, were skeptical, given all the strong personalities and egos involved.

The nine merging companies, which included Baugh's Zero Frozen Foods, trusted Baugh to evaluate their businesses and determine the number of shares in the new public corporation that each would receive. All pledged their personal wealth for three years to guarantee the corporation's success. According to Sysco history, Baugh's "good faith" plan called for all owners of the founding companies to place in escrow approximately 10% of the shares each would receive in the merger. It was envisioned that one-third of the escrowed shares could be returned over each of the three years. However, for this to occur it would be necessary that Sysco's operating results for each year (or the aggregate thereof for three years) include sales growth of at least 10% compounded annually. In addition, the company's net earnings increase would have to equal or exceed 15% compounded for the three years. Failure to reach those goals would result in the forfeiture of all escrowed shares to Sysco's treasury. So, instead of a conventional "going forward" incentive bonus arrangement for obtaining those challenging objectives, it was required that the company reach or exceed those stringent goals in order that the founders' shares of Sysco stock that had been placed in escrow be returned to them.

This performance-based, earn-out compensation philosophy institutionalized a reward for performance culture at Sysco. The dream became reality as the nine companies, with aggregate sales of $115 million in a $35 billion industry, became Sysco (an acronym for Systems and Services Company) in an initial public offering on March 3, 1970. In 1977, Sysco became the leading food service supplier in North America. Since then, it had maintained this position, increasing sales and earnings every year except 2006.

Facts

Sysco, based in Houston, Texas, sells to more than 400,000 customers annually and has over 50,000 employees. The magnitude of the Sysco operations is mind-boggling. The company offers more than 300,000 products and, on a daily basis, delivers almost four million cases of food and related food service products on time and without defect to over 360,000 customers 99% of the time. More than half of the Sysco employees are hourly warehouse and delivery people. The company also employs 14,000 sales, business-development, and marketing associates.

Although the food-distribution business is a low-margin industry, the company's financial statistics have been impressive, with its annual sales growth outpacing the food service industry's growth by two to three times. Sysco's twenty-year compounded annual growth rate through 2005 was 13.7%. It consistently has paid a dividend since its inception and has increased its quarterly cash dividend thirty-six times in thirty-five years.

Sysco products include not only the ingredients needed to prepare meals, but also numerous preparation and serving items as well as business solutions to support chefs, cooks, and restaurant owners. Products include such nonfood items as equipment and supplies, paper and disposables, and even the chemicals used to clean and sanitize kitchens. Business solutions included menu development and analysis, food-safety training, third-party back-office training, and systems.

In 2005, Sysco began the process of completely redesigning its supply-distribution system into major regional centers, simplifying supplier logistics and maximizing delivery efficiencies at significant cost savings. The company's first redistribution center (RDC) opened in 2005 in Front Royal, Virginia, serving fourteen of Sysco's broad-line distribution centers in the Northeast, and the company opened its second RDC in 2008 in Alachua, Florida. Results from the first RDC showed an 8.2% reduction in handling costs. For example, it took two hours to unload a non-RDC truck but only 20 minutes to unload an RDC truck.

Growth

In 2008, Sysco's available market space was approximately $231 billion. With sales of almost $38 billion, its market share was approximately 16%. Sysco's growth story is interesting. Since going public in 1970, the company has gone through an evolutionary growth pattern, in the following order:

- Sysco expanded its footprint geographically throughout the United States.
- Sysco expanded its product offerings to include nonfood supplies for its existing customers. Sysco segmented its customer market into four price-point segments for greater market focus.
- Sysco expanded into specialty (organic fresh vegetables and high-end meat) and ethnic foods (Chinese, Italian, Mexican, and Asian), broadening its product offerings.
- Sysco added services to help its existing customers be more successful.

- Sysco focused on cost efficiencies.
- Sysco redesigned its supply and distribution chain for additional cost efficiencies.

What is unique about Sysco? Sysco's uniqueness does not appear to be its strategy, its products, its financial expertise, or even its employees. It does not display a rah-rah culture or even a very visible culture. What is unique about Sysco is that it has figured out how, on a daily basis, to get and keep everyone—from the CEO to the truck driver—focused on doing the little things that matter to its customers.

Simply put, Sysco is an execution champion. The company understands how to balance and manage tensions between decentralized entrepreneurial autonomy and centralized controls. It also has learned how not to become complacent, self-satisfied, or arrogant. And, lastly, Sysco has figured out how to measure what is important to its success and how to reward the right behaviors all the way down the line—for example, by offering productivity incentives paid to truck drivers on a weekly basis.

Sysco is a "quiet" company without a lot of corporate cheerleading and without a lot of corporate frills. It is run more like a farm than a Wall Street corporation, with its farmers getting up every day, going to the fields, tilling the soil, watering, fertilizing, pulling the weeds, harvesting some crops, and getting up the next day and doing the job again, always very well. Sysco goes about its business in the same determined, engaged, and methodical way.

Private Labels

Other evidence of Sysco's growth strategy is the development of the Sysco brand, which was the number-one brand in food service. According to a NameQuest survey ranking top consumer brands, Sysco brand sales, in fiscal year 2002, ranked fourth, behind Coca-Cola, Kraft, and Kleenex, a testament to the strength of the brand's recognition and acceptance.

Sysco introduced its own Sysco brand products in 1975, and, at that time, more than 36,000 products carried the Sysco name. The original four quality levels included Supreme, Imperial, Classic, and Reliance. The company has added expertise in such niche-product areas as specialty meats, value-added and exotic produce, hotel and lodging industry supplies, Asian cuisine food service distribution, and domestic and international custom chain-restaurant distribution.

Because Sysco does not manufacture its food products, a quality-assurance team of more than 180 professionals determines specifications for each Sysco brand item and also sets the criteria for raw materials and the standards that manufacturers and processors are required to follow for food safety, quality, and consistency, as well as social responsibility and supplier code of conduct. The quality-assurance team identifies and establishes supply sources and audits those suppliers to enforce Sysco's strict standards for such factors as facility conditions and sanitary measures. Inspectors are at the plants when bacon comes off the production line, and they follow produce from the field to cooler to ensure that proper holding temperatures and product integrity are maintained.

Sysco's program is unmatched in the food industry. The number of people (approximately 180) and resources committed to supporting the integrity of its products is far superior to its industry competitors, who usually devote a handful of personnel to these tasks, if they are undertaken at all.

The Role of Acquisitions

Sysco's last large acquisition was in 1988, when it acquired CFS, a large food distributor that allowed Sysco to complete its national geographical platform. Sysco has been acquiring companies basically since it was formed. Often, people believe Sysco's growth has been primarily because of acquisitions. Although acquisitions have been important to establish critical geographical footholds, Sysco has grown faster internally than through acquisitions. Table 2.2 shows its organic growth in contrast to its growth by acquisition.

TABLE 2.2 Organic Growth Versus Growth by Acquisition

FISCAL YEAR	ORGANIC GROWTH	ACQUISITIONS	TOTAL GROWTH
2005	4.5%	.8%	5.3%
2004	9.1%	.9%	10.0%
2003	6.7%	5.2%	11.9%
2002	3.8%	3.4%	7.2%
2001	8.4%	4.5%	12.9%

That Sysco has had the resources and the internal structure to support its acquired companies in achieving continued growth has been its strength. When making an acquisition, Sysco usually has sought out the premier distributor in a particular market. Often, entrepreneurs have been willing to sell in order to keep their businesses intact as they have gotten close to retirement, have wanted to monetize, and have realized the value they have built in a tax-efficient manner. Sometimes, they have had no heirs who are willing or able to step in and run the business. By selling to Sysco, they have been able to realize a return on their investment while continuing to grow the business and maintain it as a viable entity. Typically, Sysco has structured its acquisitions with an earn-out provision over a period of years, which has motivated the seller to stay involved and thus has maintained profitability during the assimilation.

A critical metric for Sysco shareholders has been not only that the acquisitions have been non-dilutive to earnings but, typically, they have been expected to be accretive to earnings within the first couple of years. Acquisitions have been chosen based not only on their position in the market but also on what they could bring to the table, or the synergies that could be gained by joining with Sysco or vice versa. Perhaps it is a location that fills a particular geographical gap or a particular product base. Since going public, Sysco has made 145 acquisitions.

Foldout Companies

A suitable acquisition candidate often has not been available in a particular market that Sysco has been serving from remote locations. In a search for an alternative, in 1995 Sysco determined that once a specific sales level has been established—approximately $100 million to $125 million—a market then could support a stand-alone operation. The business in that marketplace could then be carved away from the existing remote Sysco company (or companies), and a new entity, known as a foldout, could be created.

Some advantages of this strategy have been that the foldout facility could be built to Sysco specifications, with Sysco technology systems and a custom-molded, homegrown management team, imported from other Sysco facilities that have enough knowledge of the industry and the Sysco culture to create a new operation. It has given both companies an opportunity to grow in their respective markets. And experience has shown that the 16 foldouts have grown faster than Sysco's overall growth rate.

One of the primary benefits of expanding in this manner is that it puts operations as close to the customers as possible, so that their needs are addressed quickly. Being closer to customers also means Sysco drives fewer miles, reducing fuel usage. Foldouts often are easier to assimilate than acquisitions, as many of the associates hired for a new foldout have been employed in other Sysco companies and are familiar with the company's culture. In addition, the technology systems put in place are Sysco-proven, and the facility can be built or modified according to Sysco specifications.

Helping Our Customers Succeed

Sysco's mission statement is "Helping Our Customers Succeed." Beginning with a promise to assist food service operators in building their businesses, many customer relationships have been nurtured, and countless dining trends have evolved along the way. Consuming meals prepared away from home has become as much a necessity as a choice.

Sysco employees, from the CEO to warehouse workers, understand the mission. Nearly 50% of Sysco employees are customer-facing. There are many stories about Sysco salespeople pitching in and helping its customers by washing dishes, waiting tables, and performing other duties when their employees unexpectedly have failed to show up. Sysco salespeople have taken their own families to the eating establishments of customers, building both business relationships and friendships. Sysco has created a new business review function, which features in-depth business reviews with Sysco's most valued customers. This review, unrelated to a sales call, has been used to determine the wants and needs of customers. It also has determined what works or what does not work, resulting in recommendations to help the customers' businesses become more profitable.

In fiscal 2006, Sysco performed 39,000 business reviews that, on average, increased sales to those customers by more than 15%. The business-development teams also focused on acquiring new customers by targeting the competitors' accounts with high potential and demonstrating the greater breadth and higher quality of Sysco products and services that could be tailored to the unique nature of each customer's business.

Sysco continues to develop customer-centric sales and marketing strength through its approximately 14,000 sales and marketing professionals. The company has the largest sales force in the industry, and this initiative was designed to focus its sales and marketing resources on customers and customer segments where it adds the most value, deepens partnerships, and increases profitability. Sysco's sales force is bigger than those of the next nine largest competitors combined. Sysco salespeople visit their key accounts three times a week, on average.

CARES

Sysco has designed a relationship-management initiative called Customers Are Really Everything to Sysco (CARES) to ensure that its customers receive the best service in the basic functions that customers need to run their businesses. This initiative ensures that companies receive all the products ordered, on time, and in undamaged condition. It makes sure that customers receive accurate invoices as well as the Sysco brand products that reflect the quality assurance inherent in the company and that they are served by helpful and knowledgeable sales and delivery associates.

The CARES program has evolved into a second phase, iCARE. Through this initiative, marketing associates have been trained to be more effective business consultants for customers by understanding a food service operation's profitability model, enabling them to analyze and develop menus, control inventories, and provide food-safety training. Through the Sysco Web site, customers may access a variety of third-party services to help them drive and increase customer traffic. These services include access to HR services, operational advice, financial services, food safety, music, pest control, and potential lenders to fund expansions or restaurant upgrades. Other services include assistance in creating guest birthday cards, table tents, banners, and posters as well as access to insurance carriers, credit-card services, and other services that have been unavailable to individual restaurants on a cost-effective basis. In this way, Sysco has aggregated its customers' buying power.

Culture

Sysco's entrepreneurial culture is emphasized on a daily basis in various ways:

Ownership: Sysco employees (approximately 65%) own stock (a share of the results of their hard work) in the company.

Autonomy: Its operating units have day-to-day autonomy to operate in their market, subject to strict central financial controls. Tom Lankford, Sysco's former president, stated, "Our units have complete autonomy relating to the front-of-the-house, customer-facing actions, and very little autonomy on the back of the house—financial controls, accounting, supply chain, ordering, and supplier relationships."

Responsibility: Sysco employees service customers in a way that gives them ownership and autonomy with respect to customers.

Open-door policy: Transparency, information sharing within and across business units, and a best-practices mentality all contribute to the excellent employee-retention rates: approximately 82% for sales and drivers, the key customer-facing positions, and more than 99% at the officer level, with the average tenure greater than twenty years.

Promotion from within: Sysco fills more than 95% of its promotions from within the company, and many of its top seven executives have been former line operators within their own business units, with intimate knowledge of the details. Sysco's new CEO, who took over in June 2009 is a twenty-plus year Sysco employee.

Rick Schnieders, the retiring chairman and CEO of Sysco, commented on the entrepreneurial culture:

> This culture was self-replicating. Our people feel good because many own stock, and they see results when everyone works hard and performs. Many, including our truck drivers, are on incentive-bonus programs and see compensation results directly and weekly. All this makes people work harder—they feel good about the results in which they share, and they feel good about working hard tomorrow, etc.

The Sysco entrepreneurial culture has produced three important results: (1) an entrepreneurial, iterative do-it-better mentality; (2) an openness to change, which Tom Lankford, the former president, called NIHBIDITA ("Not Invented Here, But I Did It Anyway"); and (3) a passionate focus on the details of execution day in and day out.

This passionate focus on daily execution is necessary when daily orders for more than 3.6 million cases of products that have to be sourced, loaded, and delivered the next day, on time, and defect-free are received, and the food preparer needs the food and other products in order to operate the business. As former CFO John Stubblefield remarked, "We are only as good as our last delivery."

In summary, Sysco is founded upon values that included integrity, reliability, autonomy, quality, and entrepreneurship, which have been the essence of the company's culture throughout its history. Its autonomous, entrepreneurial, decentralized culture, with its performance-based reward system, is one of the keys that has made the company successful as well as an integral part of the founding father's vision.

John Baugh knew from the beginning that running local businesses from a central location would not be effective in the food service business. Because all the company's operating subsidiaries have the autonomy to manage and operate themselves in an entrepreneurial fashion, they can respond quickly to customer needs. In other words, while Sysco has allowed its business units to operate the front of the house autonomously, the back of the house has remained centralized and controlled with a sophisticated measurement system.

The company's emphasis on metrics is evidenced by the meeting that Sysco's top executives attend every Wednesday afternoon to review the previous week's performance through the several hundred metrics for each one of its operating units. Sysco measures everything related to the receipt, movement, and delivery of products and services to customers, new-business development, every expense and capital expenditure, and its return on equity on a weekly basis.

Technology

Beginning in 1995, Sysco began working on the design and implementation of a new, all-encompassing technology system that would impact every aspect of the business: the Sysco Uniform System (SUS). Prior to that, there was no appropriate off-the-shelf package that met all the company's needs. So with the help of a consulting group, the company has developed its own system.

The first module of SUS was the Sysco Warehouse Management System (SWMS), which was installed in two phases: SWMS I, a nondirected put-away/locator system, and SWMS II, a fully directed warehouse-management system. SWMS directs the movement of products through receiving, storing, and shipping to optimize product rotation and freshness.

Modifications to the system have continued to be infused as methods and processes have improved. In 1998, the Sysco Order Selector (SOS), another module of SUS, was installed to improve order accuracy and inventory control. A wrist-mounted scanner verifies, at the touch of a finger, that the product selected is indeed what the customer has ordered, and virtually eliminates the opportunity for visual errors. Use of this unit has improved the accuracy of products selected from one error in 800 to one error in every 3,000 or 4,000 items picked by the product selector, significantly improving efficiency and customer satisfaction and reducing restocking costs.

Another enhancement, the Sysco Loading System (SLS), confirms the accuracy of products selected and then generates a map detailing the precise order of locations so that they are placed on the delivery trucks in the correct temperature area, stabilized, and easily accessible to the driver. Once the trucks are loaded, deliveries are made according to a Roadnet system that assigns optimum delivery routes to minimize driving distances and schedule deliveries within customers' desired time frames.

The building of the SUS system has given Sysco the ability to mine data on customers and use that data to provide better service, while using its resources more efficiently. With the new data, the company also has been able to stratify its customer base and determine which customers are the most profitable.

Controls

With its performance-based system, which demands strong financial controls, Sysco has maintained a tight rein, requiring that operating-company financial results and a myriad of operational and performance metrics be reported to executive management on a weekly basis. While the units are operated autonomously, they benchmark extensively on performance and operational metrics and share best practices in all areas of the business with peer operating units within the corporation, as it is difficult to find external comparables. The operating units compete with each other for operational recognition and rewards, and try to avoid being placed on the weekly Wednesday watch list of "underplan" performers.

The Sysco measurement system implements its pay for performance-based culture. It determines rewards and reinforces local autonomy and entrepreneurial spirit. The culture and the measurement system go hand in hand. As an example, its top five executive officers have 86% to 89% of their compensation incentive based with their base salaries being in the 25th to 50th percentile of its defined peer companies.

Conclusion

What can we learn from Sysco? First, it should be noted that nothing Sysco sells (products or services) is unique. What is its competitive advantage? Most compellingly, its competitive advantage is its internal growth system, which seamlessly, consistently, and in a self-reinforcing manner links its structure, strategy, work ethic, and entrepreneurial spirit to its execution process, leadership philosophy, people policies, and measurement and reward programs. Getting that right took years and Sysco constantly tries to perfect it. Sysco has taken advantage of a growth market, but even when that market began to flatten, it has focused relentlessly on executing more efficiently. At one point its CEO described Sysco as a logistics distribution company.

Sysco is a Smart Growth company. It has so far selected leaders who are operators, not financial engineers. Its growth story is a good learning template for young companies.

Notes

1. Edward D. Hess and Robert K. Kazanjian, eds., *The Search for Organic Growth* (Cambridge: Cambridge University Press, 2006), 147–148.
2. Ibid., 148.
3. Mark Lipton, *Guiding Growth: How Vision Keeps Companies on Course* (Boston: Harvard Business School Press, 2003), 36–37.
4. Ibid., 38–39.
5. Sven Smit, Caroline M. Thompson, and S. Patrick Viguerie, "The Do-or-Die Struggle for Growth," *McKinsey Quarterly* 3 (2005): 35–45.
6. Matthew S. Olson and Derek van Bever, *Stall Points: Most Companies Stop Growing—Yours Doesn't Have To* (New Haven, CT: Yale University Press, 2008).
7. Hess and Kazanjian, *Organic Growth*, 103–123.
8. Robert R. Wiggins and Timothy W. Ruefli, "Schumpeter's Ghost: Is Hypercompetition Making the Best of Times Shorter?" *Strategic Management Journal* 26, 10 (2005): 887–911.
9. Robert R. Wiggins and Timothy W. Ruefli, "Sustained Competitive Advantage: Temporal Dynamics and the Incidence and Persistence of Superior Economic Performance," *Organization Science* 13, 1 (2002): 100.

10. Larry E. Greiner, "Evolution and Revolution as Organizations Grow." *Harvard Business Review* 76, 3 (1998): 55–64.

11. Edward D. Hess, "SYSCO Corporation" (Case Study UVA-S-0140, University of Virginia Darden School Foundation, Charlottesville, 2007). This case has been updated for material events. All quotes directly from case.

CHAPTER 3

....

Economics

THEORIES OF GROWTH

IN THIS CHAPTER, I explore the field of economics, looking for empirical evidence supporting or questioning the validity of the Growth Mental Model.

Neoclassical and New Growth Economics

Much of economics involves the creation of algebraic macro-production theories that mathematically model inputs and outputs to achieve system equilibrium.[1] Growth means growth of output, and the model theoretically shows the relationship of how much input is needed to produce a specific output. This mathematical formula can be used to create as much or as little growth as desired. So, theoretically, an economist can create a formula that results in smooth and continuous growth. My question is not whether such a theoretical formula can be created. Rather, my question is, how well does such a formula represent the real world?

Of course, mathematical models of the economy are somewhat abstract as noted by Robert M. Solow, one of the three founders of modern neoclassical economics and a Nobel Laureate. When describing the ability to create a formula to model relatively smooth trendlike growth, Solow notes, "There is no implication that either sort of path ever occurs in its pure form in actual economies."[2] It is the case, however, that smooth trendlike growth is exactly what the Growth Mental Model calls for. Although economics can model smooth and continuous growth, Solow's statement challenges the model's scientific validity because it does not represent real-world behavior. The six studies in Chapter 2 are further evidence that the Growth Mental Model neither describes how companies actually operate nor represents a realistic goal for performance. Few companies can produce such smooth and continuous growth.

Neoclassical economics has evolved as economists look at different inputs to the production model, with the most recent advancement being the work of Paul Romer and others concerning the impact of technological innovation as an input.[3] The ability of neoclassical theory even to model smooth and continuous growth became suspect with the theory of Diminishing Marginal Returns adding a variable input into the production model. This theory states, basically, that at some point adding one more unit of input will not increase the output a corresponding amount. That is, at some point the return diminishes, making the formula no longer smooth and continuous. As Professor Solow stated above, these theoretical production models are merely models and not proof that the real world behaves that way.

Industrial Economics

The field of industrial economics has produced relevant empirical, firm-level research about corporate growth rates, their persistence, and their predictability that is useful in assessing the validity of the Growth Mental Model. Professor Paul Geroski of the London Business School reports that corporate growth rates are extremely hard to predict and that a period of growth is just as likely to be followed by a period of decline as it is by growth.[4]

In a study of corporate growth rates involving a sample of 147 large U.K. companies during the period 1955–1985, Professor Geroski with others noted that "somewhat to our surprise, we find that very few companies display any systemic, predictable patterns of growth even over the long run."[5] This is an important observation. One outcome of adherence to the Growth Mental Model's insistence on continuous growth as a measure of corporate success is Wall Street's focus on quarterly earnings reports. A defense of the Growth Mental Model could be that even if it does not work well in that short-term scenario, it is, nonetheless, valid in the longer term. However, Geroski's work shows that very few companies demonstrate systematic patterns of growth even over the long run. That is consistent with the research findings discussed in Chapter 2.

Additionally, Geroski notes that corporate growth is only weakly correlated with profits.[6] Because the underlying rationale for the Growth Mental Model is that growth *equals* profits, this finding is particularly troubling. According to Geroski, this unpredictability of corporate profits with corporate growth should not be surprising: "Unpredictability arises from several sources, and it has its roots in the fact that it is often difficult to predict the magnitude, effects, or timing of events that affect the size (growth) of a firm."[7]

Likewise, Eugene Fama and Kenneth French, confirming three previous studies, reported that dividend and earnings growth rates for 1950 to 2000 are largely unpredictable.[8] Underlying corporate growth is the complex interaction of many factors, both external and internal to the business. Basically, most business is not conducted through or reflected in the mathematical formulas of economics. Rather, most business is conducted with, by, and through people, and people are not rational predictable actors. When you add in this gumbo of potential human unpredictability, it is not surprising that growth is difficult to predict and challenging to manage in order to generate a smooth and continuous growth line. This common-sense result underlies much of the new theories in both behavioral and complexity economics and Smart Growth.

Another compelling piece of research dealing with the level and persistence of corporate growth rates is that done by Professors Louis Chan, Jason Karceski, and Josef Lakonishok, who studied the persistence and predictability of growth.[9]

Chan and his colleagues studied the growth in net sales, operating income before depreciation, and income before extraordinary items of more than 2,900 firms over a forty-six-year period, from 1951 to 1997. Their findings show that while there is some reliability in predicting sales growth there is no predictability in earnings growth. They also confirm Fama and French in their findings that the relationship of growth and profitability is largely unpredictable.

With respect to sales growth, Chan and his colleagues found that only 10% of the firms studied were able to grow sales greater than the median rate for four consecutive years and fewer than 10% of the firms were able to grow sales more than average for five or ten years. With respect to operating income before depreciation, only 7% of the firms studied were able to grow that variable greater than the median for four years; and 1% or less were able to do so for seven, eight, nine, or ten years.

The authors conclude: "To sum up, analysts and investors seem to believe that many firms' earnings can consistently grow at high rates for quite a few years. The evidence suggests, instead, that the number of such occurrences is not much different from what might be expected from sheer luck."[10] Their findings about the rarity and unpredictability of above-average growth applies across stock classifications: technology stocks, value stocks, growth stocks, large cap, mid-cap, and small cap stocks. Out of the 2,900 firms studied, only forty-three firms were able to put together a run for the preceding five years in growing income before extraordinary items and follow that with five succeeding years of above average growth. They found that the average real growth rate for the firms in their study, excluding stock dividends, was the same magnitude as the growth in GDP.

Considering the six studies discussed in Chapter 2 plus the above studies, one can conclude that the Growth Mental Model is more fiction than a representation of achievable reality.

Penrose: A Resource-Based View of the Firm

If the Growth Mental Model is a fiction, where can we look for a better understanding of how companies grow? In 1959, Edith Penrose published a seminal work in economics focusing on the firm and its growth.[11] She believed that growth is an evolutionary process that does not occur smoothly or continuously but rather occurs in spurts.

Penrose rejected the theory that a firm has an optimal size or profit potential. In her view, growth is dependent on the ambitions of the managers, their ability to recognize and actualize opportunities, on market conditions, and on the managers' abilities to deal with uncertainty and risk. As importantly, Penrose viewed a firm's ability to grow as dependent on it having excess managerial capacity. That is, growth requires managers to have the time to focus on growth and those managers, as a team, need to experience growth together and learn how to work together through the growth process.

Penrose's theory of growth focuses on the dynamics of managerial personal relationships, believing that the people side of the business significantly impacts the ability to grow. To make this point, she cited the legendary neoclassical economist R. F. Harrod for the proposition that the reason an entrepreneurial business cannot grow as fast as the opportunity presents itself is because a firm is a delicate organism with myriad complicated labor and management relationships. Once again, we find that people make growth complex and difficult. The movement from mathematical models to the real world brings people into play, and peoples' behaviors are not easily mathematically modeled.

Penrose contended that growth depends on people having the time and learned knowledge to grow. She saw growth as a messy process, a view that does not fit well with the assumptions of the Growth Mental Model.

Joseph Schumpeter: Creative Destruction

Professor Schumpeter fled Europe to escape Nazi rule and became an esteemed professor at Harvard University. He believed the capitalist system, while not perfect, was superior to the socialist system. He also believed the capitalist system needed oversight to prevent abuses.[12]

According to Schumpeter, the backbone of capitalism is entrepreneurship and it is through entrepreneurship that advances are made that can raise the standard of living of more people. These advances occur through innovation and innovations could occur from new goods, new markets, new production or transportation processes, or new ways of organizing or managing businesses. He believed that the capitalist system would thrive when enough innovation occurs so that the forces of innovation destroy the old way—a process he called Creative Destruction.

Like Penrose, Schumpeter viewed the economic world as being more complex and evolutionary than represented by the neoclassical linear production models. Schumpeter's focus was not on growth per se; he talked about innovation. Schumpeter's views do not directly confirm or disprove the Growth Mental Model. Nonetheless, an argument can be made that he would substitute the rule that a firm must "innovate or die" for the Growth Mental Model's imperative of "grow or die." In addition, he would likely reject the goal of smooth and continuous growth, because he talked in terms of the gales and waves of innovation, which does not suggest smoothness or continuity. Both Penrose's and Schumpeter's views of growth or innovation as a change process and a learning process fit more comfortably with the new field of complexity economics, which I discuss next.

Complexity Economics

All branches of economics are trying to do the same thing: model real-world behavior. The difference is some economic theorists build a model and then go test it against reality and others view reality and try to make sense of it through a model of what they view. Complexity economics does the latter.[13]

Complexity economics has grown out of complexity systems theory, behavioral and cognitive psychology, and evolutionary biology. Complexity economics rejects the theory that an economic system is a linear, smooth, balanced system and instead posits that economic systems are dynamic, interactive, adaptive, evolving systems that act in unpredictable ways and, in some cases, with significant unpredictable results.

Complexity economics views growth as evolutionary improvement resulting from constant experiments, tests, and forays into new directions. Organizations that thrive in this type of environment are able to exploit existing opportunities while also exploring new opportunities. This fits well with Penrose's view that growth can only occur when a firm has excess managerial capacity and the time to explore new opportunities.

Unlike industrial economics, complexity economics theorizes that at some point in an organization's life cycle, size or scale reaches a point where size has diminishing returns. This is because the complexity brought on by size creates costs in excess of the benefits of such marginal increases in size. Complexity economics posits that at some point every organization reaches a maximum productive size and so rejects the assumptions of the Growth Mental Model. Rather than accept the belief that firms must grow or die, complexity economists probably favor the belief that firms must adapt or die or evolve or die.

Although unlikely to endorse grow or die, what is interesting to consider about Penrose, Schumpeter, and complexity economists is that all would also likely reject the view that an organization can remain static and thrive. Learning, adapting to outside events (such as markets and competition), internal knowledge sharing, improving, innovating, and exploring all require businesses to change to remain relevant in their environments. However, the dynamics of this learning, improving, and innovating does not require growth in size or revenue. Growth can occur without improvement. And improvement can occur without growth. Growth by itself will not prevent a company's death. Business survival may be more an issue of constant improvement than growth.

My research findings and applied consulting experience are more compatible with complexity economics theories of growth—a complex change process built upon an experimental model—and are the basis for my Smart Growth concept.

Ecological Steady-State Economics

Ecological steady-state economics rejects the theory that growth has no limits because the world has a finite amount of resources or inputs that can be used for production.[14] Herman Daly, the founder of this branch of economics, believes that growth has to be limited and that the planet cannot support a Western standard of living for everyone. His theory advances the view that growth should reach a steady state where the earth's resources are sustained and not depleted. Growth has its limits in this branch of economics and it would arguably reject the assumption of unlimited growth and grow or die.

Given the broader environmental and economic issues facing the global market today, Daly's view of growth is both prescriptive (businesses should find ways to establish their niche with an eye toward diminished access to resources and markets and find a comfortable steady state) and practical (at some point in the not-to-distant future the hard constraints of the planet's resources will curtail growth). In both cases, Daly's views question both the wisdom and viability of the Growth Mental Model.

Behavioral Economics

Behavioral economics, led by the work of Professor Daniel Kahneman, questions many tenets of neoclassical economics, especially the belief that the economic system is made up of rational actors who, with complete information, will act to create perfect competition, resulting in efficient markets and predictable economic equilibrium.[15] Behavioral economics posits that people can and often do act irrationally and in ways that do not maximize value. Further, they act inconsistently and unpredictably, failing to learn, and look for relative comparisons as much as absolute comparisons. Once you inject human irrationality and failure to learn into the mix (and this is true of both customers and managers), it is not surprising that business growth is not the smooth, continuous, linear ideal that neoclassical economics mathematically model but, rather, one characterized by spurts, zigzags, cycles, and upward and downward spikes.

Conclusion: Economics—Theories of Growth

The closest theoretical support for the Growth Mental Model appears to be the neoclassical school of economics, whose mathematical description of the economy produces a linear production model that suggests, in theory, that smooth and continuous growth is possible. However, even neoclassical economists, including Robert Solow, one of the founders of the neoclassical school, note that the linear production model has little direct application in the real world. There are simply too many other variables to consider. So at its most basic level, the Growth Mental Model's demand for smooth and continuous growth is only a theoretical construct. There is even less support for the Growth Mental Model in other fields of economics, which look at how businesses actually behave. For example, research on growth rates and business size in industrial economics concludes that predictable business growth is no more than a chance event and that continuous above-average growth is rare.

So, in the real world, businesses only rarely, and briefly at best, are able to generate continuous growth numbers, even with an array of creative accounting tools available. Why is this the case? Penrose's resource-based analysis of business, Schumpeter's creative destruction view of innovation, complexity economics, and behavioral economics all contribute to an explanation of why smooth and continuous growth is unrealistic. A key missing variable in the Growth Mental Model is one that includes human beings who bring unpredictability, irrationality, and personal relationship dynamics into play.

Given the rarity of any company meeting the Wall Street Rules of continuous growth, and ample research about how companies really grow, what can explain the dominance of the Growth Mental Model? Adherence to it, in spite of the evidence against its usefulness, continues to fuel the Earnings Game, producing opaque earnings statements, short-term myopia, and the premature reallocation of capital. The dynamics generated by the Growth Mental Model also result in the premature destruction of businesses, negatively impacting innocent employees, their families, and their communities. The Growth Mental Model should be discarded.

We have learned that growth is rarely continuous and that it is a dynamic complex process. Even in good companies, growth can be difficult. Growth is both a learning process and a change process, and both of those processes are hard and take time. An example of this can be found at McDonald's Corporation. As you read the McDonald's case, ask yourself: How has McDonald's tried to remain entrepreneurial? Since 2000, how has McDonald's tried to reignite growth? Why has McDonald's focused on being better not bigger? Why is it so hard to execute growth strategies? How does McDonald's achieve high employee engagement in franchised stores?

McDonald's Corporation Case

Incorporated in 1955, McDonald's rapidly became the largest fast-food-restaurant organization in the world.[16] At the end of 2007, its 31,377 stores served nearly 50 million people every day in 118 countries. Some 78% of McDonald's stores were operated by franchisees or by affiliates, and 22% were operated directly by the company. The McDonald's system employed nearly 465,000 people, and in 2008 its revenue was $23.5 billion. In February 2009, McDonald's had a market capitalization of $58 billion.

McDonald's strategy in 2009 continues to be "Plan To Win," with a focus on "being better, not just bigger" and delivering better restaurant experiences to its customers. McDonald's evolution to this strategy shows how its growth has been neither smooth nor continuous, especially in its U.S. operations. McDonald's hit a growth plateau and had to adjust its focus and redefine what growth meant at McDonald's. McDonald's is a story of growth resiliency.

Brief History

In 1955, Ray Kroc, a fifty-two-year-old milkshake-machine salesman, opened his first McDonald's restaurant in Des Plaines, Illinois, as a franchising agent for Maurice and Richard McDonald, who operated a successful fast-food restaurant in San Bernardino, California. After years of trial and error, the McDonald brothers had devised a fast-food-operation system that offered a ten-item menu. Customers lined up for cheaply priced hamburgers, french fries, and milkshakes in a clean environment that offered prompt service.

Originally, Kroc's primary interest in the burgeoning fast-food industry had been to maximize his milkshake-machine sales to McDonald's franchises. But the McDonald's operating system attracted customer-oriented salesman Kroc's attention and triggered his idea to turn McDonald's into a fast-food chain that appealed to young families.

Kroc believed that McDonald's would be profitable if it delivered quality, service, and cleanliness (QSC) to its customers, with the long-range goal of perfection. Kroc bought out the McDonald brothers for $2.7 million in 1961 and improved the operating and franchise system further. He was relentless in his pursuit of complete operational compliance from his franchises. His commitment to creating an exceptional customer experience did not stop at the edge of the store parking lot, either; Kroc was known to pick up McDonald's product–related rubbish around its stores whenever an opportunity arose.

In the 1960s and 1970s, suburbanization greatly contributed to the company's growth, both in sales and in the number of stores in the United States. In 1963, McDonald's opened its 500th store and sold its billionth hamburger. Skillful marketing and new products helped growth. For example, in 1962, McDonald's introduced the Golden Arches and Ronald McDonald through mass-media marketing campaigns and created a nationwide brand image, introducing such new products as the Quarter Pounder (1962), Filet-O-Fish (1963), Hot Apple Pie (late 1960s), Big Mac (1968), Egg McMuffin (1973), and the Happy Meal (1979), all of which grew sales. McDonald's went public in 1965.

International growth for the fast-food chain started with a store in British Columbia, Canada, in 1967. In 1971, McDonald's opened stores in Australia, Germany, Guam, Holland, and Japan. Over the years, the system evolved into five global-market regions: the United States; Europe; Asia/Pacific, Middle East, and Africa (APMEA); Latin America; and Canada.

The Franchise System

Kroc's background in sales helped him develop a franchise system that was different. In the 1950s, franchisors commonly profited by selling territorial rights, equipment, and supplies to their franchisees. But Kroc saw an inherent conflict of interest in such an arrangement. Under his system, McDonald's did not sell supplies to its franchisees because Kroc firmly believed that his long-term success depended on the success of his franchisees, who he considered and treated as business partners.

Originally, Kroc sold single-store franchises for an initial fee of $950 and a royalty of 1.9% of annual gross sales. He did not allow absentee ownership. He offered extensive support and training to his franchisees so they could attain excellence and optimize their earnings. His commitment to support and train his franchisees led to the establishment, in 1961, of McDonald's first Hamburger University, which later spawned regional training departments and was duplicated in seven other countries around the globe.

In addition to franchise stores, Kroc decided to have company-operated stores for experimental and training purposes. He capped the number of company-operated stores at 30% of all stores because he believed that the company's "vitality depend[ed] on the energy of many individual owner-operators."[17]

McDonald's also provided extensive support in advertising and marketing to its franchisees. Each store was required to spend at least 4% of its gross sales annually for advertising and promotion, but the franchisees had the freedom to create their own advertising through local advertising agencies and regional advertising cooperatives. The company and franchisees also had the option to combine their resources through the National Advertising Fund to purchase national mass media advertising. As for the qualifications of franchisees, Kroc noted: "McDonald's doesn't confer success on anyone. It takes guts and staying power to make it with one of our restaurants. At the same time, it doesn't require any unusual aptitude or intellect. Any man with common sense, dedication to principles, and a love of hard work can do it."[18]

Besides the hard work, Kroc encouraged franchisees to create grassroots innovations necessitated by competition in local markets. Franchisees had the latitude to test ideas in their local markets, and McDonald's had the corporate resources to commercialize promising new ideas that could benefit the system.

As McDonald's grew, however, centralization and bureaucracy began to stifle innovation, and franchisees became frustrated. To decentralize management decision making and keep innovation alive across the system, Kroc instituted some major restructuring—starting in the late 1960s, when McDonald's restaurants numbered about 650—by dividing the country into autonomous regions because he believed that "authority should go with a job" and the people closest to customers should make management decisions.[19] When Kroc handed the company over to Fred Turner in 1974,

Turner, following the same philosophy, decentralized the corporate structure and increased regional managers' authority. Another restructuring took place in 1999 because franchisees complained about poor communication and excess bureaucracy.

Kroc also believed that McDonald's had a responsibility to give back to the community, and he made community service part of the McDonald's franchise system. He started the first Ronald McDonald House in 1974, to house families who needed a place to stay close to the hospital where their sick children were receiving medical treatment. To foster community spirit, Kroc mostly recruited mom-and-pop franchisees and encouraged them to get involved with grassroots service activities in their communities. After Kroc died in 1984, Ronald McDonald House was turned into Ronald McDonald House Charities (RMHC). RMHC's activities were expanded to include other programs that focus on improving children's health and well-being.

In 2007, McDonald's had about 2,400 franchisees in the United States, and 83% of them owned more than one store. McDonald's also had the largest number of minority and female franchisees in the fast-food industry, with women and minorities making up more than 37% of all its franchisees. The McDonald's selling pitch to prospective franchisees, "You are in business for yourself, but not by yourself," symbolized the wide support offered by the McDonald's system.

Franchisees paid an initial fee of $45,000 and an ongoing royalty fee of 12.5% of gross sales (i.e., 4% service fee, 4% advertising and promotion, rent, and fees for audit, inspection, software maintenance, etc.). The company's initial investment for a traditional store ranged from $730,750 to $1,549,000, and determined the rate for annual rent, which varied between 8.5% and 14% of the initial investment. Because McDonald's leased or subleased store properties to franchisees, revenue from the sale or lease of real estate and services represented about 41% of its total revenue in 2006. The annual sales volume per U.S. store ranged from $332,000 to $7,933,000, averaging $2,114,000. For a store with a $2 million sales volume, operating income before rent and other occupancy costs averaged $561,000, or 28.1% of sales.

After Kroc

In 1976, under Fred Turner's leadership, McDonald's sales reached $3 billion, and it opened its 4,000th store. By 1980, McDonald's had over 6,000 stores, and in the early 1980s, the fast-food chain survived the "burger wars" against its two major competitors, Burger King and Wendy's. Mc-Donald's continued to grow its sales and market share, again by diversifying its menu to satisfy changing customer tastes (e.g., introducing Chicken McNuggets and ready-to-eat salads for health-conscious customers).

In March 1987, Turner was succeeded by Michael Quinlan as CEO, under whose leadership McDonald's pursued aggressive high-growth strategies around the globe. Even in what was believed to be a saturated market, it expanded the number of U.S. stores, from 9,000 in 1991 to 12,500, in 1997—a nearly 40% increase. This strategy cut into the sales of existing stores and frustrated franchisees, with the result that same-store sales went flat in the mid-1990s.

So, by the late 1990s, some financial analysts viewed McDonald's as a solid company afflicted with inertia largely because of its sluggish U.S. business. In June 1998, responding to the decline in revenue, McDonald's eliminated a little over 500 jobs—about 23%—at its headquarters, the first job cut in its history.

Jack Greenberg (August 1998–December 2002)

Jack Greenberg was charged with turning around the sluggish U.S. business eighteen months before he even became CEO, in August 1998. Greenberg, an affable and self-effacing accountant from the firm of Arthur Young, joined McDonald's as its CFO in 1982. He learned the fundamentals of the McDonald's operation while serving concurrently as a regional manager and as CFO. Greenberg saw a need for McDonald's to go back to its roots: growth through new menu selections and operational innovations.

Armed with his financial and field expertise, Greenberg launched four major initiatives as CEO. First, in an attempt to improve quality and encourage innovation, he introduced a new, flexible, computerized food-preparation system called "Made-for-You." Second, he expanded the menu for revenue growth. Third, he extended the McDonald's brand to McCafe, McTreat Spot, and McSnack Spot. Finally, he started to operate several fast-food chains under such brand names as Boston Market, Chipotle (Mexican), Donatos Pizzeria (thin-crust pizza), Pret A Manger (upscale sandwiches), and Aroma (British coffee shops). This multibrand expansion was an experiment to capture new "meal occasions." According to an industry analyst, "Under Jack Greenberg, McDonald's [was] starting to act like other really smart global companies."[20]

Knowing the difficulty franchisees had in attracting and retaining good employees and remaining consistent with Kroc's belief that McDonald's was a people business, Greenberg made people one of the company's major areas of strategic focus: "We've always prided ourselves on training, but I think we're at a different level of commitment to our people, at all levels of the organization, to develop them and train them and orient them better to McDonald's."[21]

The company's relationships with its U.S. franchisees were perceived to be fairly adversarial in 1996–1997, owing to its aggressive store expansion. Still, Greenberg's people-focused initiatives improved the company's relationships with its franchisees, customers, and competitors. Recognizing his efforts, *Restaurants & Institutions* magazine selected Greenberg as its 1999 Executive of the Year.

In 2001, McDonald's eliminated 700 jobs in the United States, including some through store closings, while it extended its array of benefits, such as discounts for day-care centers and homeowners' insurance, to hourly workers. Numerous attempts to innovate for revenue growth failed, and quarterly profits kept declining because of sluggish U.S. sales, negative publicity related to mad-cow disease in Europe, and weakened global economies, especially in Latin America and Asia. In the United States, the Made-for-You kitchen backfired for two reasons. The first was its installation cost of $25,000 per store, about half of which McDonald's subsidized. The second was slow service. McDonald's mystery shoppers—an undercover, self-diagnostic program initiated in February 2002—found that its stores "were meeting speed-of-service standards only 46% of the time." They also reported "complaints of rude service, slow service, unprofessional employees, and inaccurate service."[22] The company's relationships with its franchisees and customers were declining.

In the third quarter of 2002, U.S. same-store sales fell 2.8%, and European same-store sales fell 1.3%.[23] The low-cost Dollar Menu, introduced in October 2002 to boost U.S. sales, was a failure. These sales results led McDonald's to dramatically reduce restaurant openings to 600 worldwide, down from a high of about 2,000 in 1996.[24] In the last quarter of 2002, McDonald's reported its first quarterly loss, $343.8 million, reflecting the closure of more than 700 stores—primarily in the United States and Japan—and the associated charge of $853 million. To reinvigorate its business, the board appointed James Cantalupo as CEO to replace Greenberg, effective January 2003. On March 11, 2003, the company's stock price plunged to $12.42—the lowest since the 1999 split at $45.31.

James R. Cantalupo (January 2003–April 2004)

Cantalupo ascended to the CEO position from his position of president, after serving twenty-eight years at McDonald's. Under Cantalupo's leadership, McDonald's adopted three comprehensive and synergetic revitalization strategies: a return to the operational excellence and leadership marketing that resonated with people around the world, system alignment around the customer-centered Plan to Win, and financial stewardship for strength. In essence, as Cantalupo put it, the revitalization strategies were designed to "grow by being better rather than being bigger" and to build brand loyalty.

The Plan to Win was designed to "deliver operational excellence and leadership marketing" and contained "aggressive goals and measures for success on the five drivers of exceptional customer experience—people, products, place, price, and promotion ('5Ps')."[25] These 5Ps became the corporate mantra for McDonald's. For each driver, McDonald's set specific criteria and measurements to gauge its improvement. The criteria for people were service, hospitality, and pride among employees. Measures for people included "increase in speed-of-service and friendliness scores, and a reduction in service-related complaints." Most important, the Plan to Win clearly stated that the company's "restaurant staffs are responsible for delivering exceptional customer experiences."[26]

McDonald's introduced cashless payment and extended hours to better serve its customers. To better train crews, McDonald's developed e-learning programs, emphasized hospitality training, and simplified the operational environment for efficiency. It also introduced new, "hipper" restaurant designs to appeal to young adults and explored more favorable pricing from its suppliers.

Cantalupo's tenure as McDonald's CEO abruptly ended on April 18, 2004. He died of a heart attack a few hours before he was scheduled to address hundreds of franchisees from around the world at the company's biennial owner-operator convention in Orlando, Florida. One executive who was at the convention recalled the moment when he and others learned of Cantalupo's passing: "[W]e pulled together and gave each other hugs and held hands. That's when [the power of the McDonald's family] really hit me—any and all of our success is because of the people we work with and work for."[27] Tapping into the deep talent bench on the McDonald's management team, the board appointed Charlie Bell as CEO within hours of Cantalupo's death.

Charlie Bell (April–November 2004)

Bell was an energetic, forty-three-year-old Australia native who started at a McDonald's as a part-timer in Sydney at the age of fifteen. He had broad international experience and was known for his fresh thinking (e.g., the introduction of McCafe in Australia). Prior to his appointment as CEO, Bell, as president and chief operating officer, had worked closely with CEO Cantalupo and was instrumental in implementing both the back-to-basics strategy at store level and the award-winning global campaign "I'm lovin' it."[28]

Bell stayed the course with the Plan to Win. Unfortunately, in May 2004, Bell was diagnosed with cancer and underwent surgery sixteen days after Cantalupo died. He never fully recovered and resigned his CEO position in November 2004 to fight his cancer. The board acted immediately to replace him, elevating sixty-year-old Vice President James Skinner to CEO.

James Skinner (November 2004–Present)

Skinner initially worked as a crewmember for seven months at a McDonald's restaurant in 1962. He then served in the U.S. Navy for over nine years and in 1971 joined McDonald's as a restaurant manager-trainee in Carpentersville, Illinois. Thereafter, Skinner spent most of his McDonald's career overseas. Mourning the loss of his friends and leaders, Cantalupo and Bell, Skinner considered his ascent to CEO bittersweet. "Change in leadership does not mean change in strategy. We know—and our sales results prove it—that when we focus on our customers and our restaurants, McDonald's can't be beat. . . . [I will serve as CEO] as long as I can make a meaningful contribution."[29]

In fact, despite unprecedented leadership turmoil—three CEOs in nine months—the Plan to Win continued to generate results. In March 2005, Skinner listed his priorities as "driving long-term, sustainable profitable growth, talent development, and succession planning; and playing a leadership role in promoting balanced, active lifestyles to McDonald's customers."[30] In 2005, commenting on McDonald's fiftieth anniversary, Skinner stated:

> I see a company that remains true to the values that got us here over all these years as we grew from one restaurant to more than 31,000 today. Focusing on our customers and our restaurants and on giving

back to the communities and the "quality, service, cleanliness and value" [philosophy] have caused us to be so successful. I look at how far the company has come, yet realize how far we have to go with our contributions to communities, customers, and society. . . . [W]hat I am most proud of is that I've stayed committed to McDonald's for these 33 years because of the commitment McDonald's made to me. [McDonald's] has Midwestern values: integrity, credibility, honesty, and an overwhelming sense of fairness in how we treat our customers, employees, franchisees, and suppliers.[31]

Today, like Skinner, twenty of McDonald's top executives started working for McDonald's in a restaurant, and 67,000 of McDonald's restaurant managers and assistant managers started as restaurant staff. Today 41% of McDonald's franchisees are minorities or women.

In 2005, Skinner put renewed focus on employees. McDonald's enhanced its medical-insurance coverage for its part-time and full-time workforce and encouraged its employees to participate in 401(k) plans. Managers' 401(k) enrollment more than doubled, to approximately 90%, while hourly employees' participation doubled to more than 20%. Individual franchisees improved employee benefits as well. For example, to build trusting relationships and reduce turnover, Steve Bigari, who owned nine McDonald's restaurants, implemented McFamily Benefits, which included access to transportation, education, health care, housing, child care, and even stock options. He was able to offer these programs because of collaboration among state, nonprofit, and private agencies. All employees qualified after ninety days.

To redefine "McJob," the term coined in the 1980s to describe an unstimulating, low-paying job with few prospects, McDonald's launched the recruiting campaign "At McDonald's You Can Go Anywhere!" Contrary to the general perception of McJob, more than 40% of the company's top fifty officers had started as restaurant crewmembers.

To better identify and train high-potential job candidates who were suited for customer service and teamwork, McDonald's created a screening questionnaire and upgraded its orientation process. In 2007, about half of its U.S. stores required job applicants to take the questionnaire.

The Plan to Win's holistic approach to recruit, train, develop, and retain people was intended to enhance employees' pride in working at McDonald's and strengthen their commitment to their work. Various efforts helped reduce manager turnover to 10%–20% in 2004, well below the restaurant-industry average of 33%. In 2004, the crew-turnover rate at McDonald's was

90% (down from 150% a few years earlier), compared with the industry average of about 111%. The ninety-day crew-turnover rate was reduced to 40%–45% in 2004, down from 50% in 2001.

Skinner has also focused on food quality, nutrition, and supply chain standards. McDonald's now claims to sell only 100% beef, 100% chicken, and Grade A eggs and that it audits and inspects its suppliers regularly. Each McDonald's restaurant goes through over seventy safety protocols every day.

Today, McDonald's continues to prosper from its focus on being better not being bigger and has set growth targets of increasing sales and revenue between 3% and 5% a year and because of continued operating efficiencies increasing average operating income between 6% and 7% a year.

McDonald's demonstrates that a company can reenergize itself after growth slips and that at some point the focus on expansion has to turn to a focus on running the existing business better with more modest top-line growth.

Notes

1. Robert M. Solow, "Perspectives on Growth Theory," *Journal of Economic Perspectives* 8, 1 (1994): 45–54; Robert M. Solow, "The Last 50 Years in Growth Theory and the Next 10," *Oxford Review of Economic Policy* 23, 1 (2007): 3–14; Richard Nelson, "How New Is New Growth Theory?" *Challenge* 40, 5 (1997): 29–58; Paul M. Romer, "Why, Indeed, in America? Theory, History, and the Origins of Modern Economic Growth," *American Economic Review* 86, 2 (1996): 202–206; Paul M. Romer, "Increasing Returns and Long-Run Growth," *Journal of Political Economy* 94, 51 (1986): 1002–1037.
2. Robert M. Solow, "The Neoclassical Theory of Growth and Distribution," *BNL Quarterly Review* 215 (2000): 349.
3. Paul M. Romer, "The Origins of Endogenous Growth," *Journal of Economic Perspectives* 8, 1 (1994): 3–22.
4. Paul A. Geroski, "Understanding the Implications of Empirical Work on Corporate Growth Rates," *Managerial and Decision Economics* 26, 2 (2005): 129.
5. Paul A. Geroski, S. Lazarova, G. Urga, and C. F. Walters, "Are Differences in Firm Size Transitory or Permanent?" *Journal of Applied Econometrics* 18, 1 (2003): 48.
6. Geroski, "Understanding the Implications," 129.
7. Ibid., 135.
8. Eugene F. Fama and Kenneth R. French, "The Equity Premium," *Journal of Finance* 57, 2 (2002): 640.

9. Louis K. C. Chan, Jason Karceski, and Josef Lakonishok, "The Level and Persistence of Growth Rates," *Journal of Finance* 58, 2 (2003): 643–684.

10. Ibid., 655.

11. Edith Penrose, "The Theory of the Growth of the Firm," in *The International Encyclopedia of Business and Management*, ed. Malcolm Warner (Oxford: Oxford University Press, 1996), 2440–2448.

12. Joseph A. Schumpeter, *Capitalism, Socialism and Democracy* (New York: HarperCollins, 2008); Thomas K. McCraw, *Prophet of Innovation: Joseph Schumpeter and Creative Destruction* (Cambridge, MA: Harvard University Press, 2007).

13. Eric D. Beinhocker, *The Origin of Wealth: The Radical Remaking of Economics and What It Means for Business and Society* (Boston: Harvard Business School Press, 2006).

14. John Attarian, "The Steady-State Economy: What It Is, Why We Need It," Negative Population Growth, 2004, www.npg.org/forum_series?steadystate.html; Richard W. England, "Natural Capital and the Theory of Economic Growth," *Ecological Economics* 34 (2000): 425–431.

15. Daniel Kahneman, "Maps of Bounded Rationality: Psychology for Behavioral Economics," *American Economic Review* 93, 5 (2003): 1449–1475; Daniel Kahneman and Alan B. Krueger, "Developments in the Measurement of Subjective Well-Being," *Journal of Economic Perspectives* 20, 1 (2006): 3–24.

16. Edward D. Hess, "McDonald's Corporation" (Case Study UVA-S-0147, University of Virginia Darden School Foundation, Charlottesville, 2008). This case has been updated for material events. All quotes are directly from the case.

17. Ray Kroc, *Grinding It Out: The Making of McDonald's* (New York: St. Martin's Press, 1987), 109.

18. Ibid., 111.

19. Ibid., 143.

20. Patricia Sellers, "McDonald's Starts Over," *Fortune*, June 22, 1998, 35.

21. Scott Hume, "Jack Greenberg's New Populism," *Restaurants & Institutions*, July 1, 1999, 60–66.

22. David Stired, "Fast Food, Slow Service," *Fortune*, September 30, 2002, 38.

23. Shirley Leung, "McDonald's Posts 11% Drop in Net; Fewer Restaurants to Be Opened," *Wall Street Journal*, October 23, 2002, B3.

24. Ibid., B3.

25. McDonald's Corporation (March 5, 2004), *McDonald's Corporation's Annual Report*, retrieved August 30, 2009, from U.S. Securities and Exchange Commission's EDGAR database, www.sec.gov/Archives/edgar/data/63908/000119312504035282/d10k.htm.

26. McDonald's Corporation (November 3, 2003), *McDonald's Corporation's Current Report*, retrieved August 30, 2009, from U.S. Securities and Exchange Commission's EDGAR database, www.sec.gov/Archives/edgar/data/63908/000104746903035700/a2121466z8-k.htm.

27. Amy Garber, "The Golden Anniversary of the Golden Arches," *Nation's Restaurant News*, April 4, 2005, 37.

28. *Advertising Age* named McDonald's the Marketer of the Year for 2004.

29. Amy Garber, "New MCD Chief: Strategy to Stay the Same," *Nation's Restaurant News*, December 13, 2004, 1–2.

30. McDonalds Corporation, "Report on the Corporate Responsibility Committee of the Board of Directors of McDonald's Corporation: Regarding the Adequacy and Effectiveness of McDonald's Policies, Plans and Strategies to Support Balanced Lifestyles," www.aboutmcdonalds.com/mcd/investors/corporate_governance/ board_report_on_strategies_to_support_balanced_active_lifestyles.html? DCSext.destination=http://www.aboutmcdonalds.com/mcd/investors/ corporate_governance/board_report_on_strategies_to_support_balanced_ active_lifestyles.html.

31. Scott Hume, "Interface: Jim Skinner," *Restaurants & Institutions*, March 1, 2005, 17.

CHAPTER 4

Organizational Design and Strategy

THEORIES OF GROWTH

THIS CHAPTER FOCUSES on research in organizational design and corporate strategy in a search for evidence that supports or challenges the validity of the Growth Mental Model. This research looks at corporate half-truths, strategic sustainable competitive advantage, hypercompetition, how growth progresses or occurs in good growth companies, and company life cycles. Although none of the research deals directly with the Growth Mental Model, this research calls into question the underlying assumption that business growth should be smooth and continuous over long periods of time and challenges the axiom of "grow or die."

Corporate Half-Truths

Management consulting firms, some academics, and the business press continually espouse the newest theory for business success to help companies grow. Professors Jeffrey Pfeffer and Robert Sutton, in their outstanding book on the need for more evidence-based management decisions and less fad following, contend that many slogans and new theories of growth are only half-truths: "Change and innovation are nasty double-edged swords. When companies try something new, it usually fails."[1]

Based on their extensive research, Pfeffer and Sutton report that the failure rates for mergers and acquisitions, business process improvements, new human resource systems, large technology system implementations, and new product rollouts are actually much higher than most managers think.[2]

They conclude that businesses' efforts to change, grow, and innovate are as likely to fail as they are likely to succeed, which would make smooth and continuous growth hard to manage and predict. They recommend bringing experimental rigor to corporate theories by requiring proof, for example, that companies either grow or die. I hypothesize that in many cases companies are likely to grow and die if they fail to manage their particular risks of growth. Growth can stress a business's leadership, culture, and employees; its quality and financial controls; and its execution processes. Further, as becomes evident, it can dilute a business's customer value proposition. Starbucks, Harley-Davidson, and JetBlue are recent examples of how growth is not always good, and they are discussed in Chapter 7.

Businesses can try new things and new strategies but they, and the market, should be aware that there is as much chance those efforts will fail as succeed. So, given that evidence, how can Wall Street, boards of directors, managers, and shareholders reasonably expect most businesses to successfully choose and execute the right growth strategy, and do so repeatedly, which is what smooth and continuous growth would require?

One reason smooth and continuous growth is so difficult to achieve is because growth represents change. New products must be developed, new markets explored, new stores opened, and new personnel hired and trained. For companies to grow, their people must grow. And there are limits to the amount of change that can be assimilated at any one time. This point was made to me by several private company CEOs who participated in my 2008 study on the private company managerial challenges of growth. As one of the study's CEOs stated: "My business can grow much faster than my people can grow."[3]

What theorists forget, as do some strategy consultants, is that good strategies are not good unless people can execute them. That fact brings to bear the people limitation: people can only change so much, so fast, and so often, and any change will generate mistakes.

The Growth Mental Model assumes smooth and continuous growth. That assumption creates a standard that, based on the research discussed in prior chapters, fewer than 10% of the companies can achieve for any significant period of time.

Sustainable Competitive Advantage

Business strategy's primary objective is to identify how an organization can successfully compete in the marketplace. Strategy guides what a company should and should not do. Competing in the marketplace requires a company to take into account its external environment, as evidenced by Michael Porter's "5 Forces," and its internal environment as evidenced by its resources and core competencies.[4] All strategy models, whether their focus is external or internal to the business, have the same goal: to create a competitive advantage. As Porter states, "The fundamental basis of above-average performance in the long-run is sustainable competitive advantage."[5]

For years, strategists have espoused the view that successful companies need a sustainable competitive advantage in order to be successful. The key word to focus on is "sustainable" because it seems to fit well into the Growth Mental Model assumption that growth, as the metric of success, needs to be continuous and smooth. Strategists would argue that for that result to occur one needs a sustainable competitive advantage.

Strategy theory, however, has evolved over the past fifteen years. Now many strategy theorists, led by Professor Richard D'Aveni, argue that in an age of hypercompetition brought about by globalization and technology no competitive advantage is sustainable, and the most a business can hope for is short-term competitive advantage.[6] Furthermore, the only way to compete over the long term is to string together a series of short-term competitive advantages. The challenge of creating a competitive advantage in the age of hypercompetition is significant. Researchers have found that the incidence and velocity of hypercompetition continues to increase, making any competitive advantage more fleeting and thus the continuity of advantage harder to sustain.[7]

Robert Wiggins and Timothy Ruefli have conducted extensive research asking whether the time period of a competitive advantage is shrinking and whether businesses need to link together over time smaller competitive thrusts to maintain their advantage.[8] To answer these questions, Wiggins and Ruefli examined over 6,700 firms in forty different industries over a twenty-five-year period. They also examined over 13,800 business units in more than 8,800 firms over a seventeen-year period.

Summarizing their review of superior economic performance in economic and strategy research, Wiggins and Ruefli state:

Neoclassical economics argues that persistent superior economic performance is an anomaly, a temporary condition that will vanish when equilibrium is reached. Industrial organization economics argues that any persistence is the result of industry structure, with mechanisms such as entry barriers preventing the equilibrium of neoclassical economics from being achieved. Evolutionary economics as well as the related Austrian school of economics both argue that persistent superior economic performance is the result of cycles of entrepreneurial innovation and imitation that create a continuing disequilibrium where some firms can achieve persistence of performance although it will be eventually eroded. Organizational and strategic management theories have incorporated most of these ideas and added the concept of sustained competitive advantage that can lead directly to persistent superior economic performance.[9]

They then summarize twenty-seven empirical studies that focus on how quickly companies lose their superior profits and converge back to the industry average. They differentiate those studies from their work based on both research design and statistical methodology. They then test the hypotheses that

1. periods of persistent superior performance have gotten shorter in time;
2. hypercompetition occurs in most industries, not just high-tech; and
3. in a hypercompetitive environment a series of short-term advantages is the best one can achieve.

Their findings, although statistically significant, do not completely obliterate some contradictory findings, which they attempt to distinguish. Their findings do confirm that periods of consistent superior performance are decreasing across industries. They conclude that hypercompetition is on the increase and, as a result, the concept of sustainability is suspect.[10]

This challenge to the theory of long-term strategic supremacy has evolved to chip away even more from the view that prolonged periods of superior performance are possible with the right strategy. In the last few years some strategy scholars have espoused the theory that gaining only a relative competitive advantage is the appropriate objective of strategy.[11]

The work of Professor L. G. Thomas and Professor D'Aveni, in 2004, documented the spread or increase in hypercompetition in the U.S. manufacturing industry during the time period 1950 to 2002.[12] With respect to the validity or reasonableness of the expectations of the Growth Mental Model, Thomas and D'Aveni write that:

> the most prominent consequence of hypercompetition is volatility in corporate performance and a shift toward temporary advantage. The timing of new competitive positions against depreciated old positions will not be smooth or stable. The matching of new and old positions across firms will similarly be disorderly and unstable.... Typically, there will be only a few winners and many losers from hypercompetition, because the adjustment cost of continuous change will weigh down average profits (even for adaptive firms).[13]

Thomas and D'Aveni contend that smooth and continuous growth is rare in a hypercompetitive environment, and they, along with Wiggins and Ruefli, argue that hypercompetition and volatility are predominant in today's business environment.

Thomas and D'Aveni's study looks at the prevalence of hypercompetition and its results in the U.S. manufacturing industry for the time period 1950 to 2002. They conclude that

1. hypercompetition is real and pervasive in the manufacturing industry;
2. sustained resource-based competition is limited; and
3. seeking temporary advantages can be a viable course of action.

Arguably, creating and linking together successive short-term competitive advantages is a more difficult task than executing a tested successful advantage for a longer period of time. In the latter case, execution processes are easier to control and manage than the challenge of choosing new competitive thrusts and changing employees' work activities often. Clearly, hypercompetition makes smooth and continuous growth more difficult and questions the reasonableness of the Growth Mental Model.

Hypercompetition suggests that growth is unlikely to be smooth and continuous. In addition, the Pfeffer and Sutton findings that most corporate change efforts fail to produce the desired results suggests more choppy growth should be expected. As a result of the forces of hypercompetition and the usual outcomes of corporate change efforts, to meet the goals of the Growth Mental Model one would have to assume that successful corporate leadership teams are able to consistently defy the odds and not only choose and execute the right short-term hyper-competitive strategic move but also repeat this success over and over. Unlikely.

Growth Progressions

Other areas of interest in examining support for the Growth Mental Model are two lines of research that discuss growth in those rare companies that have been able to put together a string of years of consistent superior performance. The first is a study done by McKinsey & Company called the "Staircases to Growth," published in 1996, in which the researchers studied 40 global high-growth companies to learn how they grew. Interestingly, they found that these companies grew not by leaps and bounds but primarily by a series of small steps that built upon themselves, leading McKinsey to label the growth process as a staircase.[14] Each step led to other steps in an iterative fashion and not according to a premeditated master plan.

The Staircase to Growth model starts with selling more of a business's current products to existing customers. It then progresses successively to acquiring new customers with existing products to creating new products for existing customers, to improving business processes, to making core-related acquisitions, to expanding geographically, and, finally, to diversifying.[15] Even with this process, McKinsey found that only 10% of companies with above average growth are able to sustain it.

I published the second finding in 2007 in *The Road to Organic Growth: How Great Companies Consistently Gain Marketshare*.[16] In that book I describe research on twenty-three companies that were winners in my Organic Growth Index (OGI) studies for the years 1996 to 2003 and examined how those companies were able to accomplish consistent high organic growth. What I found was contrary to my hypotheses. Based on my finance and strategy background, I thought each of these companies characteristically would execute complex diversified strategies, employ the best talent, foster visionary leadership, offer unique products or services, be very innovative, and be the lowest cost provider. Surprisingly, I found that none of these practices was necessary to produce consistent high organic growth.

I found that most of the winning companies studied have disciplined, focused strategies. Instead of having the best talent, they get the most out of the talent they have. Their leaders are humble, passionate operators, most of whom have grown up in the company. Furthermore, few of these companies produce anything unique but they are inspired copiers and imitators. And, the winning companies are execution champions focused on iterative incremental improvements. More important, these companies over years have built an internal, seamless, consistent, self-reinforcing system linking strategy, culture, structure, execution processes, people policies, measurements, and rewards to drive desired behaviors. I also found that these companies seem to grow in the same Growth Progression.[17]

Such Growth Progression generally occurs as follows:

1. Geographical expansion;
2. Introduction of complementary products to existing customers;
3. Expand to new customer segments with existing products;
4. Add complementary services for existing customers;
5. Focus on cost efficiencies;
6. Focus of technological productivity in the supply chain, logistics, and manufacturing functions;
7. Add or acquire (usually on a small scale) strategic new products, customer segments, or services;
8. Move from product-centricity to selling solutions; and
9. Start over at step one and simultaneously improve in all areas.

McKinsey's Staircase and my Growth Progression are consistent with D'Aveni's assertion that hypercompetition drives strategy to a series of small thrusts and counterthrusts and that a successful strategy is always evolving. This is also consistent with recent work on innovation and growth experimentation by Jeanne Liedtka and Edward Hess, by Peter Skarzynski and Rowan Gibson, and Alexander van Putten and Ian MacMillan.[18] All of this work views growth as a portfolio of initiatives managed across timelines with the objective of producing new S-curves of income that can be scaled broadly across customer segments or geography.

The goal of a growth strategy is to create a large number of testable growth initiatives, with the ultimate aim of creating a diverse portfolio of growth initiatives that are managed like a venture capital fund. The goal is to produce a few new big S-curves of income. Since we know that not all initiatives will succeed, the system is based on probability theory and options theory and requires the generation of a pipeline of initiatives to fuel the testing process.

Darden Growth/Innovation Model

At the Darden Graduate School of Business, Professor Liedtka and I have formulated this process into a seven-step Darden Growth/Innovation Model.[19] The seven steps build upon previous steps, and the Model acts both as a pipeline and as a funnel. The Model assumes failures will occur. Failures are learning opportunities and companies such as Best Buy, which uses a version of this growth portfolio methodology, understand and accept mistakes and failures as learning opportunities.

In summary, the seven steps of the Darden Growth/Innovation Model are:

Step 1: Enabling Internal Growth System seamlessly, consistently, and in a self-reinforcing manner links and aligns a company's strategy, culture, structure, leadership model, execution processes, HR policies, and measurements and rewards to drive the desired behaviors. Evidence of such a system can be found in the Best Buy, Sysco, Room & Board, and UPS cases in this book. To create and maintain this System all, not most, of the components must be aligned to motivate and enable the desired behaviors and not just financial metrics. The System is designed to create high employee engagement.

My research and consulting have convinced me that high employee engagement (promoted by humble, passionate servant leaders) is critical for consistent high performance. Examples are Best Buy, UPS, Room & Board, Tiffany, U.S. Marine Corps, the San Antonio Spurs NBA team, Synovus Financial, TSYS, Ritz Carlton, Southwest Airlines, Outback Steakhouse, Sysco, Chik-Fil-A, Starbucks, and Levy Restaurants. I would add P&G and McDonald's to this list because of their current CEOs.

High employee engagement results in high employee retention, productivity, loyalty, and emotional engagement in the daily pursuit of improvement and execution excellence. This type of deep emotional engagement does not just happen; it is the result of consistent policies and beliefs and leadership and managers' behaviors that result in employees believing they have ownership of their careers and jobs and that if they play by the rules, they will be treated fairly and have the opportunity to be all they can be, achieving a better life for themselves and their loved ones. What helps? Stock ownership; promotion from within policies; humble, passionate servant leaders; and fairly applied, transparent, stable HR policies.

In the companies I studied, not only are most of the leaders humble passionate stewards, but also most have spent almost all of their careers in the company and have not forgotten what it is like to be a line employee. Most have been able to transform their ambition and focus from "me" to "them." Most are not visionaries or charismatic but they are into the details of their business and lead the daily fight against elitism (other than in compensation), arrogance, and complacency. They understand and manage the tensions between employee centricity and high accountability, centralization and decentralization, bureaucracy and entrepreneurial behavior, and success and group think.

Step 2: Strategic Ideation is a continuous process engaging employees and customers in the creation of new ideas that attempt to leverage strategic capabilities to create differentiating customer value propositions over time.

Step 3: Ideation Management Process is a transparent ideas evaluation process. A review team has the responsibility for communicating with participants, evaluating their ideas, giving meaningful feedback, educating participants on how decisions are made to ensure trust in the process and continued employee engagement. This step also includes an idea database for future use.

Step 4: Learning Launches is a critical step and resulted from Professor Liedtka's research on growth leaders. It is an experimental methodology to test a set of chosen ideas quickly and cheaply to see if they are worth pursuing.[20] The purpose of Learning Launches is to test critical customer value, execution, and defensibility assumptions, which have to be true for the idea to warrant further investigation, time, and investment. The goal here is to learn critical information quickly and cheaply. Learning Launches are a learning-by-doing process that is customer-centric. We have taught this process to over 500 managers in the last eighteen months.

Step 5: Learning Launch Project Tracking and Portfolio Evaluation Process is the process that manages, sets milestones, and holds people accountable for each Learning Launch; allocates resources among Learning Launches; and decides on a portfolio basis which initiatives to kill and which to continue. This process is the gateway for a subset of Learning Launches to move on to become part of a Growth Initiatives Portfolio.

Step 6: Growth Initiatives Portfolio is a diversified portfolio of growth initiatives managed on both a timeline basis and top-line-versus-bottom-line basis. That means that some initiatives will produce short- to medium-term results whereas others will be long-term oriented, and likewise, some initiatives will be revenue focused whereas others may be business process initiatives that will produce bottom-line impacts.

Step 7: Growth Portfolio Management/Review Process manages the portfolio of initiatives in order to make sure scarce resources are being effectively utilized, understanding that not all the growth initiatives will produce the desired results. This step includes not only rigorous individual project management processes but also portfolio management processes, so that the strategic corporate objectives can be accomplished from timing and business unit perspectives.

What the work discussed above emphasizes is that growth is a process of balancing exploitation and exploration; balancing short-term needs against long-term needs; and creating a pipeline of growth initiatives that need to be managed actively. This process is one of enhancing the probability of success by constantly trying new things, some of which the company hopes come to fruition as new major revenue streams replacing declining revenue streams. But this experimental process is unlikely to yield smooth and continuous growth, at least in the short run, as the Growth Mental Model desires. Professor Liedtka's research found that corporate leaders have the ability to act like entrepreneurs and my research found that good growth companies have a "small company soul" in a large company body.

One company that has done a good job with such an experimental growth process is Best Buy Co., Inc. Best Buy competes in a hypercompetitive industry and in a hypercompetitive market segment: retail electronic products. How have they been able to stay a market leader? As you read the case, please note the changes Best Buy has made to its culture, leadership philosophy, structure, and measurement and reward policies in order to implement its new Customer Centricity business model. What drives constant improvement at Best Buy? What is the Best Buy Growth System?

In 2005, Best Buy undertook a major redesign of its business model in an attempt to change from a centralized top-down product-pushing organization to a decentralized customer-centric solutions organization. This required the company, over a period of years, to roll out a new system and retrain over 100,000 employees, which proved a major undertaking. Not surprisingly, there were bumps in the road that resulted in earnings estimates being missed for a few quarters, which resulted in stock price declines.

Best Buy Co., Inc. Case

Best Buy was the leading electronics retailer in the United States in 2008, with more than 1,341 stores, revenue totaling $40 billion, and a market cap of $12 billion in February 2009.[21] Since 2000, Best Buy has expanded into Canada, Mexico, China; adding new customer segments with the acquisition of Geek Squad, Magnolia Hi-Fi, Pacific Sales Kitchen and Bath Centers, Inc., and acquiring a 75% interest in Jiangsu Five Star Appliance Co., Ltd., China's third-largest chain of electronics and appliance stores. In the last ten years, Best Buy has doubled sales every five years and is currently expanding in Europe and entering Turkey. Its mantra is "Learn slowly and carefully. Then scale fast."

In 2005, Best Buy adopted a new business model, culture, and customer-segmentation template called Customer Centricity. This move created volatility in the price of Best Buy stock during 2005–2007 because of the higher-than-expected employee costs that went with this new way of doing business and the difficulty of executing the old and the new business models simultaneously while the new model was rolled out.

Best Buy adopted its Customer Centricity business model to differentiate its offerings from its competitors and to avoid being in a commodity-based business. And, based on the results, their new model is working. Nonetheless, Wall Street has no patience and arguably has remained focused on the short-term.

History

TABLE 4.1 The Five Eras of Best Buy

Era one:	Humble beginnings
Era two:	Growth and challenges
Era three:	Forging new paths
Era four:	Unprecedented growth
Era five:	Reaching new heights

ERA ONE: 1966-1971 Best Buy's humble beginnings can be traced to 1966 when Richard Schulze and a business partner opened a Sound of Music store in St. Paul, Minnesota. This store had gross sales of $173,000 in its first year. Encouraged, the partners bought two more companies in 1967, opened two more Sound of Music stores, and then went public in 1969, as an over-the-counter stock. By 1970, revenues had reached $1 million.

ERA TWO: 1972-1982 The growth-and-challenges era took off in 1972, with expansion, new facilities, and a grand total of nine stores. In 1974, the stores expanded, offering video products and video- and laser-disc equipment. After a tornado hit the Rockville, Minnesota, store in 1981, Schulze held a "tornado sale," with low prices in a no-frills retail environment; it was the introduction of what would one day be Best Buy's successful strategy.

By 1981, Best Buy had expanded its products to include photography, home office equipment, video equipment, and televisions. In 1982, Sound of Music held its Second Annual Tornado Sale, further embracing the retail concept of name brands, low prices, and a no-frills environment.

ERA THREE: 1983-1990 In the era of forging new paths came the company's new name, Best Buy, and the opening of its first superstore. In 1985, Best Buy raised $8 million in a stock offering on NASDAQ to fund the opening of three more superstores. A twelve-store expansion was financed by a $33.6 million stock offering, also in 1985. In 1989, Best Buy changed its format once again to offer customers pressure-free shopping in a warehouse-style store with the yellow-tag logo and noncommissioned sales personnel.

ERA FOUR: 1991-1999 The era of unprecedented growth saw geographical expansion outside Minnesota that began in Texas and Chicago in 1991. By 1995, Best Buy had implemented a major operating platform to focus more on technology, operating efficiencies, and productivity, together with its efficient enterprise initiatives. With the acquisition of Magnolia Hi-Fi, a high-end retailer, Best Buy added a new customer segment.

ERA FIVE: 2000 TO PRESENT In 2001, Best Buy made what turned out to be its first acquisition mistake, buying Musicland Stores, which it sold in 2004, at an after-tax loss of $66 million. But by 2002, Best Buy had bought Future Shop, Ltd., in Canada. Also in 2002, Best Buy purchased the Geek Squad in its first foray into the home and commercial service business. These were small, concept acquisitions. Best Buy continued the expansion path in 2003, when it established a Shanghai office for sourcing electrical products, and in 2005, it adopted the new Customer Centricity business model. It rolled out this new model to sixty-seven stores in 2005 and to 233 more stores in 2006. The year 2006 was also all about China, with Best Buy's acquisition of a 75% interest in Jiangsu Five Star Appliance Co., Ltd., and the opening of the first Best Buy store in Shanghai that December.

Best Buy announced another concept acquisition in 2007, buying Pacific Sales Kitchen and Bath Centers, which operated 14 showrooms catering to customers interested in home remodeling. In 2008, Best Buy opened its first store in Mexico and formed a 50-50 joint venture with a UK company to use as its base for expansion throughout Europe.

Store Growth

Best Buy has grown through a combination of store openings, geographical expansion, and concept acquisitions (see Table 4.2).

TABLE 4.2 Best Buy Co., Inc.
Store Numbers, 1999–2008

FISCAL YEAR	TOTAL STORES (ALL BRANDS)
1999	311
2000	357
2001	432
2002	589
2003	679
2005	838
2006	941
2007	1,177
2008	1,341

Chairman and founder Richard Schulze stated, "Most changes at Best Buy, whether moving from commissioned salespeople to noncommissioned or to a large-box format, were done to make the shopping experience better for customers. Best Buy earns its business one customer at a time."

In 2005, Best Buy's adoption of its new business model, Customer Centricity, required the company to adopt a new operating structure, culture, leadership model, and employee-training program. This move made it necessary for Best Buy to shift to a decentralized structure, where each store was a separate business unit and each store manager had control over the unit.

Customer Centricity grew out of Best Buy's analysis of customer segments and its subsequent decision to require all matters concerning capital, inventory mix, and format size to be governed by the profitability of the portfolio of its customers. Instilling an owner/operator mentality in each store manager required financial training. It also required teaching managers how to grow their product mix for profit as well as manage the cost side to maximize margin. Instead of managing traffic, conversion, and revenue, store managers were trained to optimize a customer portfolio and business outcome, and new employees were trained to meet customers' needs and not just sell products.

This new customer-segmentation approach led Best Buy to create a customer model based on five customer prototypes:

- Barry—The affluent professional
- Buzz—The younger male wanting the latest gizmo
- Roy—The family man and practical buyer
- Jill—The suburban mom wanting products to enrich her kids' lives
- Small-business customers

All of this had the objective of identifying the right customers—the profitable ones—and becoming closer to them so they are more likely to spend more money at Best Buy over a longer period of time.

Best Buy defined Customer Centricity as follows:

Our customers are at the core of all of our business strategies. Customer centricity has moved beyond an initiative and is how we do business. Customer centricity means treating each customer as a unique individual. It is meeting their needs with end-to-end solutions, and engaging and energizing our employees to serve them.

Mass merchants, direct sellers, other specialty retailers, and online retailers are increasingly interested in our product categories because of rising demand. If we can understand our customers better than our competitors do, and if we can inspire our employees to have richer interactions with customers, then we can compete more effectively.

Customer centricity has been, and will continue to be, a growth driver for us.

We began our customer-centricity work three years ago, starting with a few lab stores that created an energized new culture. Before long, we saw positive indicators from these lab stores, higher comparable-store-sales gains, and a richer mix of products. While the expenses associated with this more labor-intensive model also were higher, the lab stores demonstrated potential to expand their overall profit contribution.

We observed improvements in customer loyalty, employee retention, and market share. Over time, we also noticed new growth ideas coming from our employees, such as possible real estate locations across North America.

Other growth ideas included a faster method for customizing personal computers, new services we could offer, and ways to reduce returns/exchanges of flat-panel TVs. Given these positive indicators, we made the decision to accelerate this work, and we called fiscal 2006 our tipping point.[22]

Richard Schulze added, "At Best Buy, we built the business on what we thought was best for the customer. Now we have to grow the business based on what the customer tells us."

Culture

Best Buy's corporate culture is defined by four goals:

1. Have fun while being the best.
2. Learn from challenges and change.
3. Show respect, humility, and integrity.
4. Unleash the power of our people.

How does a best-of-class business keep its people energized and prevent their becoming satisfied, arrogant, and complacent? The answer is its culture. "That culture has been defined as a culture of paranoia, which has a healthy appreciation for learning, of not being afraid to make mistakes nor admit mistakes," explained Darren Jackson, former executive vice president and CFO. "In the Best Buy DNA, failure is not an option. Mistakes are made, dealt with openly so we can learn. Best Buy's success is not dependent on a small team. We engage as many people as possible in open debate to find the best answers," said Shawn Score, senior vice president of Sales Development.

In 2005, under its new business model, the redefinition of Best Buy's culture called for treating customers like kings and queens, for referring to store employees closest to customers as royalty, and for store employees to consider headquarters employees as servant leaders. According to an article in the *Wall Street Journal*, this concept of servant leadership was illustrated by President and CEO, Brad Anderson, when he turned down substantial stock options and had those same options put into a pool for Best Buy headquarters employees.[23]

This servant-leader, employee-centric culture was illuminated further by Vice Chairman Al Lenzmeier:

> Our mission as leaders is to put in place something that will live on—be sustainable. It is a constant battle of paradoxes; entrepreneurial vs. bureaucracy; fighting complacency and self-satisfaction, which results from success; and to keep rejuvenating the core business and to look for new geographics or concepts for the future. Managers have to live our values—20% of their annual option grant is dependent upon whether they walk the talk. If you want to work at Best Buy, leave your ego at the doorstep.

Anderson added: "I was a lousy high-school student. I was written off—told not to go to college. At Best Buy, we do not write people off. Respect and opportunity to be all you can be is what Best Buy stands for."

Best Buy was intensely focused on becoming a talented company by revamping its rewards system to better enhance and mirror its values and culture and its new customer-centric model. "With the help of the Gallup Organization, Best Buy adopted the employee-strengths concept. And the company became more scientific in recruiting for FIT, managing employee careers to play to their strengths, and helping people to find their inner flame," said Randy Ross, vice president of Human Resources (HR).

Just as marketing had drilled down to segment customers according to their needs, HR implemented a most ambitious plan to segment employees into five different groups, depending on what matters most or draws people to be engaged at a consistently high level of performance. Different training, different rewards, and different work environments for those five employee segments are the result of the initiative. As Ross remarked, "We are a very energized company, but we have to be even better at getting people focused on getting the right results. Wouldn't it be great if we could help every employee at Best Buy find his or her passion and give them opportunities that excite them and energize them even more?" Store-employee turnover decreased from 81% in fiscal year 2005 to 69% in fiscal year 2006. Former CFO Jackson commented: "Best Buy's single most watched metric is employee engagement. Because we find that when employee engagement is up, so is our profitability, so is our customer satisfaction, so is our bottom line."[24]

Best Buy has a policy of promoting from within—about 50% of its store managers come from within, and more than 75% of promotions above store management are filled from within. And 75% of full-time employees own stock in the company.

Best Buy is a company designed down to the smallest detail for energy, interaction, and collaboration. Every officer or manager's office is small (very small) and windowless because Best Buy wants its officers out of their offices. There are many break rooms, conference rooms, and community areas for meetings, discussions, and problem solving. The CEO's office is also small and windowless and has a tiny conference room next door big enough for only a round table and four chairs.

U.S. Store Operations

In 2008, Best Buy had more than 165,000 employees and operated 923 superstores in the United States with an estimated 21% market share. Best Buy's U.S. store operations are organized into eight territories, with each one divided into a district under the management of a retail field officer who oversees store performance through the district managers.[25] District managers monitor store operations and meet regularly with store managers to discuss merchandising, new-product introductions, sales promotions, customer-loyalty programs, employee-satisfaction surveys, and store-operating performance. Advertising, merchandise buying and pricing, and inventory policies are centrally controlled.

Best Buy's U.S. stores are generally open seventy-eight hours a week, seven days a week, with extended holiday hours. An average store typically has one general manager and five managers. In fiscal 2006, the average staff size per store was approximately 132 employees.

Best Buy's U.S. stores follow a standardized, detailed operating procedure called Standard Operating Platform (SOP). SOP includes procedures for inventory management, transaction processing, customer relations, store administration, product sales and services, and merchandise display. All stores operate in the same manner under SOP. "At Best Buy, technology is an agent of change. Every business process has been mapped onto the Business Operating Blueprint ("BOB"), and is being changed to fit new best-of-breed technologies in order to create more transparency, reduce costs, and increase efficiencies," explained Bob Willet, CFO and executive vice president of Operations.

Results of New Business Model

The results of implementing the new business model at Best Buy initially created some short-term earnings volatility that tested Wall Street's patience. Best Buy discussed this matter in detail in its 2006 Annual Report.

In retrospect, we moved too quickly in some areas. In the fiscal third quarter, the volume of changes peaked, leading to a dispersion of results. Specifically, the performance of customer centricity stores converted in our fiscal third quarter was modestly below our expectations. We stopped conversions for 90 days, and our analysis indicated that we had overestimated our capacity for change.

We had asked stores to implement customer centricity, hire more services personnel, introduce Image Labs, reset their entertainment software space, and implement a new approach to appliance sales. Most stores had executed well on one or more of these dimensions. Yet no store was able to demonstrate the same level of success with all of these dimensions.

These results indicated to us that the overall strategy was intact, but we simply had asked too much of our people within the third quarter.

Naturally, along with the benefits of our transformation came new challenges. For example, our current product-centric organization could not effectively support the new business model.

In the interest of speed, we created parallel groups to support customer centricity in store management, finance, legal and marketing. Supporting two operating models was costly; yet our plan was to focus on efficiency after we had implemented customer centricity in all markets. We believed that speed to market was more important.

In the fourth quarter, we slowed the pace of changes, and we focused on simple outcomes. In addition, stores that had received only the cultural aspects of customer centricity made major strides.[26]

Other Growth Challenges

Best Buy's new business model was designed to create innovation and position it to continue to compete against Circuit City and Wal-Mart. In an interview, CEO Brad Anderson made the following two points:

Question: Where do you find new business ideas?

Answer: I believe that some of our best ideas have come from the people who are furthest removed from the CEO's office—those line-level employees who interact with our customers each and every day. We've got a wonderful team of eccentric people working in our Manhattan store on 44th Street and Fifth Avenue. Now, there's a large Brazilian community near the store, and the manager said, "Hey, we don't do anything to cater to them."

So he hired folks who spoke the language in the store. They wound up discovering that there are cruise ships of Brazilians that come to New York City, so they contacted the travel company and found that the store was a desirable stop for them. So all of a sudden, we have buses of tour groups pulling up on Sundays. If we waited for someone in Minnesota to come up with that idea, we'd still be waiting.

Question: Best Buy forced Circuit City to change its business model in order to compete. How are Wal-Mart, Target, and Costco forcing you to adapt?

Answer: The first thing we did to differentiate ourselves was taken directly from discount-store chains. [We created] well-lighted stores with noncommissioned salespeople. We did not invent that. Today, if you look at the standards we are using to improve our supply chain—reducing the time from manufacturer to consumer—they are taken from Wal-Mart, Tesco, and Target. In those cases, we are a fast follower. In our world, the way you win the game isn't the price of the TV—which is about the same for all retailers—but the experience you give customers once they are in our stores.[27]

Best Buy Lessons

The Best Buy story shows the difficulty of predicting growth results to the penny every quarter. Best Buy demonstrates the complete inadequacy of the Growth Mental Model and Wall Street Rules. Best Buy also illustrates the difficulty of making changes while the company is public. On the positive side, Best Buy is a good example of my theory that growth is much more than just a strategy. Smart Growth is an internal system linking growth strategies to culture, structure, execution processes, people policies, leadership model, measurement, and rewards in a seamless self-reinforcing manner so as to drive desired behaviors.

When Best Buy decided to change its business model it made consistent reinforcing changes to its leadership model, culture, structure, metrics and rewards. It aligned these to change from a centralized top-down product-centric model to a decentralized servant leadership inverted pyramid culture that is customer-centric. It is a good lesson in organizational design.

The Best Buy case also illustrates the limits of a myopic sole focus on smooth and continuous quarterly earnings growth. The market penalized Best Buy because it was not able to estimate to the penny the costs of implementing this difficult change initiative. These types of changes are hard and messy, and no one can estimate the costs to the penny. Was it reasonable for the market to demand a flawless, smooth, 100% successful rollout of a new business model that required the retraining of over 100,000 employees and the redesign of the Best Buy culture, operating systems, and reward systems? I hope by now you agree—the answer is no.

The analysts should have evaluated whether the preliminary results of the rollout were producing competitive improvements that could be replicated across the organization over time and whether the improvements would produce more revenue in excess of the costs that would normalize over time. And the analysts also should have reviewed and formed judgments about Best Buy's growth portfolio, which Best Buy published broken down by geography, product, and services, and new initiatives as compared to their competition to determine the probability of Best Buy maintaining their market leading position over time.

The Best Buy experience shows that the market wants corporate infallibility. As Henry Mintzberg, a leading strategy theorist and professor stated: "Maybe we have to put up with the cycles of success and failure, growth and decline, which of course is the 'natural' human condition."[28]

Corporate Life Cycles

Another area of research that merits review concerns understanding the corporate life cycle. The CEB Stall research shows that 87% of the companies studied experienced a growth stall and that most of the firms experiencing a growth stall were not able to recover or reenergize growth. This volatility and difficulty of sustaining high performance is further buttressed by the hypercompetition studies.

Corporate life cycle research has tried to model the different stages of a business's life. This research has generated many different models of corporate life cycles that have detailed from three to nine stages, most encompassing stages of birth, growth, maturity, and decline in some form.[29] Although lifecycle research varies in detailing the timing of its stages or evidence about whether a company can safely skip or repeat stages, it is consistent in finding that most companies go through different periods characterized by either growth or stability or, as Professor Larry Greiner has stated, evolution and revolution.[30]

Professor Greiner's work has stood the test of time, over thirty-six years, and adds to our discussion in the following way. He states: "Smooth evolution is not inevitable or indefinitely sustainable; it cannot be assumed that organizational growth is linear."[31] He theorizes that as companies move back and forth through evolutionary stages and revolutionary stages, the management solutions (strategy, structure, processes, people) that solve the challenges in one phase often become or create the problem to be solved in the next stage.

The turbulence espoused by Greiner and other life cycle or stages of growth work adds further to evidence challenging the view that growth can be smooth and continuous. The external environment and the internal dynamics within firms create a complex multitude of interacting interdependent variables that cannot be fine-tuned, controlled, or predicted.

The Organizational Design and Strategy business disciplines offer no support to the validity or reasonableness of the Growth Mental Model as a driving force in business. So far there is no convincing support for the Growth Mental Model in Economics or Business research.

Notes
....

1. Jeffrey Pfeffer and Robert I. Sutton, *Hard Facts, Dangerous Half-Truths, and Total Nonsense: Profiting from Evidence-Based Management* (Boston: Harvard Business School Press, 2006), 159.

2. Ibid.

3. Edward D. Hess, "Darden Private Growth Research Project," 2008, based upon research funded by the Batten Institute, Darden Graduate School of Business Administration, and the Darden School Foundation.

4. Michael E. Porter, *Competitive Strategy: Techniques for Analyzing Industries and Competitors* (New York: Free Press, 1980).

5. Michael E. Porter, *Competitive Advantage: Creating and Sustaining Superior Performance* (New York: Free Press, 1985), 11.

6. Richard A. D'Aveni, *Hypercompetition* (New York: Free Press, 1994).

7. Robert R. Wiggins and Timothy W. Ruefli, "Schumpeter's Ghost: Is Hypercompetition Making the Best of Times Shorter?" *Strategic Management Journal* 26, 10 (2005): 887–911.

8. Ibid.; Robert R. Wiggins and Timothy W. Ruefli, "Sustained Competitive Advantage: Temporal Dynamics and the Incidence and Persistence of Superior Economic Performance," *Organization Science* 13, 1 (2002): 81–105.

9. Wiggins and Ruefli, "Schumpeter's Ghost," 889.

10. Ibid.

11. Interview with Professor Ming-Jer Chen, February 2009.

12. Richard D'Aveni and L. G. Thomas, "The Rise of Hypercompetition from 1950 to 2002: Evidence of Increasing Structural Destabilization and Temporary Competitive Advantage" (Working Paper, Tuck School of Business, Dartmouth College, October 11, 2004).

13. Ibid., 10.

14. Mehrdad Baghai, Stephen C. Coley, David White, Charles Conn, and Robert J. McLean, "Staircases to Growth," *McKinsey Quarterly* 4 (1996): 38–61.

15. Ibid., 46–48.

16. Edward D. Hess, *The Road to Organic Growth* (New York: McGraw-Hill, 2007).

17. Ibid., 64–69.

18. Jeanne M. Liedtka and Edward D. Hess, "Designing Learning Launches" (Technical Note, University of Virginia, Darden Business Publishing UVA-BP-0529, 2008); Peter Skarzynski and Rowan Gibson, *Innovation to the Core: A Blueprint for Transforming the Way Your Company Innovates* (Boston: Harvard Business Press, 2008); Alexander B. van Putten and Ian C. MacMillan, *Unlocking Opportunities for Growth: How to Profit from Uncertainty While Limiting Your Risk* (Upper Saddle River, NJ: Wharton School Publishing, 2009).

19. Edward D. Hess and Jeanne Liedtka, "Darden Growth/Innovation Model," 2008.

20. Jeanne M. Liedtka, Robert Rosen, and Robert Wiltbank, *The Catalyst: How You Can Become an Extraordinary Growth Leader* (New York: Crown Business, 2009).

21. Edward D. Hess, "Best Buy Co., Inc." (Case Study, UVA-S-0142, University of Virginia Darden School Foundation, Charlottesville, 2007). This case has been updated for material events. All quotes are directly from the case.

22. Best Buy, 2006 Annual Report, www.sec.gov/Archives/edgar/data/764478/000110465907034935/a07-11419_110k.htm.

23. Joann S. Lubin, "A Few Share the Wealth,"*Wall Street Journal,* December 12, 2005, B1.

24. Daren Jackson, 12th Annual Global Retailing Conference, September 9, 2005.

25. Best Buy, 2006 Annual Report.

26. Ibid.

27. Matthew Boyle, "Q&A with Best Buy CEO Brad Anderson," *Fortune,* April 18, 2007, http://money.cnn.com/magazines/fortune/fortune_archive/2007/04/30/8405481/index.htm (accessed August 31, 2009).

28. Henry Mintzberg, Bruce Ahlstrand, and Joseph Lampel, *Strategy Safari: A Guided Tour Through the Wilds of Strategic Management* (New York: Free Press, 1998), 317.

29. Robert K. Kazanjian and Robert Drazin, "An Empirical Test of a Stage of Growth Progression Model," *Management Science* 35, 12 (1989): 1489–1503; Robert Drazin and Robert K. Kazanjian, "Research Notes and Communications: A Reanalysis of Miller and Friesen's Life Cycle Data," *Strategic Management Journal* 11 (1990): 319–325.

30. Larry E. Greiner, "Evolution and Revolution as Organizations Grow," *Harvard Business Review* (July–August 1972): 37–46.

31. Ibid., 4.

CHAPTER 5

. . . .

Biology

THEORIES OF GROWTH

UNLIKE ECONOMICS, the science of biology is not concerned with under-standing and modeling economic systems or activity. Nonetheless, it is interesting to look at theories of growth, growth rates, the relationship be-tween animal growth and predators, and the theory of finite energy alloca-tion in living organisms. Will we be making leaps in applying this to busi-ness growth? Yes, of course, but interestingly, several theories in biology raise questions for business growth that are worth considering.

Biology does not directly deal with the Growth Mental Model. Biology as a science is different in fundamental ways from economics. Most eco-nomic theory assumes a mechanistic, deterministic world driven to equi-librium by rational actors using complete information to produce perfect competition, resulting in profits regressing to the mean. Such a world is predictable and linear.

In contrast, biology assumes change, evolution, adaptation, changing en-vironments, predators, and feedback loops, which produces nonlinearity and unexpected results. A biological view of the world has produced a group of new theories about change and growth called Complex Adaptive Systems (CAS) and Complex Evolving Systems (CES) that along with systems think-ing and chaos theory have created an area of science called Complexity Theory. For the purposes here, all of the foregoing complexity theories are called Complexity Theory. I explore both traditional biology and the appli-cability of Complexity Theory to the business world.

So, what does biology teach us about growth? The following findings are interesting:

1. In many species, growth is not maximized. In fact, some species increase their chances of survival by not growing to their maximum sizes.[1] Clearly, this is contrary to the business mantra "grow or die." According to biology, in certain cases continuing to grow decreases the chance of survival.

2. Increases in the size of an organism sometimes increase the risk of being eaten by predators because predators select for efficient growth. Hungry predators typically prefer the biggest prey.[2]

3. Many organisms have a finite amount of expendable energy and therefore must allocate that energy across competing physiological functions, such as reproduction, growth, maintenance, and survival. As a result growth competes for finite resource allocation.[3] This parallels Edith Penrose's theory that a firm can only grow if it has excess managerial capacity or resources allocable to growth.

4. In some species, growth requires trade-offs, resulting in periods of growth and periods of no-growth.[4] Chapter 8 highlights this concept when I look at private company growth and what I call the "gas pedal" theory of growth.

5. Growth has risks—when some species grow larger, they become slower and easier to see, reducing their ability to hide from even bigger predators.[5] Likewise, growth has risks in the business world. A premise of this book is that not enough attention is paid to those risks, and as a result growth can harm a company; Chapters 7 and 8 explore this issue.

6. In plants, there appears to be two different strategies. Growth-dominated plants invest their energy in processes and structures that enhance growth. Other plants invest in nongrowth processes and structures to make and retain resources to differentiate themselves.[6] Plants in the second category have a more nuanced strategy of growth that differentiates them and promotes their long-term survivability. Why is that not a viable business strategy, too?

7. Growth can be continuous or discontinuous, determinate or indeterminate; but few things in nature can grow without limit.[7] This makes common sense even in the business world. There has to be some size at which a business becomes so big that management is too removed from line operations, customers, and employee experiences. Thus, they are unable to perceive problems that, in the aggregate, can create material risks to the company's viability.

8. Growth curves for biological organisms vary, but the most common growth curves are S-curves.[8] Most product and organizational life cycles in the business world are S-curves, too.

As has been noted, "living organisms are complex systems, consisting of parts that often grow at different rates and display different patterns. Some parts of the body may grow faster than others, some may stop growing at certain stages while others continue to grow, and organs may grow 'on demand' during regeneration."[9]

Biology raises the question of whether growing a business sometimes increases its chance of dying prematurely—that is, "grow and die." For a business, growth that is too rapid may tax the resources it has to sustain it. Likewise, business growth in the wrong environment may generate deadly competition or invite predators. These biological examples show up in some of the comments made to me by CEOs of private high-growth companies in my research on the challenges of managing hyper-growth. Some CEOs discussed the revenue level at which their businesses would become big enough to draw the competition of industry giants, thus increasing their predator risk. For one CEO, if his business were to grow to $100 million in revenue, it would move into a different competitive space where its competition would consist of large, public, well-capitalized companies that could compete by lowering prices, resulting in his young company having to sell to its competitors, that is, be eaten.

Biological examples also address the manner of growth and suggest that the Growth Mental Model's ideal of smooth and continuous growth, that is, growth without limitation or interruption, is unrealistic. It certainly is not possible for biological organisms. First, growth in many species is not continuous and can be best modeled along an S-curve in which growth slows and ultimately declines. Second, the limits imposed by finite resources and the need to allocate those resources across growth, reproduction, maintenance, and survival needs may be applicable to businesses as well. Far too often business growth strategies outstrip the resources to successfully carry them off.

Again, the focus on resource limitations on growth sounds a lot like Edith Penrose's theory of growth in economics where growth occurs when business organizations have excess managerial capacity that is not fully occupied with running the daily business. This resource limitation constraint to growth resonates with my findings in my private company research.

Young high-growth companies are challenged to both grow and at the same time put in place the processes, controls, and people to accommodate the growth. One CEO described the challenge as "when to push down on the growth pedal and when to let up so the business can (people and process-wise) catch up with the growth." This is like the engineering concept of redlining an engine where you can only run so long at redline speed without damaging the machine. This finite resource or energy concept can apply to every company, and it requires the allocation of resources between exploitation of current opportunities and exploration for new growth opportunities. The Growth Mental Model assumes management instantaneously can fine-tune that allocation to produce continuous smooth growth.

Biology suggests two new ideas that we have not found in economics:

1. Growth can increase the risk of predator attack.
2. An alternative to grow or die is grow and die.

The work of Pfeffer and Sutton supports the proposition that many growth initiatives, if undertaken in big change efforts or as acquisitions, are as likely to fail as succeed making grow or die, at best, a half-truth. Maybe the other half of that truth is grow and die. If so, accepting that premise would shift the discussion to focus on questioning under what circumstances is growth the best strategy and what variables are critical to consider. That means it could be dangerous to assume that growth is a given or that all growth has good results.

Complexity Theory

Complexity Theory attempts to explain the behavior of complex environments. It assumes that such environments are impacted by behaviors resulting "from the inter-relationship, interaction, and interconnectivity of elements within a system and between a system and its environment."[10] Complexity Theory has been applied in the fields of biology, chemistry, evolution, physics, mathematics, and to a lesser degree, economics.

Complexity Theory states that complex organizations strive for "fitness," defined as the ability to perceive, adjust, and adapt continuously to an unpredictable evolving complex environment.[11] It rejects the Growth Mental Model's fundamental assumption of continuous growth or linearity. For example: "By far the most common methods for analyzing markets, economies, and enterprises are based on assumptions of linearity: the whole is the sum of the parts; the future is a linear projection of the past. . . . The problem is that very few things in nature or commerce behave linearly. It is the rare exception rather than the rule."[12]

The world that Complexity Theory sees is not a rational, predictable, linear world but a world more like the world Richard D'Aveni sees, as discussed in Chapter 4, which is hypercompetitive and characterized by frequent change requiring continuous competitive responses. Complexity Theory also is compatible with McKinsey's Staircase Model of Growth, which is an iterative, learn-as-you-go, adaptive approach that can result in a business ending up in a completely new and unpredictable place.

Several leading theorists have encouraged the business world to adopt Complexity Theory as a model for dealing with the unpredictable, hypercompetitive, fast-paced, changing world:

> Business organizations are also complex adaptive systems, in which the agents are people, and the interactions are relationships among them. In today's fast-changing business environment, companies will survive only if they are able constantly to adapt and evolve through operating optimally as a complex adaptive system. . . . [A]ccepting businesses as being such systems requires a mindset different from that associated with long-established business models: managers and executives cannot control their organizations to the degree that the mechanistic perspective implies.[13]

The applicability of Complexity Theory to the business world has had many esteemed missionaries, mostly from non-business academic positions. Complexity Theory challenges the fundamental historical purpose of large corporations, which has been to control and manage people and resources so they produce predictable outputs.

The applicability of Complexity Theory to the business world was advanced with the landmark work of Shona Brown and Kathleen Eisenhardt.[14] As they observed, "many firms compete by changing continuously."[15] They studied continuous product innovation in the computer industry and combined their field research with Complexity Theory and evolutionary theory to construct a model of a firm where change is endemic. Their findings are consistent with the findings of McKinsey's Staircase Study, my findings on how companies that maintain consistent high organic growth achieve those improbable results, and Liedtka's study of growth catalysts in large organizations.[16]

Brown and Eisenhardt found that companies test ideas in small experiments frequently. Companies learn from this experimentation and relate those findings to an iterative link between current reality and an evolving new reality, which can result in a new product. Brown and Eisenhardt conclude: "Continuing changing organizations are likely to be complex adaptive systems with semistructures that poise the organization on the edge of chaos and links in time that force simultaneous attention and linkage among, past, present and future."[17] This experimentation testing concept is consistent with Hess and Liedtka's findings and the Learning Launch step in the Darden Growth/Innovation Model.

As discussed in Chapter 4, Thomas and D'Aveni found the incidence of hypercompetition increasing in the manufacturing industry, which is not known as a high-velocity change industry.[18] That finding, plus Brown and Eisenhardt's finding that change is the norm in successful companies, casts grave doubts upon linear growth predictability.

How do the companies that I studied achieve long periods of continuous, market-leading growth? First, keep in mind that fewer than 2% of the companies I studied fit that description. But those that did created an Enabling Internal Growth System as defined in Chapter 4. That system typically produces each year a portfolio of twenty—thirty experiments that are managed against both short-term and long-term needs and by classification as to top-line or bottom-line earnings impact. These growth companies are constant improvement and experimentation companies that try many small learning experiments and build portfolios of growth options that they hold to rigorous metrics, milestones, and decision processes. In other words, these companies place a lot of small bets and play the odds that some will be big winners. Best Buy, whose mantra is "learn slowly and carefully but scale quickly," is one of those companies.

Procter & Gamble Company Example

Procter & Gamble (P&G) is an enduring, high-quality company whose earnings and growth history has not been smooth or continuous.[19] P&G dates back to 1837 when two brothers-in-law joined to form a company to make soap and candles. Today, that company sells over $85 billion of consumer products and is the number-one consumer product company in the world.

P&G is interesting for several reasons. First, P&G's dominance and growth have been anything but smooth and continuous. In addition, in the last twenty-eight years under the direction of five different chairmen/CEOs, P&G has changed its product portfolio, made substantial brand acquisitions, gone through two major restructurings, changed its culture from a marketing company to an innovation company, focused its strategy on brands having more than $500 million of revenue, diversified its top management team, adjusted to the dominance of Wal-Mart as its biggest customer, and changed its product or brand management structure many times.

P&G illustrates the complexity of getting all the different parts of a company aligned to produce consistent results. P&G's management has struggled managing the tensions between centralization and decentralization: it has organized its product responsibilities in recent years first by individual product, then by product category, then by geography, and now by product group along with a geographical overlay. All of these changes are complex because they modify power and individual responsibilities, reporting lines, and accountability. Having to manage a business like P&G to the penny every quarter is ludicrous.

Product Overview

Today, P&G is structured into three different product groups: Beauty and Health, Household Care, and Gillette. Beauty and Health comprises about 41% of the company's worldwide revenue and is led by eight billion-dollar brands including Head & Shoulders, Olay, Pantene, Crest, and Oral-B. Household Care comprises an estimated 47% of revenue and has eleven billion-dollar brands including Downy, Tide, Bounty, Charmin, Pampers, Iams, and Pringles. Gillette, which P&G acquired in 2005 in the largest acquisition ever made by the company at a cost in excess of $57 billion, has four billion-dollar brands including Gillette, Mach3, Braun, and Duracell.

P&G's strategy is to leverage its global marketing and distribution system and maximize the value of its top forty brands with sales in excess of $500 million each. To do this P&G spends about $8 billion a year on advertising and $2 billion a year on R&D. Wal-Mart is its largest customer, accounting for approximately 15% of P&G's sales.

P&G's oldest non-acquired billion-dollar products are Ivory soap (which dates back to 1879), Tide (1946), Crest (1955), Downy (1960), and Pampers

(1961). Major acquisitions were made in 1957, 1982, 1985, 1987, 1989, 1990, 1991, 1997, 1999, 2001, and 2005. Acquired brands include Charmin, Chloraseptic, NyQuil, Oil of Olay, Cover Girl, Noxzema, Old Spice, Hawaiian Punch, Max Factor, Gillette, Tambrands, Iams, and Clairol. Acquisitions played a major role in product expansion and entry into the beauty, health, hair, toiletries, and pet food businesses.

The Evolution

A review of P&G's evolution over the last twenty-eight years under five different chairmen/CEOs is prudent. The early 1980s was a period of turmoil at P&G induced by competitors making successful inroads into P&G's dominant positions and, according to some business writers, self-induced by P&G's assumption of continued dominance as evidenced by its slow response to competitors. In 1985, P&G posted its first earnings decline in over thirty years. P&G was described as "the long slumbering giant," with a management style of thoroughness and secrecy.[20]

During that period, P&G was a hierarchical, top-down organization, whose senior management made decisions involving even minute details of product packaging, marketing, and development. Evidence of P&G's micromanagement was shown by the rule that any management memorandum was limited to one page and that all decisions had to be made and confirmed at each level of the hierarchy. This micromanagement was cumbersome, significantly impairing P&G's agility in the marketplace. Power in P&G was lodged with each brand's manager. This management structure dates back to the 1930s, when it was established to foster internal competition, the expectation being that when brand managers compete against each other for resources, better results occur.

John Smale (1981–1990)

P&G's management pattern began to change in the mid-1980s as the company's competitors began taking away market shares from P&G's dominant categories: toothpaste, laundry detergent, and disposable diapers. John Smale, who became CEO in 1981 responded by (1) creating initiatives to reduce the marketing research and decision-making time so products could get to market faster; (2) cutting costs, including implementing management layoffs; (3) transferring power from product managers to category managers; (4) changing the metrics for products from sales to bottom-line profitability; (5) substantially increasing the number of acquisitions to enter more new product markets; (6) pushing decisions down one level from top management; (7) introducing the philosophy of collaborating or partnering with retailers; (8) reducing employees at all levels, including top management, a change that challenged P&G's philosophy of employment for life; (9) introducing Japanese best practices into the plant manufacturing culture; and (10) beginning the change from a product-centric company to a customer-centric company. Under Smale, P&G made major acquisitions of NyQuil, Vidal Sasoon, Oil of Olay, Clearasil, Dramamine, Bain de Soleil, Cover Girl, and Noxema.

Smale's responses to competition, especially in the areas of acquisitions, internal restructurings, power shifts, and cultural changes, would be endorsed by the next four CEOs over the next twenty years. Smale is credited with reenergizing the giant and surprised analysts in 1990 by stepping down earlier than expected at P&G's annual meeting. The second surprise announcement at that meeting was the skipping over of P&G's president, John Pepper, Jr., and, instead, the naming of the vice chairman and former head of international, Edwin Artzt, as P&G's new chairman/CEO.

Edwin Artzt (1990–1995)

Artzt was a P&G "lifer," whose claim to fame was turning around P&G's business in Japan and then going on to build its international business. Artzt's five-year tenure as CEO was marked by a focus on accountability, cost reductions, and acceleration of P&G's change from using a premium-pricing model to implementing everyday low prices. To accomplish the goal of everyday low prices required P&G to become leaner and more productive and to restructure its entire supply chain to maintain its profit margins. The consequences of these changes were results-driven accountability, plant closings, and employee reductions, including some high-level management departures of people uncomfortable with Artzt's confrontational management style.

Artzt took major steps, including closing thirty plants and terminating 12% of the workforce, which resulted in a $1.75 billion charge. These were major moves in a company that was known for lifetime employment.

P&G's external world continued to change with the consolidation of retailers, the dominance of big-box retailers, and the continued hard competition from Colgate, Unilever, and others. Artzt continued to make acquisitions to expand the health and beauty products segments and began to reevaluate the money-losing food-and-drink business.

Artzt thought Smale's team approach went too far, making individual accountability more difficult, so he reversed some of Smale's cultural and structural moves. He also fostered a renewed focus on results, accountability, and consequences. Artzt continued the theme of change inside of P&G, but he placed his own spin on what that meant. Like Smale, Artzt thought P&G had to become better, faster, and cheaper.

Artzt's tenure was deemed a success and he stepped down in 1995. P&G then appointed the previously passed over John Pepper, Jr., as chairman/CEO and named Durk Jager, an Artzt protégé, as president of U.S. operations. Pepper had been head of international since being passed over in 1989. Pepper reorganized P&G into geographical regions, each of which had products profit-and-loss responsibilities for their geography: North America, Europe, Middle East and Africa, Asia, and Latin America, with all regions reporting to Jager.

John Pepper, Jr. (1995–1998)

The business press viewed Pepper as more a team player than Artzt had been and a throwback to the "good ole days" at P&G. His main focuses were trying to double the health-care business by the year 2000 and promoting foreign expansion, especially into China. Pepper's focus on health care pushed P&G deeper into pharmaceuticals and the research, development, and regulatory approval of new drugs.

In 1997, Pepper took a significant, foretelling strategic step by announcing that going forward P&G's focus would be to expand market share in product areas where it dominated: laundry, hair care, diapers, and feminine hygiene. Pepper's goal was to double revenues over the next ten years, and this initiative required new products and faster go-to-market times. This revenue-doubling strategy was a major change from Artzt's, which focused on cutting costs to drive growth. To accomplish his revenue-doubling strategy, Pepper emphasized innovation.

However, Pepper's reign as CEO was short. In August 1998, P&G announced it would probably miss growth estimates for the next two quarters. And one month later, P&G announced Pepper's retirement, naming Durk Jager, who was P&G president, as chairman/CEO.

Only three years earlier, under Jager, P&G had created the five geographical regions, which had profit-and-loss responsibilities for all products sold in each geographical region. In the fall of 1998 P&G changed this geographical organizational structure, giving profit-and-loss responsibility to Global Product Lines. This change represented the fourth major product go-to-market reorganization at P&G in fifteen years.

Durk Jager (1999–2000)

Although Jager was Artzt's protégé, he did not adopt Artzt's focus on cost reduction. Instead, Jager took the reins at P&G with an overriding purpose—to turn P&G into an innovative company. When Jager assumed the CEO role, he also stepped into a company that had recently missed its sales targets. P&G also had lost 10% of its global market share in recent years and had seen some of its brand market leaders knocked from their longtime number-one perches by competitors. But Jager was bold. He set out to transform P&G just as Smale had done.

Jager announced a major reorganization called "Organization 2005 Initiative," which made the following changes: (1) acknowledging that P&G had not introduced a major innovation in over twenty-five years, he offered to give away or license any of its 25,000 patents to force P&G to become more innovative; (2) he set a goal of slashing by one-half the time to get a new product to market; (3) he cut 15,000 jobs at a restructuring cost of approximately $1.9 billion; (4) he changed the management power from geography to seven global brands; (5) he created innovation teams and new business managers; and (6) he instituted stretch financial goals and linked pay to performance. Most of these changes were announced in October 1999.

Jager, however, did not have time to effectuate these initiatives. Less than a year later, in June 2000, Jager was forced to resign by P&G's board of directors who, lukewarm to another significant shift in company strategy, reinstated John Pepper as chairman and installed A. G. Lafley as CEO. In explanation, Pepper stated that Jager had tried "to change too much too fast." The disruption likely under Jager's proposed changes came on the heels of the major changes made by Pepper in his earlier tenure as head of P&G.

Changing from a geography-based organization to a global brand-based organization had been a major change for P&G, causing significant job and geography dislocations. It was estimated that more than 50% of P&G executives ended up in new jobs and that 25% of P&G brand managers left the company. Geographical moves were required for many people. For example, in Europe more than 1,000 people were transferred to Geneva. The upheaval generated by this change in business organizational structure demonstrates the necessity of taking into account the impact of such decisions on the people affected. Such changes undoubtedly, at least in the short run, make smooth and continuous growth unrealistic.

A. G. Lafley (2000–Present)

In review, by the time Lafley assumed the position of CEO, P&G had had four CEOs in less than twenty years. The last two CEOs served less than two years each. During that time, P&G experienced erratic results, lost market share, undertook two massive restructurings costing over $3.6 billion, closed over thirty plants, terminated approximately 28,000 employees, and moved from brand management to category management to geography management and then to global product groups. Its earnings growth came primarily from health-care and beauty products acquisitions and cost cutting. Accountability initiatives, linking pay to performance, new innovation teams, and decentralization were attempted to make P&G faster to the market and more innovative.

Consistent themes were expansion into health and beauty products, focusing on winning brands, organizing along brands rather than products or geography, and innovation. Both Smale and Jager had attempted massive strategic changes. Artzt succeeded in his restructuring and bottom-line focus but his protégé, Jager, installed after Pepper's short reign, reversed Artzt's bottom-line focus and, surprisingly, adopted Pepper's top-line growth goals. But in less than two years, Jager was out. This is the P&G history that fifty-two-year-old, career P&G employee Lafley inherited when he became CEO in 2000.

After several years of turmoil at P&G, Lafley adopted a low-key team player approach. He did not make any quick, big moves. Nonetheless, he continued the focus on innovation and believed that P&G should focus on its big leading brands, on big markets, and on big customers. Lafley continued many of Jager's initiatives but did so with a different manner and style. By 2002, P&G was generating positive results.

Under Lafley's leadership, P&G focused on its big brands and sold off brands that did not fit into his strategy: gone were Jif, Crisco, and Folgers Coffee. Lafley also announced that P&G was getting out of the drug development business. He acquired Clairol and Wella and in January 2005 announced P&G's largest ever acquisition: the Gillette Company. The Gillette acquisition increased P&G's product breadth, advertising scale, geographic reach, and its market shelf power with Wal-Mart, its largest customer.

As evidenced in P&G's 2008 annual report, P&G once again has reverted back to making innovation its differentiator and growth driver. This time Lafley is doing it differently by looking outside as well as inside P&G for innovation. In addition, he is defining innovation broadly to include customer experience, business processes, consumer communications, product incremental enhancements, and packaging—not simply the development of new products. Lafley has made innovation a strategy, a disciplined process, and the role or job of every P&G employee. Under Lafley, P&G views innovation as creating a pipeline of growth opportunities. It also builds into its processes rigorous go/no-go decision making so that resources can be reallocated quickly to better opportunities. P&G's innovation process has many of the characteristics of the Darden Growth/Innovation Model I discussed in Chapter 4.

Lafley exemplifies of the type of CEO my research uncovered in companies that have been able to maintain consistent high organic growth: a humble but passionate operator engaged in the details of the business who has not forgotten where he came from or where the real work gets done. In that regard, Lafley is like many of the high-performance leaders in my organic growth study: Brad Anderson of Best Buy, Rick Schnieder of Sysco, Mike Eskew of UPS, John Brown of Stryker, Phil Tomlinson of TSYS, Mike Kowalski and Jim Quinn of Tiffany & Co., and the founders of Outback Steakhouses. When I taught at Goizueta Business School, Lafley spoke to our students. He arrived without an entourage, wearing an open shirt collar and no tie, and was simply "A. G." to our students. He was soft spoken, invited questions, and was a better listener than a speaker. He came across as humble, understanding the magnitude of his duty, and acknowledged not having all the answers. He did not come across as a visionary nor was he particularly charismatic, but everyone in the room understood why he had brought inner calm, focus, and renewed energy to P&G and why he was a great leader. Many lessons can be gleaned from Lafley's example.

Next is a look at a private growth company that has evolved and adapted over its ten-year history from a start-up to a successful company with $150 million of revenue. Defender Direct is both a personal and business evolutionary and growth story. Its founder, Dave Lindsey, has an interesting view of business growth.

Defender Direct, Inc. Case

Defender Direct, Inc. (Defender), headquartered in Indianapolis, Indiana, is a privately held company that sells and installs ADT security systems and Dish Network Satellite TV to homeowners across the United States.[21] Its president and CEO, Lindsey, started the business out of his home in 1998, making a transition from new product development at Medeco Security Locks, Inc., to entrepreneur. He used $30,000 of his and his wife's personal savings to fund the start-up, which he called Defender Security Co.

Since its humble beginnings in the Lindseys' spare bedroom, Defender has become one of the largest security and satellite dealers in the Midwest, experiencing an average annual growth rate of 60% over ten years. In 2008, Defender generated $150 million in revenues and earned the rank of 387 on the Inc. 500 list of America's Fastest-Growing Companies. With 1,500 employees, the company had a national footprint of 120 offices in forty states.

Defender's stellar growth was fueled by an aggressive direct-marketing focus and national expansion, but Lindsey, who was fond of saying that "businesses don't grow—people do," credited the Defender culture, which fosters continuous employee development. As he said, "Defender has grown faster than its peers not because we are better at selling and installing security systems, but because our people have grown. Our sales have doubled because the capacity and talents of our leaders have doubled. A few years ago we stopped trying to double our business and realized the way to grow was to double our team members' enthusiasm, optimism and skills. Send people to seminars, leadership conferences and self-help programs. Build a culture on purpose, not by accident."[22]

The Founder

Lindsey was born in 1969 and grew up in the Midwest. He graduated from Indiana University with a B.S. with honors in Business-Finance and an MBA in Marketing and Finance. While working for various companies in the lock and door hardware industry, he became interested in security systems. A turning point for Lindsey came when he was passed up for a promotion while working for Medeco Security Locks in Salem, Virginia. "We're going to start a business," he said to his wife, "because I don't want to ever be in this spot again, where it's office politics controlling my career."

At Medeco, Lindsey had been involved in a program called 2x, which was a set of business processes inspired by Michael Gerber's best-selling book, *The E-Myth Revisited: Why Most Small Businesses Don't Work and What to Do About It.*[23] As Lindsey put it, "It was a way for a mostly traditional type of locksmith to double their business, using the 2x process and then up-selling. We would teach it to our locksmith dealers, and I saw it work, and decided, 'I've always wanted to own my own business, why not buy a locksmith shop, double it and create value?'"

Opportunity Knocks

Lindsey and his wife started looking for a locksmith business for sale, but having found none at a price they were willing to pay, they decided to move to Indianapolis, Indiana. "That's where my family was and my support structure, and where I really wanted to be permanently," said Lindsey. Reflecting on his days as a freelance locksmith, he commented, "I began changing locks and installing deadbolts, which was pretty horrible because every psychological test I've ever taken says that me and a power drill should stay as far apart as possible. I have some great stories about taking out my friends' locks and not being able to put them back on. . . . So that's how I began, pretty ugly, and my intention was to never do installation, because I'm not technical. But I had to get out and learn."

While his wife took over the role of a family breadwinner, Lindsey researched the security industry. "I was, like, if someone needs a lock, maybe they want an alarm system? And in the mid-nineties the alarm industry really exploded." Lindsey jumped at an opportunity when ADT Security Systems and other brands began offering $99 start-up packages for homeowners, making home security systems more affordable to a wide group of homeowners. "We wrote a business plan, got ADT to take a chance on us, and we began as an ADT Authorized Dealer ["Dealer"], and from that point, we never looked back. I never did another lock job once we signed our ADT contract."

Learning the Ropes

For the first three months as a Dealer, Lindsey focused on meeting the sales quotas. A failure to sell fifteen systems per month not only led to possible difficult business issues; it also resulted in a financial penalty, which would have swallowed much of the Lindseys' start-up capital. A devotee of Gerber's principles laid out in *The E-Myth Revisited*, Lindsey said he "was looking for that Gerber-type repeatable system, something that could be McDonaldized."

Lindsey took advantage of a sales-training program offered by ADT. "The Dealer Program I came into was 90 percent door-to-door sales," said Lindsey. "ADT was teaching guys to knock on doors. They threw me in a van with a bunch of other guys and put me on the street and I'd sell ADT systems door-to-door."

That day Lindsey, who had never sold an ADT system before, made his first sale within a couple of hours. "I saw it work," he said. He immediately called his wife to tell her he was going to buy a fifteen-passenger van. As he recalled, "I had seen a repeatable process, which involved a van; when you go door-to-door you have to have that team environment—when you drive together in one car, you've got to pick the people up so they can't leave, until they get a sale. When everybody drives individually, they end up getting back in their cars and leaving."

The first month of knocking on doors, Lindsey sold six security systems and the second month, with the help of a friend, fifteen, which was a cause for a huge celebration; they fulfilled ADT's monthly quota. The third month, with the first hires onboard, was even better: thirty systems sold.

The ADT Sales Contest

By September 1998, Lindsey had assembled a team of ten salespeople. "I really wanted to start the team out with a bang," he said. "I needed a catalyst, a point of focus." ADT's sales contest with a $15,000 prize was exactly what Lindsey needed to fire up his team. "Each dealer's quota was based on the previous three months' sales," he said. "I believed we had a great opportunity to win since our previous three months' quota would be only 17 units." The team launched a sales blitzkrieg. As Lindsey recalled,

> My living room was converted into our Sales Meeting War Room, my artwork was covered up with a makeshift sales board and my entertainment center became an employee mailbox system. Administrative paperwork was handled from my back bedroom, complete with a board stretched out on the bed to form a desk, a computer and a borrowed fax

machine. Side meetings and training sessions were held on the front lawn. We were entrepreneurs, making the rules up as we went.

We had no fear and knew we had a great product and wanted to meet as many people as possible. We went out together each day, feeding off each other's energy.

One day in mid-September, while his sales team was gathered in his living-room, Lindsey went to the back bedroom to call ADT's headquarters to find out how his team ranked among other Dealers. His surprise turned to shock, as he learned that as a new Dealer he had his sales quota increased from seventeen to forty-five. Shaken, Lindsey stared at his reflection in the bedroom mirror, weighing his options.

What happened next was what Lindsey referred to as "an inflection point in the company" and "the moment of truth" for him as a leader. He took a few minutes to compose himself and went back to the living room to face his sales team. He candidly related the news, and then spent a few minutes rallying his troops. "We're going to blow through this," he said.

With forty-five sales under its belt already and two more weeks to go, Defender still had a shot at winning the contest. "We took it up a notch or two during those last two weeks and worked long hard days," said Lindsey. Defender's installation crew tripled capacity to make sure all the systems Defender had sold were installed the next day. By the end of the month, with 142 systems sold and installed, Lindsey and his sales team were 316% above their quota and 835% above their three-month historical average.

Having defeated hundreds of other Dealers across the United States, the upstart Defender snatched the top prize in the sales contest. "September was crazy," said Lindsey. "After four months of knocking on doors, we had a system and we knew what we were doing. Soon after, we sold 200, 300 systems, and we ran pretty quickly to the 600 range a month. And it kind of skyrocketed from there."

The Entrepreneurial Mindset

For the first few months of operation, Defender subcontracted all systems installations. "You know the old adage, nothing happens until a sale happens," said Lindsey. "So we focused on creating demand." In September, when the sales hit 142 systems, however, Lindsey hired his first installation technician. At the beginning, Defender hired technicians with minimal industry experience who were able to install a wireless alarm system that was easy to install.

Around the same time, Lindsey hired his first sales manager, who took over driving the van with the sales team, freeing Lindsey's time and allowing him to try to "get the paperwork done to support this," as he put it. "I was able to stop and go back and put some processes in place." Reflecting on building the business early on, he recalled, "We kept in mind Gerber's three roles in a business: the entrepreneur's job is to create the process, the manager's job is to assure the process is used, and the technician's job is to follow the process and use it. And that has dominated my thoughts for the past ten years. Every time we're trying to grow something, we are very clear about who is playing these roles and we make sure somebody's doing each of these. In the beginning, I played all those different roles, but I was conscious that I was ultimately the entrepreneur, and for the first three or four years all I did was build processes."

Thinking Big—With a Clear Focus

In November 1998, Defender opened a second office that sold 125 systems the first month. Lindsey's sales team made a pledge to open a new office every ninety days, ending their first year of operation with four offices. "I lived by, and we still do," said Lindsey, by Gerber's tenet—"big business is just a small business that thought big. And we wanted to be much bigger. In those days we'd always remind ourselves that it's not okay to put a mom-and-pop system in place, because that's just going to keep us small forever."

Looking for ways to grow his business, Lindsey considered expanding into the commercial security market, but after some thought he decided that the residential market would be Defender's staple. "We weren't so much a security company as a home market and installation company." Lindsey said. "We found another product that could be marketed in a mass way and be installed in homes."[24] That product was satellite TV, which Defender added to its offerings in 2001, and quickly became one of the top Dish Network dealers.

Since making the decision to concentrate on the residential market, Lindsey has stayed true to course and steered his company away from potential distractions. "We have a saying posted all over our offices—'focus equals growth.'" As he elaborated: "Today we still only have 13 part numbers in our inventory room, the same 13 we had 10 years ago. We have not added things. We keep doing more of the same better, trying to Mc-Donaldize it. We understood focus as the goal early on, constantly using an ABC format to prioritize. I coach all of our new leaders, 'We don't pay you to get everything done—we pay you to get the most important things done.'"

Defender's Circle of Life

Another practical tool, which Lindsey and his leadership team used on a weekly basis, was the so-called Circle of Life. It was a visual representation of their understanding of how their business worked. "Imagine a clock face," said Lindsey. Twelve o'clock is marketing, three o'clock is sales, six o'clock is installation and nine o'clock is admin and finance. It used to be just sales, door-to-door, but it all starts with marketing. So I spent my energy on really ramping it over the last five years."

Whenever Lindsey noticed a bottleneck in any of the four quadrants of the circle, he would focus his full attention on that particular area to alleviate the bottleneck. He explained how he and his direct reports used the Circle of Life as follows:

First, I'd work with marketing until we had enough leads. But we didn't have enough salespeople, so I'd jump over to sales, and make sure we close all the leads until we didn't have enough technicians. Then, I'd go down to installation and make sure we're getting all the systems installed, and it would flow back up, and then we'd have a paperwork backup, so I'd make sure ADT was paying us. And then as soon as that is all released, we say that the money flows around that. Marketing takes a dollar and starts it as 12 o'clock, and you hope that two dollars come up when you spin around the circle. So then I'd go back to marketing and say, okay, we've got some more marketing programs: let's go. And I just kept running around that circle. The faster you spin the circle, the faster we grow.

I've had my direct reports come to me and say, "You're focusing on my part of the circle right now. You've been to my office every day this week," and I'm, "Yeah, I'm going to be in your part of the circle until our install rate or our backlog is down." Today, I'm backing up from that a little bit as I'm changing my role.

To keep a close eye on his business's financial performance, Lindsey used a scorecard, which he introduced a year after he had started Defender. "It's a concise Excel spreadsheet," said Lindsey, "with weeks' and months' worth of history and then this week's numbers, like, what's the close rate? We want to get that scorecard more automated and we want that to be a live dashboard." Lindsey held weekly Friday meetings with his direct reports, during which they thoroughly reviewed all metrics on the scorecard. The meetings started in the afternoon and lasted more than four hours.

The Evolution of the Business Model

For the first three years, Defender's sales force consisted of "full-commission door-knockers," as Lindsey put it. "It was a great way to start, because there's no marketing and you're only paying someone when the sale was made. Then we realized we could set appointments instead of knocking on doors and we became 100 percent telemarketing based."

Around the time Defender was making a transition to telemarketing, Lindsey's acquaintance introduced him to Marcia Raab, who owned a small call center in Indiana. Soon after, Defender became Raab's exclusive customer. "She did a great job, was such a servant to our business—she really did it at an exchange rate with us," said Lindsey. "Terrific marketing and sales person. She grew the twenty-person call center to 200 people in two centers, and she owned that."

Defender eventually bought Raab's call centers, and Raab became Defender's vice president of sales and marketing. "She was an absolute dynamo," said Lindsey. "She started coming to our staff meetings when she was our outsource partner with her own call centers, which she ran like it was a division of ours. And then we formalized it and put her in the VP spot."

The telemarketing operation had to be scrapped in 2001, when "the no-call list hit," as Lindsey put it, allowing consumers to limit unwanted telemarketing pitches. "We reinvented the business for the third time. Now it's 100% direct mail and the Internet, so our call centers handle only incoming calls."

Lindsey's Biggest Challenges

From the time Lindsey launched his own business, he had been challenged to continually evolve his relationship to the company, transforming himself from a door-to-door salesman, to sales manager, to controller, to regional manager, to president and CEO in ten years. As he reflected on his changing role,

> My biggest struggle has been constantly reinventing my relationship to the business. You go from a business that's in an extra bedroom, to 200 employees nationwide, $150 million in sales, and that is a huge challenge in itself, both in terms of process, skill, and psychologically. Every year I say to my wife that I have to reinvent my relationship to the business. It started with hiring the first sales manager to go take these guys to knock on doors for me, to then jumping to be an admin lead and putting someone else in my place. I feel like I kept filling a hole and then leaving somebody behind. And then taking it from being in Indianapolis to being a regional presence and all the skills that it takes. And today I'm evolving even more into being—I think of it as a chairman, a shareholder, investor, as well as business strategy and new products.

Managing People

As Lindsey's relationship to his business evolved, so did his management philosophy. At first, he found it hard to delegate. "It was hard to release control," Lindsey admitted. "At one time I thought I could do it better than anybody else. All it took was to hire a couple of people and understand they could do it better than me."

After six months of driving a van with his door-to-door sales team, Lindsey found a sales manager—the second one he hired—who he could trust and who, eventually, became the number-one ADT sales rep in the country, rising through the ranks to VP of sales. Similarly, the first installation technician Lindsey hired grew to become Defender's VP of installation. When Defender was generating $20 million revenues, he was in charge of installation for the whole company. "When the job started to outstrip him, he was put into a regional role, which was still almost a $10 million region," said Lindsey. "I always say to people whose jobs outstrip them, 'You still have the same level of responsibility, or more.'"

A manager who never had much tolerance for mistakes, Lindsey described himself as a proponent of "tough love." As he said, "I kind of manage with a Bobby Knight type of mentality with my direct reports. I've always said I need people with thick skin who themselves did not tolerate mistakes."

In 2008, Lindsey had three direct reports: a chief operations officer (COO), chief marketing officer (CMO), and chief financial officer (CFO). They are partners in the business.

Defender's Culture

Lindsey attributed Defender's success to its culture, which he had built around each employee's "personal growth." As he said, "Another word is 'terrific.' We talk about being terrific every day, and we choose to be that way."

Lindsey, who believes in continuously learning and growing, started to encourage his employees to do the same early on, sending them to various self-improvement seminars, such as the Dale Carnegie Training Program and Ed Foreman Successful Life Course. "We coined a saying, 'Businesses don't grow—people do,'" said Lindsey. "I don't want this to become a cliché around Defender because it's been our secret sauce. All of us had to grow. We've accomplished this reinvention through good books and good tapes and networking with good people."

Over the course of ten years, Lindsey reinvented Defender's business model three times, reinvented himself and his role, but, most important, redefined the purpose of his business, which had evolved from making money to growing people. "Our growth plan is that you have to reinvent yourself this year," Lindsey told 1,500 Defender employees at an annual Self-Improvement Day, which was held in April 2008 in Indianapolis. This company-wide commitment to personal growth and continuous reinvention is the linchpin of the corporate culture, and the Self-Improvement Day provides an opportunity to reaffirm it every year.

Lindsey was particularly proud of "Defender Advantage," the company's four-year-long initiation program into the Defender culture, where employees received leadership training, participated in a company-wide book club, and traveled with their families on mission trips abroad to volunteer. In addition, every newly hired installation technician attended Defender University, a complete training program that prepared them to be successful in the field. Part of the Defender University's curriculum was the Culture Day, during which all new hires heard from Defender's senior managers, including Lindsey, via satellite. The main purpose of Culture Day was to drive the following message: "We are asking you to work harder on yourself than on your job."

Besides focus and drive, Lindsey listed forgiveness as one of his greatest strengths as a leader. As he told his staff, he believes that "our ability to forgive each other really [has] built a culture around here. It's the glue that allows us to stay at this breakneck speed." Lindsey, who described himself as a "student of leadership," stressed that his "basic belief in forgiveness comes from my Faith and having learned from Jesus, who was a servant leader." Reflecting on his entrepreneurial journey, Lindsey commented, "It's been a humbling learning experience for me as a business owner. It's not about having a better plan or a widget. It's about helping your employees, because every time they grow, I grow. And that's what keeps me going, that's my calling in life—to build and develop leaders. . . . We don't want to be in the business of buying and selling businesses. We want to be in the business of growing and developing leaders. We have a platform to do that. So that's what my goals are."

Notes

....

1. Jeffrey D. Arendt, "Adaptive Intrinsic Growth Rates: An Integration Across Taxa," *Quarterly Review of Biology* 72, 2 (1997): 149–177; Stephen A. Arnott, Susumu Chiba, and David O. Conover, "Evolution of Intrinsic Growth Rate: Metabolic Costs Drive Trade-Offs Between Growth and Swimming Performance in *Menidia Menidia*," *Evolution* 60, 6 (2006): 1269–1278; Karl Gotthard, "Increased Risk of Predation as a Cost of High Growth Rate: An Experimental Test in a Butterfly," *Journal of Animal Ecology* 69, 5 (2000): 896–902; Stephan B. Munch and David O. Conover, "Nonlinear Growth Cost in *Menidia Menidia*: Theory and Empirical Evidence," *Evolution* 58, 3 (2004): 661–664.
2. José M. Gómez, "Bigger Is Not Always Better: Conflicting Selective Pressures on Seed Size in *Quercus Ilex*," *Evolution* 58, 1 (2004): 71–80.
3. Arseniy S. Karkach, "Trajectories and Models of Individual Growth," *Demographic Research* 15, 12 (2006): 347–400.
4. Arnott, Chiba, and Conover, "Evolution of Intrinsic Growth Rate"; Munch and Conover, "Nonlinear Growth Cost," 661–664.
5. Gotthard, "Increased Risk of Predation"; Munch and Conover, "Nonlinear Growth Cost."
6. Arendt, "Adaptive Intrinsic Growth Rates."
7. Karkach, "Trajectories and Models of Individual Growth."
8. Ibid.
9. Ibid., 348.

10. Eve Mitleton-Kelly, "Ten Principles of Complexity & Enabling Infrastructures," in *Complex Systems and Evolutionary Perspectives of Organisations: The Application of Complexity Theory to Organisations*, ed. Eve Mitleton-Kelly (New York: Elsevier Science, 2003), 5.

11. John Henry Clippinger III, ed., *The Biology of Business: Decoding the Natural Laws of Enterprise* (San Francisco: Jossey-Bass, 1999), 7.

12. Ibid., 13.

13. Roger Lewin, *Complexity: Life at the Edge of Chaos* (Chicago: University of Chicago Press, 1999), 198.

14. Shona L. Brown and Kathleen M. Eisenhardt, *Competing on the Edge: Strategy as Structured Chaos* (Boston: Harvard Business School Press, 1998); Shona L. Brown and Kathleen M. Eisenhardt, "The Art of Continuous Change: Linking Complexity Theory and Time-Paced Evolution in Relentlessly Shifting Organizations," *Administrative Science Quarterly* 42 (1997): 1–34.

15. Brown and Eisenhardt, "Art of Continuous Change," 1.

16. Merhdad Baghai, Stephen C. Coley, David White, Charles Conn, and Robert J. McLean. "Staircases to Growth," *McKinsey Quarterly* 4 (1996): 38–61; Edward D. Hess, *The Road to Organic Growth* (New York: McGraw-Hill, 2007); Edward D. Hess, "Organic Growth—Lessons from Market Leaders" (Working Paper, 2007); Jeanne M. Liedtka, Robert Rosen, and Robert Wiltbank, *The Catalyst: How You Can Become an Extraordinary Growth Leader* (New York: Crown Business, 2009).

17. Brown and Eisenhardt, "Art of Continuous Change," 32.

18. Richard D'Aveni and L. G. Thomas, "The Rise of Hypercompetition from 1950 to 2002: Evidence of Increasing Structural Destabilization and Temporary Competitive Advantage" (Working Paper, Tuck School of Business, Dartmouth College, October 11, 2004).

19. The P&G story is based on these primary sources: Daniel Bogler and Adrian Michaels, "Attempting to Shift the Stretch-Goal Posts," *Financial Times,* June 9, 2000, 32; Daniel Bogler and Adrian Michaels, "How a Stumble Became a Headlong Fall Over the Cliff," *Financial Times,* June 9, 2000, 18; Katrina Brooker and Julie Schlosser, "The Un-CEO: A. G. Lafley Doesn't Overpromise. He Doesn't Believe in the Vision Thing. All He's Done Is Turn Around P&G in 27 Months," *Fortune,* September 16, 2002, http://money.cnn.com/magazines/fortune/fortune_archive/2002/09/16/328576/index.htm; Neil Buckley, "P&G Chief Puts Smiles Back on Investors' Faces," *Financial Times,* May 6, 2002; Harlan S. Byrne, "A Return Visit to Earlier Stories—A Little Leeway: Procter & Gamble CEO John Pepper Is Being Patient in Pharmaceuticals," *Barron's,* January 1, 1996, 12; Brian Dumaine, "P&G Rewrites the Marketing Rules," *Fortune,* November 6, 1989, 34; "Taking It on the Chin," *Economist,* April 16, 1998, www.economist.com/business/displaystory.cfm?story_id=E1_TGDVNS; "Proctor & Gamble—Jager's Gamble," *Economist,* October 28, 1999, www.economist.com/business/displaystory.cfm?story_id=E1_PNGTNV; "Procter's Gamble," *Economist,* June 10, 1999, www.economist.com/business/displaystory.cfm?story_id=E1_PNNVDJ; "A

Marriage Made in Heaven—and in the Bathroom," *Economist*, January 28, 2005, www.economist.com/agenda/displaystory.cfm?story_id=3619402; "The Rise of the Superbrands—Consumer Goods," *Economist*, February 3, 2005, www.economist.com/displaystory.cfm?story_id=3623265; "Staying Pure," *Economist*, February 23, 2006, www.economist.com/business/displaystory.cfm?story_id=E1_VVQVVJD; "Face Value: A Post-Modern Proctoid," *Economist*, April 12, 2006, www.economist.com/businessfinance/displayStory.cfm?story_id=6795882; "Brand Management," *Economist*, March 1, 2007, www.economist.com/business/displaystory.cfm?story_id=E1_RSSGPSN; "Proctor & Gamble: Will She, Won't She?" *Economist*, August 9, 2007, www.economist.com/business/displaystory.cfm?story_id=9619074; "Starbucks v. McDonald's," *Economist*, January 10, 2008, www.economist.com/business/displaystory.cfm?story_id=10498747; "Starbucks Runs into Trouble," *Economist*, January 8, 2008, www.economist.com/business/displaystory.cfm?story_id= 10490218; "Comeback Kings?" *Economist*, January 8, 2009, www.economist.com/business/displaystory.cfm?story_id=12896749; Andrew Edgecliffe-Johnson, "P&G Cuts 15,000 Jobs in Attempt to Pep Up Sales—Group to Focus on Reviving Innovation," *Financial Times*, June 10, 1999, 1; Andrew Edgecliffe-Johnson, "P&G Cautions Over Recovery Before 2001," *Financial Times*, August 2, 2000, 30; Sarah Ellison, Ann Zimmerman, and Charles Forelle, "Sales Team—P&G's Gillette Edge: The Playbook It Honed at Wal-Mart; Consumer-Products Giant Helps Huge Retailer Make Specialty Items Mainstream; Coffee Beans for Beginners," *Wall Street Journal*, January 31, 2005, A1; "Procter and Gamble—After Artzt," *Financial Times*, March 21, 1995, 21; "P&G to Get Ahead by Marketing," *Financial Times*, June 5, 1997, 29; "Growth Pains Take Their Toll on P&G," *Financial Times*, August 5, 1998, 27; "Companies & Finance—the Americas—the What, Not the Where, to Drive P&G," *Financial Times*, September 3, 1998, 34; "Procter & Gamble Succumbs to Wall Street Blues," *Financial Times*, September 10, 1998, 40; "P&G Prepares for Thorough Shake-Up," *Financial Times*, June 7, 1999, 30; "LEX Column—Procter & Gamble," *Financial Times*, June 10, 1999, 22; "Howard Schultz's Starbucks Memo," *Financial Times*, February 23, 2007, http://us.ft.com/ftgateway/superpage.ft?news_id=fto022320071839455856&page=2; Jeremy Grant, Louisa Hearn, and Ian Bickerton, "Deal Forces New Realities on Competition," *Financial Times*, January 28, 2005, http://us.ft.com/ftgateway/superpage.ft?news_id=fto012820050069008406&page=1; Steven Greenhouse, "A New-Found Pep at P&G," *New York Times*, February 3, 1985; Carol Hymowitz and Gabriella Stern, "Taking Flak: At Procter & Gamble, Brands Face Pressure and So Do Executives—Amid Harsh Public Criticism by CEO, Some Bail Out; Artzt Calls It Training—Cutting Prices, Cutting Jobs," *Wall Street Journal*, May 10, 1993, A1; Emily Nelson, "Rallying the Troops at P&G—New CEO Lafley Aims to End Upheaval by Revamping Program of Globalization," *Wall Street Journal*, August 31, 2000, B1; Proctor & Gamble Company, 2008 Annual Report, The Proctor & Gamble Company—Financial and Strategic Analysis Review, Reference Code: GMDCPG32329GSA;

Bill Saporito and Ani Hadjian, "Behind the Tumult at P&G," *Fortune*, March 7, 1994, http://money.cnn.com/magazines/fortune/fortune_archive/1994/03/07/79047/index.htm; Zachary Schiller, "Marketing the Marketing Revolution at Procter & Gamble—Its 50-Year-Old Way of Selling Competing Products Gives Way to a New Concept: The Category," *BusinessWeek*, July 25, 1988, 72; Zachary Schiller, "The Corporation—No More Mr. Nice Guy at P&G—Not by a Long Shot," *BusinessWeek*, February 3, 1992, 54; Zachary Schiller, "Top of the News P&G's Worldly New Boss Wants a More Worldly Company—Edwin Artzt's Procter Will Be Savvier, Pushier, and a Lot More Global," *BusinessWeek*, October 30, 1989, 40; Zachary Schiller, "Procter & Gamble Heads for the Medicine Cabinet," *BusinessWeek*, August 7, 1995, 28; Jolie B. Solomon and John Bussey, "Cultural Change: Pressed by Its Rivals, Procter & Gamble Co. Is Altering Its Ways—Firm Trims Its Work Force, Sets Up Project Teams; Some in Union Are Irked—One-Page Memo Loses Clout," *Wall Street Journal*, May 20, 1985, Section J; Alecia Swasy, "Slow and Steady: In a Fast-Paced World, Procter & Gamble Sets Its Store in Old Values—Rules, Habit, Hierarchy Seem to Work for Soap Giant Despite Hot Competition—No More Monopolies, Though," *Wall Street Journal*, September 21, 1989, Section J; Richard Tomkins, "International Company News—P&G Chief Artzt to Step Down in July," *Financial Times*, March 15, 1995, 32; Richard Tomkins, "Heirs Apparently as Different as Chalk and Cheese," *Financial Times*, March 21, 1995, 21; Richard Tomkins, "Pepper Preparing to Step Down from Top Job at P&G," *Financial Times*, September 10, 1998, 31; Richard Tomkins, "P&G Clouds the US Corporate Mirror," *Financial Times*, June 10, 1999, 28; Winston Williams, "Personality Change for P&G," *New York Times*, March 23, 1984, Section D.

20. Greenhouse, "New-Found Pep."
21. Edward D. Hess, "Defender Direct" (Case Study UVA-G-0623, University of Virginia Darden School Foundation, Charlottesville, 2009). All quotes are directly from the case.
22. "Defender Security Co." *Indianapolis Business Journal*, September 15, 2003.
23. Michael E. Gerber, *The E-Myth Revisited: Why Most Small Businesses Don't Work and What to Do About It* (New York: HarperCollins, 1995).
24. Terri Greenwell, "*IBJ*'s Fastest Growing Companies," *Indianapolis Business Journal*, September 17, 2007.

CHAPTER 6

....

Smart Growth

AUTHENTIC GROWTH

I **HAVE FOUND** no empirical support for the axiom "grow or die" or for the Growth Mental Model. My research and the predominant views in various fields support an alternative way to think about growth, which I call Smart Growth.

Smart Growth rejects the assumptions that every business must grow, that all growth is good, and that bigger is always better. It also rejects the Growth Mental Model tenet that growth should be continuous and smooth. These assumptions are neither true nor based on science or business reality. Smart Growth rejects the Earnings Game and believes that business health should be measured by Authentic Earnings.

Smart Growth rejects the axiom that every business must grow or die. In many cases growth can cause the death of a business. Smart Growth rejects the assumption that the primary objective of a business is to continue to grow. Smart Growth replaces the axiom of grow or die with "improve to remain competitive." Smart Growth rejects the tenet that big is always better and believes that being better is more important than being bigger.

The primary objective of Smart Growth is to build enduring businesses, which continue to meet the needs of their customers, employees, owners, and the communities in which they operate by being good corporate citizens. Smart Growth is not anti-growth; but Smart Growth believes that improvement is more important than growth. If a business improves, it is likely it will have the opportunity to grow.

That opportunity to grow requires that a business approach growth not as a given but rather as a conscious decision to be made with rigorous analytical thinking, weighing the pros and cons of growing versus the pros and cons of not growing. Smart Growth believes that growth is change and growth is a complex process that is enabled and hindered by human dynamics; as such, growth creates risks, which need to be illuminated and managed. This complex process rarely happens smoothly or continuously without mistakes, bumps in the road, or detours. Smart Growth changes growth from an assumed given to a rigorous decision and risk management process.

Smart Growth comprises two different components. The first is Authentic Growth: growth generated by either selling more services and products in arm's-length transactions to more customers or by operating more efficiently and productively. Authentic Growth does not include earnings generated by the Earnings Game. Authentic Earnings are qualitatively different from those produced by the Earnings Game. Earnings Game results do not represent the same type of information about the viability, competitiveness, and strength of a business's business model or customer value proposition. Rather, Earnings Game numbers represent intellectual machinations and financial engineering, usually the intellectual capital of the CFO or advisors from accounting and investment banking firms. The second component is risk: Smart Growth believes that all growth creates risks that need to be managed, which is discussed in Chapters 7 and 8.

Smart Growth companies do make acquisitions but those acquisitions are driven by strategic reasons and not by Earnings Game reasons. In many cases such acquisitions add capabilities or new customer segments, such as Best Buy's acquisitions of the Geek Squad and Magnolia Hi-Fi and Sysco's acquisitions that geographically expanded the company.

Disclosure/Transparency of the "Earnings Game"

A significant problem in public financial SEC reporting requirements is that a company is not required to clearly disclose how it generates its earnings and, in particular, how much to the penny of its earnings are Authentic Earnings versus Earnings Game earnings. This lack of transparency about the quality and source of the earnings reported can mask company problems, which can impact investors' judgments and stock values. Without transparency, the market has no basis to assign different values to different quality or types of reported earnings. Although companies are required to disclose quarterly earnings and annual earnings along with management discussion of material results and risks, it is difficult to look at those reports and understand how a company generated its results to the penny. This enables the Earnings Game.

What Is the Impact of the Earnings Game?

Chapter 1 shows that business leaders such as John Bogle, Warren Buffett, Arthur Levitt, organizations such as the U.S. Chamber of Commerce, the Aspen Institute, the CFA Centre for Financial Market Integrity and the Business Roundtable Institute for Corporate Ethics all acknowledge the Earnings Game's existence and its negative consequences, but little has been done to change the game. I contend the Earnings Game is alive and well today and that it has the potential to corrupt our public markets and our financial system.

Although knowledge that companies manage earnings is widespread, no one knows the magnitude of the Earnings Game or the degree to which it conceals fundamental weaknesses in companies. It is surprising that these questions have not been the subject of rigorous academic research.

With the current lack of complete transparency, could the earnings created by the Earnings Game be creating the illusion of value for a company? Recall from Chapter 1 that the average tenure of a public company CEO is about six years and the average holding period of a company's stock is about one year. And remember the fees earned by accounting firms, law firms, and investment banks by helping companies play the Earnings Game and the potential positive impact of the Earnings Game on stock options.

This mutuality of short-term interests by those players may not only result in a short-term mentality, which can hinder, postpone, or even destroy long-term value creation, but also it may be appropriating a disproportionate amount of financial wealth from the system based on the Earnings Game. The Wall Street Rules may be driving short-term behaviors, which may disproportionately create immense wealth for the short-term players. This potentially large wealth extraction does not increase a company's competitive advantage or its sustainability, nor does it inure in most cases to long-term stockholders, such as employees who own company stock in their 401(k) plans.

Does the Earnings Game serve the public interest? Does it increase global competitiveness? Does it increase economic national security? Does it contribute to long-term societal, family, and job stability? Does it help create enduring high-quality businesses?

When a significant number of public companies materially play the Earnings Game, they run the risk of creating an earnings bubble. Why should our financial system take that chance? As a country we should not be running that risk. Therefore, the SEC should require companies to clearly let the sun shine on how they create their earnings. Why not require full disclosure of Authentic Earnings and Earnings Game earnings to the penny?

There are two fundamental rules of managing a business: (1) if you want something done, measure it; and (2) if you want it done well, measure and reward it. So, why not establish systems to measure and reward Authentic Earnings? Boards of directors can do that now without SEC action. Also, companies can choose not to play the earnings guidance quarterly game. Companies whose earnings are authentic can try to circumvent any negative market reaction of rejecting the Wall Street Rules by disclosing how they create their earnings and their strategic growth portfolio initiatives. This notifies investors where the company plans to go and how it intends to get there. Best Buy has done the latter for years on its Web site.

The issue of earnings management, which is part of the Earnings Game, has drawn the focus of noted investors and business commentators. Warren Buffett discusses the issue this way: "I can't tell you how much I hate managed earnings in terms of what they do to people. The nature of managed earnings is that you start out small. It's like stealing five bucks from the cash register and promising yourself you'll pay it back. You never do. You end up the next time stealing ten bucks. Once you start that kind of game it draws everybody in."[1]

Another noted investor, John Bogle, questions the myriad of ways to create earnings by noting that the incidence of corporate earnings restatements has risen nearly eighteen-fold from 1997 to 2006 to more than 1,570.[2]

In his May 21, 2008, column, Steve Pearlstein, Pulitzer Prize–winning business columnist for the *Washington Post*, writing about General Electric (GE), stated: "Unfortunately, under his [CEO Jeff Immelt] predecessor, this wonderful reputation got transformed into a solemn promise to deliver double-digit earnings growth every quarter, and to do so in a way that precisely matched the earnings guidance provided by the company. To meet those expectations, GE has become suspiciously adept at booking revenue and expenses and timing asset sales to meet earnings estimates with amazing precision and consistency." Pearlstein then exhorts Immelt to opt out of the "mindless earnings expectation game" and get back to GE's roots of creating new products and operating more efficiently.[3]

As described in Chapter 1, the Earnings Game leads many companies to make short-term decisions solely to meet earnings expectations even if they have long-term negative value creation consequences. The only way out of this Earnings Game is disclosure of the nature and source of the earnings. The Coca-Cola Company provides an interesting look at the Earnings Game. Under the leadership of Roberto Goizueta, Coca-Cola became a great growth company, but some of that remarkable growth was produced by buying and selling bottlers, spinning off its distribution system, and controlling the sales price of its syrup to its bottlers. Warren Buffett served on the board of directors of Coca-Cola for seventeen years until 2006. In Buffet's authorized biography, *The Snowball,* the author had this to say about the Earnings Game:

> Buffett had had enough of "managed earnings" that underlay these Coca-Cola problems, in which the Wall Street analysts' predictions of what a company would earn enticed managers to dig behind the sofa cushions in order to "make the numbers" thereby meeting or beating "consensus" to please investors. Because the vast majority of companies had tried to set, then surpass Wall Street's expectations instead of simply reporting what they earned—making the practice uniform—even a penny per-share shortfall made them look as though they were having problems and often led to precipitous declines in stock prices. Thus, companies claimed they must manage earnings, in a vicious, self-fulfilling game. But "earnings management" was sort of Ponzi-ing.[4]

Coca-Cola Company Case

Coca-Cola is the world's largest manufacturer and distributor of nonalcoholic beverage syrups and concentrates.[5] In 2008, it sold more than $31 billion worth of products in more than 200 countries. Coca-Cola sells its syrups and concentrates directly to fountain purchasers and consumers through wholly owned or independently or partially owned bottlers and canning or distribution companies.

Coca-Cola owns approximately 35% of Coca-Cola Enterprises (CCE), the world's largest marketer, producer, and distributor of Coca-Cola products, which operates in U.S., Canadian, Belgian, French, British, and Dutch markets. Coca-Cola became a high-growth company under the leadership of Roberto Goizueta, who served as president and later chairman and CEO from 1980 until his death in 1997. Under Goizueta's leadership, Coca-Cola's market cap grew from $4.3 billion to $180 billion. But after his death, Coca-Cola's market cap declined to under $115 billion, and by 2006, for the first time in their long competitive history, Pepsi-Cola gained the larger market cap. This decline took place under three CEOs: Doug Ivester, Doug Daft, and Neville Isdell. In early March 2009, Coca-Cola's market cap exceeded $92 billion, or about half of what it was at its peak under Goizueta, whereas PepsiCo's market cap was $73 billion.

Without Goizueta at the helm, Coca-Cola was plagued by internal political issues and international business and public-relations issues in Belgium, the United Kingdom, India, France, and Colombia. It also faced charges of racial discrimination, whistle-blower lawsuits, and channel-stuffing allegations. Coca-Cola's "captive" but nonconsolidated financial relationship with CCE also came under the microscope. Furthermore, the company was playing catch-up with such noncarbonated beverages as water, tea, and energy and health drinks. Under Isdell's leadership, which ran from 2004 to 2008, Coca-Cola began aggressively making acquisitions and forming joint ventures with high-growth beverage companies. Muhtar Kent, who became CEO in July 2008, has continued this trend.

Early History

Dr. John Pemberton, an Atlanta pharmacist, developed the Coca-Cola formula and dreamed that he could make a fortune selling it as a medicine for many ailments. Inspired by a French wine concoction, he tinkered with the formula to create a mixture made of coca leaves and spices. In 1886, Pemberton first sold his medical tonic in Jacob's Pharmacy in Atlanta for five cents, but Pemberton was unable to turn Coca-Cola into a business by himself and had to turn to investors for money. Although his syndication of the Coca-Cola product was alleged to have been haphazard, surprisingly, more than 100% of it was sold.

In 1887, Asa Candler purchased an interest in Coca-Cola and ultimately acquired 100% interest, for a total investment of $2,300. Candler then patented the Coca-Cola formula, which has remained a closely guarded secret. Candler realized Coca-Cola's potential, but he lacked the capital to expand the business quickly, so in 1899, for $1, he sold the exclusive rights to bottle and distribute Coca-Cola in most of the United States to two Chattanooga,

Tennessee, businessmen, Benjamin Thomas and Joseph Whitehead. These men enlisted John Lupton in their new venture, and by 1919, there were more than 1,000 independent Coca-Cola bottlers.

From Robert to Roberto

In 1919, the Candler family, allegedly without their father's knowledge, sold Coca-Cola for $25 million to an investor group led by W. C. Bradley and Ernest Woodruff, the father of Robert Woodruff, who would become president of Coca-Cola in 1923 and ruled Coca-Cola until 1997—almost seventy-five years. Woodruff managed Coca-Cola conservatively, and the company paid out more than 50% of its earnings as dividends and operated with little or no debt.

Robert Woodruff extended Coca-Cola's distribution reach to gasoline stations and vending machines and through global expansion. During World War II, Woodruff made sure Coca-Cola was available to U.S. service personnel worldwide. It was also during Woodruff's reign that Coca-Cola was first sold in cans, and Tab, Fresca, and Sprite were introduced. Under Woodruff, Coca-Cola was controlled from its headquarters in Atlanta, Georgia, and its board was controlled by Woodruff and its bank, the Trust Company of Georgia. By the end of the Woodruff years, Coca-Cola was bottled and distributed by approximately 400 independent bottlers.

Roberto Goizueta (1980–1997)

Serving as chairman and CEO of Coca-Cola from August 1980 until his death in October 1997, Roberto Goizueta was reputed to have created more shareholder value during his tenure than any other CEO in history. He has the distinction of being the first non-founder CEO to become a billionaire while a company CEO.

Born into a wealthy Cuban family, Goizueta graduated from Yale University. He first went to work for Coca-Cola in Cuba as a chemical engineer, but after defecting with his family to the United States during the Castro revolution, he worked for Coca-Cola in Miami. After relocating to Coca-Cola headquarters in Atlanta, Goizueta moved up the corporate ladder as a technician and then the head of legal and external affairs. Although he was not a marketing or financial person by training or experience, Goizueta learned to excel in these areas by the time he ascended to the top job at Coca-Cola, where Woodruff's selection of him as president surprised many. He beat out another well-respected Coca-Cola marketing wizard—Donald Keogh—whom Goizueta convinced to stay on as his number-two man. Together, Goizueta and Keogh created a remarkable partnership that, over the years, made both of them very wealthy. Goizueta became, in effect, "Mr. Inside" and "Mr. Wall Street," whereas Keogh became the global marketer.

Goizueta, the chemical engineer and master internal politician, became a master marketer of the Coca-Cola brand. After he became president, in 1980, he quickly maneuvered his way into the chairmanship and CEO positions, and by 1981 had changed the rules regarding board-membership qualifications to solidify his power base.

Goizueta experienced both success, with the introduction of Diet Coke in 1982, and failure, with the introduction of New Coke in 1985 to much fanfare, only to withdraw it when it proved to be a flop. He dealt with the independent bottling system by forcing the weak bottlers to sell (usually to Coca-Cola) and by buying up the strong bottlers who wanted to sell, preventing them from being bought by other corporations. Some of the purchased bottlers were resold at a profit to other bottlers, and some continued to be held by Coca-Cola, reducing the number of independent bottlers to fewer than 200.

In 1986, as financial engineers, Goizueta and Ivester saw an opportunity to consolidate the bottling operations and spin them out of Coca-Cola into CCE, thus moving significant assets off Coca-Cola's balance sheet. This move provided a second financial benefit as, in most cases, Coca-Cola was able to structure and control the price of its syrup sales to CCE. Realizing that Coca-Cola's use of equity capital to expand was more costly than debt, Goizueta led Coca-Cola's first major debt offering of $215 million. In addition, he saw the positive impact of a Coca-Cola stock-buyback program, and instituted one that bought back a significant amount at low prices. He was responsible for Coca-Cola's expansion into China, India, and Indonesia.

Also during his tenure, Coca-Cola sold off its shrimp-farming, wine, and Aqua Chem businesses, allowing the company to focus on its carbonated-beverage business. The result was that its sales grew from $4 billion to $18 billion and its market cap from $4.3 billion to $180 billion. Goizueta's reign at Coca-Cola aptly may be called the "golden years" because he led the creation of substantial shareholder value. Goizueta motivated his leaders through stock options and introduced a strategic process as well as centralized controls within Coca-Cola. His tremendous impact in Coca-Cola's base of Atlanta endures through the Goizueta Foundation, which, in addition to other donations, has made major bequests to the Goizueta Business School at Emory University.

Doug Ivester (1997–1999)

When Goizueta succumbed to lung cancer in October 1997, he was replaced by Doug Ivester, who, before his tenure at Coca-Cola, had previously worked for Goizueta as an accountant with Ernst and Young. At Coca-Cola, Ivester became Goizueta's financial-engineering partner as the company's CFO and was intimately involved in the CCE initiative and Coca-Cola's capital strategy and earnings management.

Ivester's reign was short and unsuccessful. It was marred by a major racial-discrimination lawsuit, health scares in Belgium and France, European Union antitrust issues, and botched acquisitions of Orangina in France and Cadbury Schweppes in Australia, Mexico, and continental Europe.

Doug Daft (1999–2004)

Replacing Ivester was another Coca-Cola executive, Australian Doug Daft, who was a change agent in many ways. For instance, Daft saw the need to focus on noncarbonated drinks. This was a major shift as the Coca-Cola system was built upon and engineered to market, manufacture, and bottle carbonated drinks. Daft also tackled Coca-Cola's structure, which he considered bloated, and its attitude, which he felt was complacent. He undertook Coca-Cola's first major restructuring, laying off nearly 20% of the company's workforce and forcing out or reassigning thirty of its top thirty-two senior managers. Although Daft managed to settle the racial-discrimination lawsuit for $156 million, survive antitrust investigations in Europe, and clear the company's name regarding channel-stuffing allegations and investigations in Japan, Germany, and the Balkans, several events tainted Coca-Cola's global image during his tenure: the whistleblower lawsuit exposing the Burger King drink-test manipulation and the botched introduction of Dasani into the United Kingdom.

Daft tried to move aggressively into new-drink segments by negotiating the purchase of Quaker Oats and its Gatorade product. Surprisingly, this proposed acquisition was rejected by the board as being too expensive, creating a golden opportunity for PepsiCo, which bought it and later profited when Gatorade became the dominant energy/athletic drink. Still, Daft pressed on. He tried to be innovative by forming a joint venture with Procter & Gamble regarding Minute Maid. He announced that Coca-Cola would start home-delivery service under his regime. He introduced Vanilla Coke. But after only five years Daft announced his intent to resign in 2004, setting the board on a very public search outside Coca-Cola for a new CEO.

Neville Isdell (2004–2008)

The board was unable to recruit a high-profile CEO from Kellogg, Gillette, or Home Depot or, reportedly, to lure Jack Welch out of retirement. Instead, it brought back a former Coca-Cola executive, Neville Isdell. The ascension of Isdell to CEO was described by *Fortune* magazine: "Since then [1998], with breathtaking speed, it [Coca-Cola] has become a case study in business dysfunction. In just six years this group [the board] has installed one CEO, ousted him, and installed another so inexperienced that he needed constant shoring up, and finally, after a very public search that found no outside takers, named a third—a retired Coke executive who had been passed over for the top job [before]."[6]

Dutifully, Isdell took the helm and announced that "if the system isn't broken, there's still opportunity for both Coca-Cola and the other soft drink brands."[7] Under Isdell, Coca-Cola adopted a "Manifesto for Growth" strategy, together with its mission "to refresh the world." Isdell inherited a company that was still number one in carbonated drinks, a slow-growth market, but was a distant second in the high-growth noncarbonated-beverage market. In three years, he tried to move Coca-Cola into the new-beverage market, with increased new-product development and acquisitions. The company introduced many new drinks and varieties of drinks already being marketed, including Tab Energy, Coca-Cola Blak, Full Throttle Fury, and Coca-Cola Zero, and bought Fuze Beverage and Energy Brands (maker of Glacéau beverages).

Under Isdell, Coca-Cola reorganized its North American beverage division into three groups: sparkling beverages, still beverages, and energy beverages. Isdell also tried to address Wall Street's concerns by setting the following realistic growth targets:

- Volume: 3% to 4%
- Revenue: 5% to 6%
- EPS: high single digits

In 2008, Coca-Cola expanded further by buying 40% of Honest Tea and forming a major coffee drink joint venture with IllyCafe of Italy. In July 2008, Kent took over and continued the trend by signing a distribution agreement with Hansen Natural for Monster Energy drinks. Coca-Cola's recent financial results are shown in Table 6.1.

TABLE 6.1 Financial Results

YEAR ENDED DECEMBER 31 (IN BILLIONS)	2008	2007
Net operating revenues	$31.9	$28.9
Gross profit	$20.6	$18.5
Operating income	$8.4	$7.3
Net cash operations	$7.6	$7.2

According to its 2008 Annual Report, Coca-Cola's consolidated statements show that acquisitions and consolidation of controlled bottling operations during 2008 and 2007 resulted in a substantial increase in the number of company-owned bottling plants. In the same report, 6% of the 11% increase in net operating revenue from 2007 to 2008 was attributed to currency and hedging gains.[8] Coca-Cola's stock performance is shown in Table 6.2.

TABLE 6.2 Five-Year Stock Performance

YEAR ENDED	COCA-COLA	PEER GROUP	S&P 500
12/31/07	$134	$188	$142
12/31/08	$102	$144	$90

Source: SEC Form 10-K for fiscal year ended December 31, 2008.

Products

Although Coca-Cola's distant second place in the noncarbonated-beverage market is a major issue, its product portfolio and new-product introductions make up a long list. Coca-Cola owns or licenses more than 500 brands, thirteen of which are $1 billion or more brands, including Coke, Diet Coke, Fanta, Sprite, Coca-Cola Zero, Vitamin Water, Powerade, Minute Maid, and Georgia Coffee. Four of the top five nonalcohol drink brands in the world are owned by Coca-Cola: Coca-Cola, Diet Coke, Fanta, and Sprite.

Bottlers

Candler's decision in 1899 to outsource bottling and distribution to franchised bottlers and the consolidation of bottlers in the United States resulted in CCE creating a strong stakeholder base, which had been Coca-Cola's focus for many years. A magazine article described the situation: "Over the years, Coke has sapped its bottlers' profits in order to boost its own. . . . Analysts say that Coke has increased concentrate prices 3% to 4% annually during the past decade: U.S. bottlers, with customers hooked on discounting, generally haven't been able to raise prices. The upshot: only one of Coke's ten anchor bottlers around the world . . . is believed to earn a return above its cost of capital."[9] CCE has an exclusive license to produce, market, and distribute Coca-Cola products in perpetuity in authorized containers. Coca-Cola has absolute authority to set prices and terms of payment and purchase. Bottlers cannot distribute non–Coca-Cola products, and Coca-Cola has to consent to any sale of any bottler, in whole or in part. The financial results of Coca-Cola's largest bottler, CCE, are shown in Table 6.3.

TABLE 6.3 Selected CCE Data

YEAR ENDED DECEMBER 31 (IN BILLIONS)	2008	2007	2006	2005
Net operating revenues	$21.8	$18.7	$19.8	$18.7
Cost of sales	$13.8	$11.2	$10.8	$10.2
Gross profit	$8.0	$7.6	$7.4	$7.2

Source: Coca-Cola Enterprises SEC Form 10-K for fiscal year ended December 31, 2008.

Growth: What Is the Reality?

In 2004, CEO Isdell inherited a culture created by Woodruff, a financial system developed by Goizueta, a bottling system designed by Candler, a restructured company engineered by Daft, and a new consumer marketplace. He also inherited seven years of anemic growth. Isdell formulated a "Manifesto for Growth," setting modest, realistic growth targets, depending on one's perspective. Kent inherited a company that had been actively buying brands and bottlers under Isdell. It is not clear how much of Coca-Cola's recent growth is attributable to internal Authentic Growth as compared to brand acquisitions and bottler acquisitions. We do know that over one-half of its increase in net operating revenue in 2008 as compared to 2007 came from currency and hedging gains.[10]

Buffett's biography provides fascinating information about Coca-Cola. The author describes how Coca-Cola bought and sold bottlers and squeezed CCE to manage earnings.

> But in 1997, Coca-Cola had started to set goals for itself that were so ambitious that it took—not a ham sandwich, not even Goizueta—but a lot of financial engineering to achieve them.
>
> Coke owned forty percent of CCE and tended to act as though it owned a hundred percent. The creation of CCE by rolling up a group of bottlers had been part of a larger strategy of buying and selling bottlers to time the profits and boost Coca-Cola's earnings. This was neither illegal nor technically deceitful, but it was nonetheless an illusion.[11]

Conclusion

Coca-Cola is a great brand and a good company. Coca-Cola has not done anything illegal. But it appears that it, like many other public companies, has partially complied with the Wall Street Rules by playing the Earnings Game. The Coca-Cola story illustrates that a good company can get in the habit of engaging in sales transactions or other financial transactions that produce legal reportable earnings but are not what I consider Authentic Growth.

Chapter 2 showed that continuous growth is the exception not the rule. And according to my research, less than 2% of the companies in one of my studies were able to grow primarily authentically for longer than six years.

As discussed in Chapter 4, my research of those companies produced the concepts of the Enabling Internal Growth System, which is evidenced in the Sysco, Best Buy, UPS, and Room & Board cases in this book. That research also produced the Organic Growth Progression, which is similar to the McKinsey Staircase to Growth model. My research plus the research of Professor Liedtka produced the elements of the Darden Growth/Innovation Model, which is also discussed in Chapter 4. These research findings attempt to illuminate for companies how other successful Authentic Growth companies have achieved their results.

Notes

1. Alice Schroeder, *The Snowball: Warren Buffett and the Business of Life* (New York: Bantam Dell, 2008), 778.
2. John C. Bogle, *Enough: True Measures of Money, Business and Life* (Hoboken, NJ: John Wiley & Sons, 2009), 108.
3. Steven Pearlstein, "Leap of Illogic on Wall Street Leaves GE Flat-Footed," *Washington Post*, May 21, 2008, http://washingtonpost.com/wp-dyn/content/article/2008/05/20/AR2008052001806_pf.html.
4. Schroeder, *The Snowball*, 778.
5. Edward D. Hess, "The Coca-Cola Company" (Case Study UVA-S-0145,University of Virginia Darden School Foundation, Charlottesville, 2007). This case has been updated for material events. All quotes are directly from the case.
6. Betsy Morris, "Coke: The Real Story How Did Coca-Cola's Management Go from First-Rate to Farcical in Six Short Years? Tommy the Barber Knows," *Fortune*, May 31, 2004, 84–92.
7. Dean Foust, "Things Go Better With . . . Juice; Coke's New CEO Will Have to Move Quickly to Catch Up in Noncarbonated Drinks," *BusinessWeek*, May 17, 2004, 81.
8. Coca-Cola Company, Annual Report, 2008, www.thecoca-colacompany.com/investors/form_10K_2008.html (accessed August 31, 2009).
9. Patricia Sellers, "Coke's CEO Doug Daft Has to Clean Up the Big Spill," *Fortune*, March 6, 2000, 58–59.
10. Coca-Cola Company, Annual Report, 2008.
11. Schroeder, *The Snowball*, 670.

....

CHAPTER 7

Managing the Risks of Growth

PUBLIC COMPANIES

I **WROTE THIS BOOK** to challenge how business leaders, managers, and investors think about growth. Most, having trained and worked in environments where the Growth Mental Model reigns supreme, fail to think about growth critically. For most business leaders, investment analysts, investors, and even MBA students, "grow or die" is the Holy Grail of business. Given that view, growth is assumed and it is thought to be always good.

Smart Growth rejects those views and seeks to subject growth decisions to three tools developed through my executive education and consulting projects: (1) a rigorous analytical Growth Decision Process; (2) a Growth Risks Audit Process; and (3) a Managing the Risks of Growth Plan.

Chapter 1 has already shown that the Growth Mental Model and Wall Street Rules can create a short-term mentality, which can drive bad corporate behaviors. We have learned that the Earnings Game is played by many companies and it can hide or mask fundamental business weaknesses.

This chapter focuses on how growth can be bad if it stresses too much a company's culture, its customer value proposition, its financial controls, its quality controls, its employees, or its operational controls. Growth can be bad if the risks of growth are not managed well or if the pace of growth outstrips capabilities or infrastructure, or overwhelms employees.

Growth Decision Process

I developed my appreciation for the necessity of growth decisions and managing the risks of growth not from my research of public companies but from my research of private high-growth companies. This is interest-ing because private company CEOs do not have to attend to the Wall Street Rules nor do they have the temptation to play the Earnings Game. Why were the private company CEOs I studied more aware of and concerned about the risks of growth than the public company CEOs in my other research?

I do not know the answer to that question. Could it have something to do with the fact that private company CEOs have invested their own money in their business and in most cases have invested a significant portion of their wealth?

Smart Growth advocates that business managers make careful decisions about growth only after they systematically weigh the reasons and oppor-tunities to grow against the risks of growth. For example, a management team should continually ask:

1. Should we grow?
2. Why should we grow?
3. How much should we grow?
4. Are we ready to grow? What are our preconditions for growth from cultural, structural, management, people, capital, process, controls, and technology perspectives?
5. What are our growth alternatives?
6. What are the pros and cons of each alternative?
7. Have we completed the Growth Risks Audit?
8. Have we designed a Growth Risks Management Plan to manage those risks?

Growth is change and change is risky. Growth challenges people and internal systems. When companies grow, companies change beyond simply getting bigger.

Growth Risks Audit Checklist

I have used the following Growth Risks Audit checklist in some executive education and consulting work and it has worked well, but by no means is it presented here as the "best of class" methodology. Each company has its own stresses and fault lines, so any audit checklist should be modified accordingly. The purpose of this audit is to force thinking about a range of issues to sensitize management to the proposition that managing growth includes managing opportunities as well as risks.

1. For each growth initiative, evaluate if, how, and to what extent that initiative will put material stress on your
   - culture;
   - structure;
   - management team;
   - employees;
   - execution processes;
   - quality controls;
   - customer value proposition;
   - customer experience;
   - financial controls;
   - financial safety net; and
   - image and brand reputation.
2. What specific behaviors create material business risks for you? Will growth increase the likelihood of those behaviors?
3. Based on your answers to questions 1 and 2, prioritize those risks in order of harm to your business.
4. How do you know if those risks are occurring? What is your early warning system for each material risk? How do you monitor and detect those risk-inducing behaviors? How do you manage against creeping additive risks?
5. Does your measurement and reward system encourage or discourage those risky behaviors?
6. Managing growth takes a far different mentality than managing the risks of growth. How do you put in place processes that allow your managers to do both?
7. What changes to your execution processes, quality control processes, financial and information systems do you need to make to better manage the risks of growth?
8. Do you need to balance your internal communications about growth with communications about the specific growth risks you want to avoid?
9. Do you need to pace growth?
10. Under what conditions will you slow down or pause growth?
11. What is your risk management plan for each key material internal risk?
12. Will growth change whom you compete against?

13. If so, how will your new competitors likely respond?

14. Will that new competition impact your ability to maintain current customers? How? How will you ward off those new competitors? On what basis are you at a disadvantage with respect to the new competition? Do they have the capabilities to offer a better customer value proposition than you offer? Could the new competition put your business more at risk?

15. What changes do you need to make from a strategy, structure, cultural, execution processes, quality control, financial controls, information management, measurements, and rewards perspective to manage these risks of growth? In what priority?

16. Have you created a risk management execution plan with timelines, milestones, and accountability?

17. How do you collectivize growth risk management across your management team?

Growth risk management accepts the fact that growth is change and that change can have unintended consequences on people, culture, quality, and financial goals. Some of those consequences may seem small but when they are added to other small consequences, they may result in a big negative impact, as Starbucks exemplifies.

The next step after completing the Audit is to create a plan to manage those risks. I have found working with companies that it takes a different mindset or mentality to think about growth risks and their management than to think about growth. I have found very few managers who can switch back and forth quickly from a risk management mentality to a growth mentality. As a result, one has to put in place processes that give early warnings of growth risks issues and one has to allocate specific management time to monitoring growth risks frequently. This takes discipline and focus. One has to put a team into a different mindset to do this.

This chapter examines the risks of growth from a public company perspective. Chapter 8 discusses managing growth from a private company perspective. The three management tools mentioned above can be used by both public and private companies.

First, let us look at some public companies to see how they managed or mismanaged the risks of growth. Some of these companies succumbed to the public market's pressure for continuous short-term growth, generating some unintended adverse consequences. In the case of JetBlue, the company's expansions overtaxed its critical infrastructure, which collapsed in the

Valentine's Day 2007 winter storm, stranding passengers and generating a fury of bad press. Other companies, such as Starbucks and Harley-Davidson, appear to have watered down their internal standards to achieve growth goals. Others, such as Home Depot, attempted cost savings initiatives that diluted their culture and customer experience.

I begin with Starbucks, which is a story being played out as I write this book. It is a classic example of how growth can change a company—sometimes for the worst.

Starbucks Coffee Example

Starbucks is a story of entrepreneurship, persistence, passion, great success, and recently, some poor growth risk management.[1] Howard Schultz, the founder of Starbucks, was raised in a federally assisted housing project in Brooklyn, New York. His father was a truck driver and, as a young man, Howard watched how his father's employer treated him after he was injured and unable to work, leaving him without a job, benefits, and pension—a beaten man. Schultz vowed that if he were ever a company leader he would never treat his employees that way. As a leader "he would not leave people behind."[2]

The drive to escape poverty and succeed helped make Schultz a super salesman, and his serendipitous introduction to freshly brewed coffee and the idea of becoming a purveyor of coffee became his passion. That passion led to his extraordinary persistence as he spent more than a year persuading the owners of the original Starbucks coffee roasting business first to hire him in 1982 and then to let him open a coffee café. But that was not enough for Schultz, who wanted to bring the coffee experience to even more people and to do so by his own standards for both the coffee and managing the business. To accomplish this, Schultz persisted for over a year to raise money to start his own coffee café business and to build it into a profitable high-growth company while keeping his promise to himself to treat his employees fairly.

In his book *Pour Your Heart into It*, Schultz stated that Starbucks was "living proof that a company can lead with its heart and nurture its soul and still make money."[3] In that book, published in 1997, five years after Starbucks went public, Schultz stated: "A company can grow big without losing the passion and personality that built it, but only if it's driven not by profits but by values and people."[4] However, that belief is now being tested.

Starbucks went public in 1992 with Schultz serving as CEO until 2000. When he stepped down at the age of forty-seven, he remained as chairman. During his tenure as CEO, he built Starbucks into the leading international coffee café with approximately 2,500 worldwide locations and revenues exceeding $1.6 billion, making Starbucks a model for employee engagement and partnership by offering health care and stock options widely to its workforce.

Orin Smith, who had joined Starbucks as CFO in 1990, succeeded Schultz as CEO from 2000 through March 2005. Under his leadership Starbucks grew from $1.6 billion in revenue to $4.5 billion. At the end of 2004, Starbucks operated 8,569 locations. Under Smith's five-year tenure, Starbucks added approximately 6,000 locations. See Table 7.1 for Starbucks' growth history.

TABLE 7.1 Starbucks Growth Table

YEAR	CEO	NET REVENUE	TOTAL STORES	GOAL STORES
1996	Schultz	$698M	1,015	
1997	Schultz	$975M	1,412	
1998	Schultz	$1.3B	1,886	
1999	Schultz	$1.68B	2,498	
2000	Smith	$2.17B	3,501	20,000
2001	Smith	$2.6B	4,709	
2002	Smith	$3.3B	5,886	25,000
2003	Smith	$4.1B	7,225	
2004	Smith	$5.3B	8,569	
2005	Donald	$6.4B	10,241	
2006	Donald	$7.8B	12,440	40,000
2007	Donald	$9.4B	15,011	
2008	Schultz	$10.4B	approx. 17,000	

Jim Donald, who had joined Starbucks in 2002 after a career in the grocery industry, including stints at Safeway, Albertsons, Wal-Mart, and Pathmark, succeeded Smith as CEO. Under Jim Donald's three-year tenure, the push to expand Starbucks accelerated sharply. Donald added another 6,414 locations, translating into nearly 180 stores per month. Donald opened more stores in his three years than Smith did in five and more than Starbucks did in its first ten years.

Donald's chief operating officer, Martin Coles, joined Starbucks in 2004, having come from Reebok. This is important because the two top leaders of the company came from outside the industry and from businesses with different customer value propositions than Starbucks.

At the end of Smith's five-year tenure in 2004, Starbucks had total liabilities of $916 million with $2.47 billion in shareholder equity. At the end of Donald's reign in 2007, Starbucks's total liabilities had surged to $3.06 billion—an increase of over $2 billion in debt, much of it financed as short-term debt, with total shareholder equity of $2.3 billion.

February 14, 2007, was an auspicious day in the history of Starbucks. On that day Schultz sent an e-mail to Donald, copying the other members of the executive team, entitled "The Commoditization of the Starbucks Experience." That e-mail also mysteriously appeared on the Internet and was widely read. Because of its importance, I have included it in its entirety below:

From: Howard Schultz
Sent: Wednesday, February 14, 2007 10:39 AM Pacific Standard Time
To: Jim Donald
Cc: Anne Saunders; Dave Pace; Dorothy Kim; Gerry Lopez; Jim Alling; Ken Lombard; Martin Coles; Michael Casey; Michelle Gass; Paula Boggs; Sandra Taylor
Subject: The Commoditization of the Starbucks Experience

As you prepare for the FY 08 strategic planning process, I want to share some of my thoughts with you.

Over the past ten years, in order to achieve the growth, development, and scale necessary to go from less than 1,000 stores to 13,000 stores and beyond, we have had to make a series of decisions that, in retrospect, have lead to the watering down of the Starbucks experience, and, what some might call the commoditization of our brand.

Many of these decisions were probably right at the time, and on their own merit would not have created the dilution of the experience; but in this case, the sum is much greater and, unfortunately, much more damaging than the individual pieces. For example, when we went to automatic espresso machines, we solved a major problem in terms of speed of service and efficiency. At the same time, we overlooked the fact that we would remove much of the romance and theatre that was in play with the use of the La Marzocca machines. This specific decision became even more damaging when the height of the machines, which are now in thousands of stores, blocked the visual sight line the customer previously had to watch the drink being made, and for the intimate experience with the barista. This, coupled with the need for fresh roasted coffee in every North America city and every international market, moved us toward the decision and the need for flavor locked packaging. Again, the right decision at the right time, and once again I believe we overlooked the cause and the affect of flavor lock in our stores. We achieved fresh roasted bagged coffee, but at what cost? The loss of aroma—perhaps the most powerful non-verbal signal we had in our stores; the loss of our people scooping fresh coffee from the bins and grinding it fresh in front of the customer, and once again stripping the store of tradition and our heritage? Then we moved to store design. Clearly we have had to streamline store design to gain efficiencies of scale and to make sure we had the ROI on sales to investment ratios that would satisfy the financial side of our business. However, one of the results has been stores that no longer have the soul of the past and reflect a chain of stores vs. the warm feeling of a neighborhood store. Some people even call our stores sterile, cookie cutter, no longer reflecting the passion our partners feel about our coffee. In fact, I am not sure people today even know we are roasting coffee. You certainly can't get the message from being in our stores. The merchandise, more art than science, is far removed from being the merchant that I believe we can be and certainly at a minimum should support the foundation of our coffee heritage. Some stores don't have coffee grinders, French presses from Bodum, or even coffee filters.

Now that I have provided you with a list of some of the underlying issues that I believe we need to solve, let me say at the outset that we have all been part of these decisions. I take full responsibility myself, but we desperately need to look into the mirror and realize it's time to get back to the core and make the changes necessary to evoke the heritage, the tradition, and the passion that we all have for the true Starbucks experience. While the current state of affairs for the most part is self induced, that has lead to competitors of all kinds, small and large coffee companies, fast food operators, and mom and pops, to position themselves in a way that creates awareness, trial and loyalty of people who previously have been Starbucks customers. This must be eradicated.

I have said for 20 years that our success is not an entitlement and now it's proving to be a reality. Let's be smarter about how we are spending our time, money and resources. Let's get back to the core. Push for innovation and do the things necessary to once again differentiate Starbucks from all others. We source and buy the highest quality coffee. We have built the most trusted brand in coffee in the world, and we have an enormous responsibility to both the people who have come before us and the 150,000 partners and their families who are relying on our stewardship.

Finally, I would like to acknowledge all that you do for Starbucks. Without your passion and commitment, we would not be where we are today.[5]

This is a remarkable e-mail. First, Schultz talks about the devastating effect of the creeping dilution of the Starbucks brand—several small steps taken in the interests of efficiency and productivity that diluted the brand and the customer experience. This is an important point. Several productivity enhancements were made by Schultz's successors and perhaps no one of them alone would have diluted the brand but, when added together they had enormous and, for Schultz, adverse consequences.

With the ambitious growth agenda implemented by Donald, it is unclear whether anyone seriously considered the impact of such growth on the customer experience. Where were the critical inquiry, the constructive debate, and the constructive dissent? Were Donald and Coles caught up in scoring high quarterly earnings numbers? Did Starbucks consider or debate the risks of growth? Failing to consider these questions about the consequences of growth is risky if an organization wants to avoid diluting the customer experience that made them successful to begin with.

In his e-mail, Schultz implies that the rapid growth-dilution of the Starbucks customer emotional experience made it easier for competitors, such as Dunkin' Donuts and McDonald's, to make inroads against Starbucks. Schultz's e-mail raises other issues as well: Why did Schultz put his concerns into an e-mail that could be widely distributed rather than, as chairman of the board, have a heart-to-heart with his management team? Second, he does not talk about the potential cannibalization of its existing stores that would likely result from the significant new openings. Last, Schultz was concerned that by its rapid growth Starbucks had lost its essence of who it was, which drove its customer value proposition and competitive differentiator. The drive for operating efficiencies and store opening efficiencies trumped the sight, aroma, and feel of coffee. Did Starbucks lose its essence? The same question is later posed to Home Depot.

In hindsight, Schultz's e-mail looks like a warning shot because Starbucks announced on January 7, 2008, that Schultz was returning as CEO, relieving Donald of his duties. His letter to Starbucks employees, dated January 7, 2008, stated that Starbucks had invested ahead of the growth curve and that led to bureaucracy that had taken the focus off the customer. Schultz further announced that he would slow the pace of new store openings and close some underperforming stores.[6] On January 12, 2008, *New York Times* business columnist Joe Nocera wrote: "If you are going to fix what ails Starbucks you have to forget about growth. And you have to stop thinking about your company as a sexy growth company. Those days are over."[7] On January 30, Starbucks signaled a major retrenchment, announcing that in 2008 it would reduce store openings in the United States, as compared to 2007 openings, by 34% and that 100 underperforming stores would be closed. In that announcement Starbucks said it would give the financial community a new way to measure its progress and it would not release same store sales comps. In addition, beginning in 2009, Starbucks would discontinue releasing earnings guidance to focus on making better decisions for creating long-term value.[8]

The rapid growth train had slammed on the brakes. Tellingly, on February 25, 2008, Starbucks announced it was bringing back Arthur Rubinfeld who had built Starbucks's best-of-class real estate site selection and design team. Rubinfeld had helped build Starbucks to 4,000 stores before leaving in 2001. This rehiring was the precursor to Starbucks's announcement on July 1, 2008, that it would close 600 underperforming stores in the United States, 70% of which had been opened since 2006 under Donald's tenure.

The business press hit Starbucks hard for its excesses. A *New York Times* article on July 4, 2008, titled "The Empire of Excess" asserted that Starbucks's biggest mistake and greatest challenge boiled down to three words: "location, location, and location."[9] It then reported that commercial real estate brokers who worked with Starbucks said the company was so determined to meet its growth promises that it relaxed its underwriting standards, often taking inferior sites to meet its growth expectations. The article pointed out this was particularly common in the South and Southern California. Likewise, the *Economist* on July 3, 2008, stated, "As it expanded at a breakneck pace, the company opened too many Starbucks in subprime locations."[10]

As predicted by the *New York Times* article, the 600 stores to be closed had the highest concentrations in California, Florida, and Texas, with Las

Vegas closing thirteen stores, followed by San Diego with ten and Dallas and Baton Rouge with nine each. On July 30, 2008, Starbucks announced it would close sixty-one stores in Australia.

On September 26, 2008, Schultz wrote to his employee partners and in bold type stated: "In FY09, we must view growth differently than we ever have. It means fewer, better stores reaching more customers. It means innovative offerings that complement our coffee and delight our customers. This is a new way of looking at our business."[11] Four months later, on January 28, 2009, Starbucks announced the closing of another 300 stores and a reduction of total new store openings globally in 2009 to 310.

What a story. Smith and Donald, both apparent devotees of the Growth Mental Model, had taken Starbucks on a rapid growth course with insufficient regard for the impact on the brand and the customer experience. For several years, Starbucks kept raising Wall Street's expectations by raising its goal for global stores from 15,000 to 20,000 to 25,000 to 30,000 to 40,000. In 2005, after Smith retired, Starbucks installed in the senior leadership positions Donald and Coles, both relatively new to Starbucks and to the industry. Nonetheless, they launched an aggressive growth strategy.

In only three years they opened more than 6,400 locations, nearly 75% of the total amount of 8,569 locations opened during Starbucks first seventeen years. At the same time, to push efficiencies, they made changes to the coffee machines, coffee bags, and store design, diluting rather than enriching the customer's coffee experience. And in doing this, they increased Starbucks's total liabilities during Donald's three-year tenure 340%, from $.9 million to $3.06 billion. They undertook both operational and financial risk while, in Schultz's view, diluting the Starbucks culture and customer value proposition.

Arguably, Starbucks had unwisely inflated growth expectations by raising its growth targets. To meet those targets, during 2005–2007, Starbucks was willing, either consciously or unconsciously, to run the risk of diluting the brand, diluting the coffee experience, and diluting the real estate site selection quality controls while more than tripling Starbucks's liabilities. Surprisingly, these decisions were not made in isolation. The expansions were done with the approval of its board of directors as well as its chairman, Schultz. Did Schultz or other board members ask the question: What are the risks of this substantial increase in location openings in 2005, 2006, 2007? Did anyone ask the question: How do we manage those risks so as not to lose our essence?

Starbucks shows that: (1) small changes can add up and can have a big impact; (2) rapid growth can dilute a company's culture; (3) rapid growth can dilute the customer value proposition; and (4) the pressure from the public market to grow can cause dilution of quality controls. All of these outcomes can result in a competitive position more vulnerable to attack by new competitors.

The Starbucks story is not over. Remember, in his 1997 book, Schultz wrote: "A company can grow without losing its passion and personality but only if it is driven not by profits but by values and people."[12] And, although that principle was arguably obscured during the tenure of Donald, on September 26, 2008, Schultz reaffirmed it when he told his employees that Starbucks "must view growth differently."

The long-term ramifications of Starbucks's self-inflicted growth wounds are unknown. What is known is that Starbucks faces a major challenge in reestablishing the deep, rich emotional experience it once had with its customers and its employees. As Schultz wrote in his February 2007 letter, it is the challenge of reversing the commoditization of the experience. It is not difficult to calculate the losses incurred by the store closures and compute the costs of the substantial increase in debt, but what one cannot compute is the dilution of the culture and the bond among the company, its employees, and its customers or the costs of the opportunity Starbucks has given to McDonald's and Dunkin' Donuts.

JetBlue Example

The JetBlue case shows how growth over a period of years can mask operational risks.[13] Founded by David Neeleman in 1999, JetBlue Airways made its inaugural flight on February 11, 2000. It was a stellar start-up success and grew very fast through 2006. JetBlue, however, outgrew its operational infrastructure, which imploded during a winter weather storm on February 14, 2007. During that storm and its aftermath, JetBlue experienced communication and re-ticketing system problems in addition to crew management and rerouting problems, stranding ten passenger-filled flights at JFK airport for hours on tarmacs, generating irate customers and bad press. In one case, passengers spent eleven long hours trapped on the tarmac.

As a result of this massive multilevel operational breakdown on Valentine's Day, JetBlue named both a new chief operating officer and a new vice president of JFK operations in March 2007 and, in May 2007, the board of directors asked Neeleman to step down as CEO.

In a *New York Times* article appearing on February 19, 2007, Neeleman attributed the huge breakdown in operations to "weak management and a shoestring communications system." He stated: "We had so many people in the company who wanted to help who weren't trained to help. . . . We had an emergency control center full of people who didn't know what to do."[14] When growth outstrips a company's operational processes and communications infrastructure, management must rectify those risks promptly to avoid an implosion such as the one JetBlue experienced. Storms are not uncommon, especially in February. Why didn't anyone step back in 2002–2006 during JetBlue's expansion and ask whether its systems were adequate to handle storms or other contingencies? There also should have been consideration of whether JetBlue had in place the right people, processes, and procedures to withstand such a big disruption that grounded so much of its fleet. Growth can be intoxicating, particularly when it signals the success of a new business concept. But growth creates risks that have to be managed to avoid implosion.

Now, I turn to another corporate drama that was played out over years as a new CEO tried to balance continued high growth with installing needed operational efficiencies and controls.

Home Depot, Inc. Case

The Home Depot, Inc. was founded by Bernie Marcus and Arthur Blank in 1978, after they were fired from Handy Dan, a small chain of home-improvement stores, in spite of stellar performances.[15] Home Depot became the world's largest home-improvement retailer and the second-largest retailer in the United States, at one time employing more than 364,000 associates in 2,432 stores and generating $91 billion in revenue.

In early 2009, Home Depot operated 2,275 retail stores and had sales of $77 billion for fiscal year 2007 and employed approximately 300,000 associates. Since 2002, it has repurchased about 32% of its outstanding stock for over $27 billion and has a 62% debt-to-equity ratio. Its focus now is on operating efficiency, associate engagement, and capital efficiency, predicting future sales growth of 3%–5% and new store growth of 1.5% new square footage. Its 2009 eight-person senior leadership team has, on average, 5.6 years tenure at Home Depot with only two of the eight joining Home Depot prior to 2002.

Home Depot is another sad soap opera about growth and the fragility of corporate cultures, the dependency of success on emotionally engaged line employees, and the lack of one-size-fits all business operating models. Like Starbucks, Home Depot provides a story of how outsiders brought into a company and given significant latitude to pursue growth eroded its culture, changed its management team structure, expanded into different lower-margin businesses, and sacrificed customer experience.

From 1979 to 2000, one of Home Depot's cofounders served as CEO and grew the company to $45.7 billion in revenue. But in 2000, the board decided a change was needed and replaced CEO Arthur Blank with General Electric executive Bob Nardelli, who had just lost the race to be Jack Welch's replacement at GE. Seven years later, in January 2007, Nardelli resigned after a contentious tenure, during which revenues grew to $91 billion and the number of stores to 2,100. And yet, the company's stock price dropped 6% during Nardelli's tenure.

Nardelli brought GE-style strategic planning, accountability, HR policies, operating efficiencies, and technology to Home Depot. He also built the wholesale-supply business through acquisitions and expanded the business internationally. In the process, Nardelli made significant executive changes and centralized controls, merchandising, purchasing, and inventory, all of which changed the culture of Home Depot. Naysayers called the program the "GE-ization" of Home Depot. After Nardelli's resignation, the board appointed Frank Blake as chairman and CEO. Blake, another former GE executive, had been brought to Home Depot by Nardelli.

History

Bernie Marcus, the son of Jewish immigrants, was born in Newark, New Jersey, in 1929. He grew up poor and began his career as a pharmacist, eventually owning his own drugstore. Later, he moved from his ownership position to corporate employee and, in time, became CEO of Handy Dan. Marcus hired Arthur Blank while at Handy Dan.

Blank grew up in Queens, New York, in a small, one-bedroom apartment. He went to Babson College to study accounting and worked for the Arthur Young firm before returning to work for his mother in the family business. Ultimately, Blank became CFO of Handy Dan under Marcus, until their dismissals in 1978.

Two other men played a key role in creating Home Depot: Pat Farrah and Ken Langone. Marcus, Blank, Farrah, and Langone all met through Handy

Dan. Farrah, a junior-college dropout, was the founder of HomeCo, a Southern California home-supply store with the new retailing concept of a big-box, no-frills, stocked-to-the-ceiling inventory. Langone was a successful New York investment banker whose claim to fame was taking Ross Perot's EDS public. Langone met Marcus when he became interested in buying a part of Handy Dan. Langone raised the $2 million of venture capital needed to start Home Depot, and Farrah joined Marcus and Blank when HomeCo went bankrupt.

First Stores

The first Home Depot stores were opened in Atlanta in June 1979 because favorable subleases were available on good store locations. The founders wanted to name the new business "Bad Bernies Buildall," but their bank balked. Finally, Home Depot was chosen as the name, and at the end of 1979, the company had three stores in Atlanta with $7 million in sales.

Home Depot became profitable in 1980 and went public in 1981 in order to raise expansion capital. The expansion first took place in Florida through new-store openings, and by the end of 1983, Home Depot had opened nineteen stores and made $250 million in revenue. These store expansions are shown in Table 7.2.

TABLE 7.2 Home Depot Store Expansions: 1980–1989

YEAR	NUMBER OF STORES	REVENUE
1980	4	$22.0M
1981	8	$54.5M
1982	10	$117.6M
1983	19	$256.2M
1984	31	$432.8M
1985	50	$700.7M
1986	60	$1.01B
1987	75	$1.45B
1988	96	$2.0B
1989	118	$2.76B

The number of Home Depot employees quickly grew from 300 to 17,500 and the 1990s brought more store growth and geographical expansion, as shown in Table 7.3.

TABLE 7.3 Home Depot Store Expansions: 1990–1999

YEAR	NUMBER OF STORES	REVENUE
1990	145	$ 3.8B
1991	174	$ 5.1B
1992	214	$ 7.1B
1993	264	$ 9.2B
1994	340	$12.5B
1995	423	$15.5B
1996	512	$19.5B
1997	624	$24.2B
1998	761	$30.2B
1999	930	$38.4B

During the 1990s, the ten-year compound annual growth rate (CAGR) for sales was 30.1%, and the ten-year CAGR for earnings was 35%. It was also during the 1990s that Home Depot began to think about international expansion. By 1992, Home Depot stock was selling at a price to earnings multiple of 62, and for the ten-year period from 1982 to 1992, its CAGR for revenue was 51%. Yet, in 1992, it had only a 7% market share.

Although the number of Home Depot stores almost doubled from 1993 to 1996, the stock price remained relatively flat. In May 1997, Marcus stepped down as CEO and cofounder Blank took over. Under Blank's leadership, Home Depot announced several growth initiatives in 1998, including

- a new, smaller (35,000 sq. ft.) neighborhood-convenience-store concept to compete with True Value and Ace Hardware,
- international expansion to Chile and Argentina,
- direct-mail and telephone orders,
- a professional builders' market-segment expansion called ProInitiative, and
- the launching of high-end, home-design-furnishings stores called Expo Design Centers.

Culture

Marcus and Blank created a distinctly decentralized, entrepreneurial, rah-rah "bleeding-orange culture" that was employee- and customer-centric. Marcus, considered the lead "outside" executive, refused to pay Home Depot employees, referred to as associates, on a commission basis. He wanted employees to focus on teaching customers, solving problems, giving the correct advice, and understanding that customer trust and loyalty would produce more sales in the long run than just pushing goods out the door.

Marcus also believed in an inverted pyramid and non-elitist management style. He wanted employees to be stockowners, so he established a stock-purchase program that guaranteed that employees would not lose money because the company would buy back the stock at any time for the same amount paid at purchase.

This was the same money-back guarantee that Home Depot made to its customers, who at any time—even years later—could return any product for cash with no questions asked. This entrepreneurial, decentralized structure, in effect, made each store a separate business unit and gave store management more latitude to operate each unit, including, in some cases, the ordering of merchandise. And, just as important, when Home Depot hired carpenters, painters, plumbers, and construction workers, they were inculcated with the mantra to "serve customers first and foremost." Marcus and Blank preached that Home Depot would continue to be the market leader so long as it gave the best service. This Home Depot culture created a Home Depot family atmosphere in which loyal employees worked hard because they were given financial and career opportunities. Equally as important, the employees revered Marcus.

In their book, *Built from Scratch*, Marcus and Blank, together with Bob Andelman, laid out some of the management principles they believed had made Home Depot successful: "One of the big advantages that we have over most of our competitors is being decentralized. It allows us to be close to the customers and access the best knowledge in the field. . . . Our store managers and their assistant managers have more operating and decision-making leeway than in any other retail chain in America."[16] And in describing the management structure at Home Depot in terms of an inverted pyramid, they wrote: "The people at the store are the most important—after customers—because they interface with the customer . . . and in our inverted management structure, everyone's career depends on how the associates in stores function."[17]

2000: A New CEO

In 2000, a major corporate drama was played out at General Electric: Which of three internal candidates would be chosen to succeed the legendary CEO Welch? Home Depot board member Ken Langone (the original financier of Home Depot, in 1978) also served on the General Electric board. When Welch chose Jeff Immelt over Nardelli, Langone called Nardelli and offered him the Home Depot CEO job. The Home Depot board never really explained Blank's ouster, nor did it appear to have considered anyone but Nardelli for the job, but in hiring him the board set out to follow a course of tsunami-like change.

To begin with, Nardelli was a great operator, a numbers guy who had spent almost his entire career at General Electric. At different times, he had been CEO of Transportation and then CEO of Power Systems at General Electric. He was definitely a disciple of the General Electric operating style and system.

The Home Depot board had moved quickly, offering Nardelli an extremely lucrative employment contract containing a compensation package that eventually exceeded $30 million a year, with a lucrative $100 million severance package. Nardelli was also loaned $10 million as a relocation package that was forgiven with tax abatement. Although Home Depot was the country's second-largest retailer, Nardelli had no retail business experience. At the time he took the Home Depot position, he was the first executive without retail experience to be chosen as CEO of a major nonfood business. But he wasted no time at Home Depot making important changes in the people, structure, process, and culture, all at once, and introduced GE-like strategy, operations, and HR processes. In Nardelli's first six months at Home Depot, twenty-nine of the top thirty-four Home Depot executives left the company. Some were replaced by General Electric executives.

Giving Nardelli his due, Home Depot did need more efficient controls, processes, and operations. For example, the company had more than 400 different employee-evaluation processes spread over the retail operating divisions without consistent review or promotion policies. Nardelli implemented many changes while maintaining store and revenue growth, as shown in Table 7.4.

TABLE 7.4 Home Depot Store Growth: 2001–2006

YEAR	NUMBER OF STORES	REVENUE
2001	1,333	$53.6B
2002	1,532	$58.2B
2003	1,707	$64.8B
2004	1,890	$73.1B
2005	2,042	$81.5B
2006	2,147	$90.8B

Once, when asked to describe his management style, Nardelli replied, "What I'm known for is transferring best practices. That's particularly important in this economic environment when you have to maximize revenue through existing assets."[18] He gave a longer explanation for Home Depot's growth potential.

We laid out a $900-billion-plus market opportunity. There's about $175 billion in the do-it-yourself market. There's $110 billion in installation labor only, and another $100 billion if you add material to it. There is about $290 billion in the professional small-repair and remodel area. There's another couple of hundred billion dollars in the higher-end professional. We looked at each of those segments and looked at who was a player. That's what gave us the confidence to enter new areas, such as the at-home-services business. We now have about 25 national programs where we install everything from roofing, siding, fencing, windows, decking, and sheds.[19]

By 2005, Nardelli's strategy was to improve the core stores, diversify through services and new channels, and move upstream and to international markets. Nardelli and his team focused on bottom-line cost efficiencies and the development of a wholesale-builder-supply business and a home-services business.

Nardelli also cut labor costs by doubling the number of part-time workers and by centralizing buying and inventory mix. He invested $2 billion in technology and put General Electric command and control processes in place, taking control away from store and division managers. He also reversed Home Depot's cash-returns policy and changed company policies on sales to the government.

In addition, Nardelli sold off the Chilean and Argentine stores and moved aggressively into the home-services business, buying roofing, fencing, and window-installation companies. He acquired Hughes Supply for $3.5 billion in order to bolster Home Depot's foray into the professional-builder market—a lower-margin business. In addition, he bought four home-improvement stores in Mexico.

When Nardelli joined Home Depot, its stock was selling at $39 a share. In 2001, it quickly rose to $53, but by February 2003, it was selling at only $21.

2006: The Turning Point

All of Nardelli's changes created turmoil within Home Depot, whereas Lowe's, Home Depot's largest competitor, continued to do very well. In 2006, analysts focused on how Home Depot stores were not as modern as Lowe's and that customer satisfaction was down. Also in 2006, the University of Michigan's American Customer Satisfaction Index rated Home Depot last among the major retailers. Matters came to a head that same year over Nardelli's pay package and his handling of the 2006 stockholders' meeting, when no board members attended and he limited both shareholders' question time and the length of the meeting.

During fiscal year 2006, Home Depot increased its debt-to-equity ratio from 10% to 47% by using its debt to invest $3.5 billion in its core business, make $4.3 billion in acquisitions, repurchased $6.7 billion of stock, and paid $1.4 billion in dividends. In July 2006, Nardelli reviewed his tenure at Home Depot: "We are going through a transformational period as we redefine the business, building off of our core, adding services for an aging population that has shifted from do-it-yourself to do-it-for-me and that has shifted to shopping on-line. Certainly, building off of the 30% of professional customers by extending product offerings is one of the most defining moments in our history. We will look back on this as a turning point in positioning the company for the next leg of expansion."[20] In December 2006, Home Depot acquired HomeWay, China's first home-improvement retailer, and its 12 stores.

In January 2007, Nardelli refused to make major changes to his employment contract and resigned. At the time, Home Depot stock was selling at close to the same price it sold at when Nardelli was hired seven years earlier. In 2007, Blake, who replaced Nardelli as CEO and chairman, instituted a program to increase Home Depot's leverage to repurchase stock, to sell the wholesale supply business that Nardelli had bought, and to rationalize the home services businesses. Blake changed the discussion from growth to operating efficiency and the efficient use of capital, in some ways accepting the fact that Home Depot's new-store growth potential was limited.

Home Depot Lessons

First, some questions are in order. Why did Marcus and Blank allow the operations and technology side of the business to lag too far behind new store openings and revenue growth? Was there a time when they should have played process and controls "catch-up," slowing growth while doing so? Why did Nardelli within his first six months replace twenty-nine of Home Depot's top thirty-four executives? Did Nardelli attempt to change too much too fast? After all, Home Depot was not, in the market's eyes, in a distress situation. Did Nardelli's acquisitions represent too much new growth in different businesses? Did Nardelli care enough about the Home Depot culture or the customer experience?

How carefully, if at all, did Nardelli assess the complexity of his proposed changes and the risks? For example, did he gauge the impact on Home Depot's culture, customer satisfaction, and employee engagement when he made the decision to shift to using more part-time employees? Nardelli, like Donald at Starbucks, made many changes aimed at driving cost efficiencies, but did the costs of those changes in cultural, employee, and customer experience outweigh any such gains? Nardelli, also like Donald, came in as CEO from a different industry. Both fell back on what they knew.

What is Blake saying about growth? Is he touting Home Depot as a high-growth company, or is he advocating that Home Depot become a well-run company more like Sysco? Has Home Depot adopted the McDonald's strategy of being better not bigger? Compare what Frank Blake is doing at Home Depot with what Howard Schultz says about how Starbucks has to redefine what growth means.

Next is a look at Harley-Davidson, another example of how arguably management can knowingly weaken its quality control processes in order to drive growth.

Harley-Davidson Example

Harley-Davidson (HD) is a story that is being played out in the spring of 2009 in both the financial markets and in the courtroom.[21] HD is the leading motorcycle company in the United States, with an approximate 46% market share. It derives its revenue from the sale of motorcycles to dealers, the sales of parts and HD accessories, and the financing of approximately 53% of its U.S. consumer motorcycle purchases. HD's stock sold for $12.70 per share in late March 2009, down from a high of $70 in October 2007. HD, like all manufacturers of big-ticket items, has been hurt by the U.S. recession and the securitization liquidity crisis.

But HD's financial statements raise some questions because in 2008 HD increased its provision for credit losses by $28 million; other income decreased by a $37.8 million charge to earnings based on its receivables; and it wrote down $41.4 million related to securitization interests. In addition, it took a loss of $5.4 million on a securitization transaction and it had to retain $54 million of subordinated securities from securitization pools.[22]

HD's 2008 Annual Report refers to two major lawsuits, the claims of which HD vigorously contests and which HD has asked the courts to dismiss. These lawsuits deal with the year 2004 through April 2005, and the complaints are based on interviews with more than twenty confidential witnesses who worked for HD. The lawsuits allege that (1) HD engaged in channel stuffing to inflate the sales of its motorcycles to its dealers and (2) HD Financial Services lowered its consumer underwriting standards to make loans to people who ordinarily would not qualify, artificially boosting its sales to meet Wall Street expectations. In effect, the lawsuits accuse HD of making sub-prime motorcycle loans and increasing substantially the percentage of such loans in order to meet earnings estimates. HD denies all allegations. The lawsuits further allege that there was substantial insider selling of stock while these activities were going on.[23]

Clearly, I do not know the facts. It is enough for our purposes that the detailed allegations in the HD lawsuits illuminate some ways companies can, if they choose, play the Earnings Game to meet the Wall Street Rules.

Other Examples of Risk Taking

The public market's pressure to grow continuously can drive corporate executives to take too much risk. Clearly, in some cases the executives taking on the increased risks know exactly what they are doing. Evidence of this is a statement made by rating agency executives discussing their firms' roles in the securitization frenzy that helped fuel the 2007–2009 economic crisis: "Let's hope we are all wealthy and retired by the time this house of cards falters. . . . Combined, these errors make us look either incompetent at credit analysis, or like we sold our soul to the devil for revenue."[24]

Likewise, Gretchen Morgenson, in her *New York Times* column on November 2, 2008, cites an employee of Washington Mutual who stated: "At WaMu it wasn't about the quality of the loans, it was about the numbers."[25] The numbers loved by Wall Street can, and do, drive bad business decisions.

Notes

1. The Starbucks story is based on these primary sources: Janet Adamy, "At Starbucks, A Tall Order for New Cuts, Store Closures," *Wall Street Journal*, January 29, 2009, http://online.wsj.com/article/SB123317714771825681.html; Janet Adamy, "At Starbucks, Low-Key Vet Plots Course," *Wall Street Journal*, March 18, 2008, B1; Janet Adamy, "Schultz's Second Act Jolts Starbucks—Already Intense, He Faces New Pressure: Peltz Owns a Stake," *Wall Street Journal*, May 19, 2008, A1; Janet Adamy, "Corporate News: Starbucks Keeps Sandwiches, Tweaks Recipe," *Wall Street Journal*, July 26, 2008, B5; Janet Adamy, "Starbucks Plays Common Joe," *Wall Street Journal*, February 9, 2009, http://online.wsj.com/article/SB123413848760761577.html; Howard Behar and Janet Goldstein, *It's Not About the Coffee: Leadership Principles from a Life at Starbucks* (New York: Penguin, 2007); Jonathan Birchall, "Starbucks to Cut 6,700 Jobs Amid Falling Sales," *Financial Times*, January 28, 2009, www.ft.com.cms/s/0/086fd976-47b2-11dd -93ca-000077b07658.html, Jonathan Birchall, "Starbucks to Close 600 US Stores," *Financial Times*, July 1, 2008, www.ft.com.cms/s/0/2d72f8fc-ed84-11dd -bd60-0000779fd2ac.html; Claire Cain Miller, "Starbucks to Close 300 Stores and Open Fewer New Ones," *New York Times*, January 29, 2009, 7; Joe Nocera, "Curing What Ails Starbucks," *New York Times*, January 12, 2008, www.ny times.com/2008/01/12/business/12nocera.html; Valerie O'Neil, "Starbucks Announces Strategic Initiatives to Increase Shareholder Value; Chairman Howard Schultz Returns as CEO" (Press Release, January 7, 2008), www.starbucks.com/ aboutus/pressdesc.asp?=816; Janet Adamy, "Starbucks Reveals Locations of Stores to Be Closed: Announces Job Cut," *Wall Street Journal*, July 18, 2008, B2; Howard Schultz and Dori Jones Yang, *Pour Your Heart Into It: How Starbucks Built a Company One Cup at a Time* (New York: Hyperion, 1997); Howard Schultz, "The Commoditization of the Starbucks Experience: Howard Schultz's Starbucks Memo," *Financial Times*, February 23, 2007, http://us.ft.com/ftgateway/

superpage.ft?news_id=ft0022320071839455856&page=2; Howard Schultz, "Howard Schultz Transformation Agenda Communication #1" (Press Release, January 7, 2008), Starbucks Press Room, www.starbucks.com/aboutus/pressdesc. asp?id=814; Howard Schultz, "Howard Schultz Transformation Agenda Communication #3" (Press Release, January 30, 2008), Starbucks Press Room, www .starbucks.com/aboutus/pressdesc.asp?id=822; Howard Schultz, "Howard Schultz Transformation Agenda Communication #6" (Press Release, February 11, 2008), Starbucks Press Room, www.starbucks.com/aboutus/pressdesc.asp?id= 830; Howard Schultz, "A Message from Howard—Building a Stronger Company for the Future" (Press Release, July 29, 2008), Starbucks Press Room, www .starbucks.com/aboutus/pressdesc.asp?id=884; Howard Schultz, "A Message from Howard—Fiscal Year 2009—A New Beginning" (Press Release, September 26, 2008), Starbucks Press Room, www.starbucks.com/aboutus/presc.asp?id= 900; Howard Schultz, "A Message from Howard—Difficult Decisions in a Time of Uncertainty" (Press Release, January 28, 2009), Starbucks Press Room, www .starbucks.com/aboutus/pressdesc.asp?id=982; Starbucks Annual Report 2000– 2008, www.investor.starbucks.com; Starbucks, "Starbucks Continues to Align Organization for Sustained Global Growth" (Press Release, February 25, 2008), Starbucks Press Room, www.starbucks.com/aboutus/pressdesc.asp?id=834; Starbucks, "Starbucks Increases Number of U.S. Company-Operated Store Closures as Part of Transformation Strategy" (Press Release, July 1, 2008), Starbucks Press Room, www.starbucks.com/aboutus/pressdesc.asp?id=877; Starbucks, "Starbucks Unveils New Strategic Initiatives to Transform and Innovate the Customer Experience" (Press Release, March 19, 2008), Starbucks Press Room, www.starbucks.com/aboutus/pressdesc.asp?id=850; Starbucks, "Starbucks Poises Organization for Continued Global Growth" (Press Release, July 17, 2007), Starbucks Press Room, www.starbucks.com/aboutus/pressdesc.asp?id=782; Brad Stone, "The Empire of Excess: Lax Real Estate Decisions Hurt Starbucks," New York Times, July 4, 2008, www.nytimes.com/2008/07/04/business/04starbucks.html; Jenny Wiggins, "The Trouble with Starbucks," Financial Times, December 12, 2008, www.ft.com/cms/s//aa9831ce-c266-11dd-a350-000077b07658.html; "Starbucks: Grounds Zero," Economist, July 3, 2008, www.economist.com/business/display story.cfm ?story_id=11670630; "Comeback Kings?" Economist, January 8, 2009, www.economist.com/businessfinance/displaystory.cfm?story_id=12896749; "Starbucks Runs into Trouble," Economist, January 8, 2008, www.economist. com/business/displaystory.cfm?story_id=10490218; "Brand Management," Economist, March 1, 2007, www.economist.com/business/displaystory.cfm?story_ id=E1_RSSGPSN; "Staying Pure," Economist, February 23, 2006, www.economist .com/business/displaystory.cfm?story_id=E1_VVQVVJD; "Starbucks v. McDonald's," Economist, January 10, 2008, business/displaystory.cfm?story_id= 10498747.

2. Gretchen Morgenson, "Was There a Loan It Didn't Like?" New York Times, November 2, 2008, B1; Schultz and Yang, Pour Your Heart into It, 4.

3. Shultz and Yang, *Pour Your Heart into It*, 5.
4. Ibid., 8.
5. Schultz, "Howard Schultz's Starbucks Memo."
6. Schultz, "Howard Schultz Transformation Agenda Communication #1" (2008).
7. Nocera, "Curing What Ails Starbucks," B1.
8. Schultz, "Starbucks Increases Number of U.S. Company-Operated Store Closures as Part of Transformation Strategy" (2008).
9. Stone, "Empire of Excess," C1.
10. "Starbucks: Grounds Zero" (2008).
11. Schultz, "A Message from Howard—Fiscal Year 2009—A New Beginning" (2008).
12. Schultz and Yang, *Your Heart into It*, 8.
13. The JetBlue story is based on the following primary research sources: Jeff Bailey, "JetBlue's C.E.O. Is 'Mortified' After Fliers Are Stranded," *New York Times*, February 19, 2007, www.nytimes.com/2007/02/19/business/19jetblue.html; Jeff Bailey, "JetBlue Cancels More Flights in Storm's Wake," *New York Times*, February 18, 2007, www.nytimes.com/2007/02/18/business/18jetblue.html; CBS2, "JetBlue Attempts to Calm Passenger Furor," February 15, 2007, http://cbs2.com/national/jetblue.tarmac.JFK.2.279800.html; Chris Isidore, "JetBlue Founder: Storm Cost CEO Job," CNNMoney.com, June 26, 2007, http://money.cnn.com/2007/06/26/news/companies/neeleman/index.html; JetBlue, "JetBlue Airways Pre-Cancels 23 Percent of Its Scheduled Flights for Feb. 17 and Feb. 18, 2007" (Press Release, February 17, 2007), http://investor.jetblue.com/phoenix.zhtml?c=131045&p=irol-newsArticle&ID=964503&hig; JetBlue, "JetBlue Extends Operational Recovery Through Monday, Feb. 19" (Press Release, February 17, 2007), http://investor.jetblue.com/phoenix.zhtml?c=131045&p=irol-newsArticle&ID=964506&hig; JetBlue, "JetBlue Names Russell Chew Chief Operating Officer" (Press Release, March 7, 2007), http://investor.jetblue.com/phoenix.zhtml?c=131045&p=irol-newsArticle&ID=971589&hig; JetBlue, "Alex Battaglia Named Vice President of JetBlue's JFK Operations" (Press Release, March 20, 2007), http://investor.jetblue.com/phoenix.zhtml?c=131045&p=irol-newsArticle&ID=975729&highlight=; JetBlue, "JetBlue Airways Names Dave Barger President and Chief Executive Officer. Founder David Neeleman Will Continue to Serve as Chairman of the Board" (Press Release, May 10, 2007), http://investor.jetblue.com/phoenix.zhtml?c=131045&p=irol-newsArticle&ID=998672&highlight=; "JetBlue Apologizes After Passengers Stranded," February 16, 2007, MSNBC.com, www.msnbc.msn.co/id/17166299/print/1/displaymode/1098/; David Neeleman. "An Apology from David Neeleman" (Letter to Customers, JetBlue), www.jetblue.com/about/ourcompany/apology/index.html; Stephanie Overby, "What JetBlue's CIO Learned About Customer Satisfaction," *CIO*, April 5, 2007, www.cio.co/article/print/102500/What_JetBlue_s_CIO_Learned_About_Customer_Satisfaction; Robert Smith, "JetBlue Offers Passengers Rights, Compensation," NPR, February 20, 2007, www.npr.org/templates/story/story.php?storyId=7501286.
14. Bailey, "JetBlue's C.E.O. Is 'Mortified' After Fliers Are Stranded" (2007).

15. Edward D. Hess "The Home Depot, Inc." (Case Study UVA-S-0144. University of Virginia Darden School Foundation, Charlottesville, 2007). This case has been updated for material events. All quotes directly from case.

16. Bernie Marcus and Arthur Blank, with Bob Andelman, *Built from Scratch* (New York: Times Books, 1999), 238, 240.

17. Ibid., 271, 272.

18. Patricia Sellers, "Exit the Builder, Enter the Repairman: Home Depot's Arthur Blank Is Out. New CEO Bob Nardelli Is In," *Fortune*, March 19, 2001.

19. Bob Nardelli, Patricia Sellers, and Julie Schlosser, "It's His Home Depot Now After Nearly Four Years at the Helm, Ex-GE Guy Bob Nardelli Tells Us How He's Finally Getting Results," *Fortune*, September 20, 2004.

20. Maria Bartiroma, "Bob Nardelli Explains Himself," *BusinessWeek*, July 24, 2006.

21. The Harley-Davidson example is based on these primary research sources: Matthew Boyle, "Risky Loans: Harley Hits the Slick; Its Finance Arm Pumped Up Sales with Hog Wild Lending That Could Harm Its Pristine Credit Rating," *Business Week*, October 27, 2008, 54; Susanna Hamner, "Harley, You're Not Getting Any Younger," *New York Times,* March 22, 2009; Harley-Davidson Inc., 2008 Annual Report, Part 1; James B. Kelleher, "Analysis—Harley Hits a Rough Patch as Key Execs Jump Off," Reuters, January 13, 2009, http://global.factiva.com/aa/default.aspx?napc=p&cpil=en&_XFORMSTATE=AAF7MT; United States District Court, Eastern District of Wisconsin, Milwaukee Division, "In Re: Harley-Davidson, Inc. Securities Litigation," Civil Action No. 05-C-0579-CNC.

22. Harley-Davidson Inc., 2008 Annual Report, Part 1.

23. United States District Court, "In Re: Harley-Davidson."

24. Amit R. Paley, "Credit-Rating Firms Grilled Over Conflicts," *Washington Post,* October 23, 2008, A1.

25. Morgenson, "Was There a Loan It Didn't Like?" B1.

CHAPTER 8

....

Managing the Risks of Growth

PRIVATE COMPANIES

P RIVATE COMPANIES, unless they have institutional investors, generally do not have as many external pressures to grow as do public companies, because the Wall Street Rules and SEC filing requirements do not apply to them. Nonetheless, private companies in many ways face even more risks in undertaking growth because they often have more limited resources. Limited resources include capital, people, managerial depth, managerial experience, processes, controls, information systems, and time. In many cases, private companies, unlike big public companies, do not have the capacity to absorb or withstand a growth mistake. Their resiliency to bounce back from a failed growth initiative may be limited.

Also, in most cases, private company CEOs risk their own money and the financial security of their families when they undertake growth initiatives. This personal financial risk is substantially higher than the relative financial risk taken by public company CEOs, who rarely lose their million-dollar salaries when they fail and often are escorted out the door with large financial good-bye presents.

Given the limited resources and the financial vulnerability of private companies, in general, one could hypothesize that private company CEOs would approach growth differently than public company CEOs. They do.

Darden Private Growth Company Research

In 2008, I began a research project that focused on learning how private companies cope with the challenges of growth.[1] I was curious about how managers managed simultaneously across business functions; how they executed growth initiatives with limited time and resources; how they prioritized what they focused on each day; how they balanced growth with executing existing business; whether they invested ahead of or behind the growth curve; how they learned to delegate; how they met the challenges of building a management team; whether they managed or paced growth or took whatever came through the door; and when and in what order they put in more controls and processes. I did not research entrepreneurial start-ups. Rather, I looked at companies that were part of the small group that had survived the start-up phase and had been through a high-growth phase.

I was fortunate. Fifty-four CEOs of high-growth private companies agreed to participate in my study; each participated in a recorded interview, which was later analyzed both by me and independently by my research students. Almost all of the companies had been publicly acknowledged as high-growth companies by one of the big four public accounting firms or by magazines such as *Inc.* or *Entrepreneur.* The companies were diversified across industries and were located in twenty-three different states. Twenty-one of the companies primarily produced products and thirty-three were primarily service companies. They had an average age of 9.6 years and an average estimated 2008 revenue of $60 million. Although they averaged $60 million in revenue, the range was from $5 million to over $300 million in revenue.

This research was primarily qualitative and descriptive—not predictive. So far, I have not been successful in convincing CEOs who failed the high-growth phase to discuss why they failed in order to identify the causes.

The CEOs included five females. Of the fifty-four CEOs, thirty-four started companies in an industry in which they had substantial prior experience; twenty-eight had no prior start-up experience; and twenty-six did have prior start-up experience. Forty of the companies had no institutional funding at start-up.

I looked for best practices and decision heuristics or templates. I found that growth equaled change. Growth changed the companies—their culture, their people, and how they did business. Growth changed the human dynamics of how people communicated and with whom they communicated. It challenged peoples' competencies and interpersonal skills. Furthermore, for these companies, the human dynamic of growth proved to be one of the biggest challenges of managing growth. And this challenge recurred as the companies grew because many management teams were not able to manage a bigger or more complex business. As a result, CEOs had to continuously upgrade these teams and face the difficulties of hiring and integrating new players into existing management teams, which often stirred up difficult emotional and loyalty issues for remaining team members.

These human dynamics made growth difficult to manage, and it also made smooth and continuous growth rare. Some of my other findings were:

1. Most companies did not plan for growth. In some cases, it just happened. Those CEOs regretted not thinking about what a bigger company would look like and regretted not thinking about how much growth their company could accommodate. Some companies were overwhelmed by growth and had to slow growth down in order to survive. Others understood the risks of growing too fast before they had the people and quality and financial processes in place and, thus, they turned away business until they were more prepared for growth. Many companies accepted the growth and tried to upgrade people, processes, and controls at the same time as they grew, which was challenging.

CEOs with prior entrepreneurial experience learned from that experience that they needed to plan up front for growth, and they spent time visualizing and designing what their company would look like from people, structure, and process perspectives at different sizes. Some of the companies experienced at least one life-threatening time. Causes ranged from growing too fast, poor financial controls, geographic expansion too distant from the home base of business, losing the major customer, and adopting nonfriendly customer business models that were not flexible.

Growth created real financial stresses because, in most cases, growth required the outlay of significant cash ahead of the receipt of new revenue. Many companies did not plan for that mismatch nor did they estimate it reliably, which created severe cash flow pressures. These experiences resulted in many of the CEOs becoming humble and making statements such as, "We were lucky to survive that phase" or "We nearly lost control of the ship then."

The CEOs I interviewed had beaten the odds, surviving nearly ten years and, in fifty-three cases, building profitable companies. That process seemed to have made them more conscious of the risks of growth. Several told me they learned to question why they should grow. Some CEOs stated that growth in itself was not the endgame for them. Growth became secondary to building a good company that serves customers and is a good place to work.

Several told me they learned that generating more revenue once one reached a certain stage of profitability was not a valid reason for pushing growth. Stating it another way, experiencing the challenges and complexity of managing through growth changed some of the CEOs. Many had never thought critically about growth and just bought into the "grow or die" mentality. But many were fundamentally changed by the growth process and learned that managing growth successfully was not a foregone conclusion.

2. As they learned that growth was a difficult process and was sometimes a one-step-forward-and-two-steps-backward process, they learned the need to manage the pace of growth. Many CEOs said their companies became better when they learned to say no to new opportunities. Learning to focus and being strategic in taking on business led to a "sweet-spot" strategy for many.

3. Growth changed things. Growth changed what the CEO did. Growth changed what the employees did. Growth added people and more structure. And when they added new people to the mix, they got different human dynamics than before. The chemistry changed. When the management teams expanded, the different combinations of interpersonal dynamics multiplied the people complexity, which impacted execution. Growth increased the complexity of communications and the chance of miscommunications and interpersonal misunderstandings. Communications complexities often led to mistakes, inefficiency, and a lack of focus, undermining a smooth growth process.

4. CEOs had to learn how to delegate and, as one said, "Delegation is not a natural act." Delegation was a consistent difficult issue for CEOs. How do you learn to delegate? Who teaches a course in "letting go"?

5. Most companies had difficulties in building a management team because of multiple hiring mistakes. These mistakes were financially and emotionally costly. CEOs had particular difficulty in evaluating expertise outside their functional domains. Multiple hires were common for senior finance, HR, and technology positions. Many experienced hires from big companies could not adapt to the entrepreneurial environment of a smaller, private company, and many hires from small companies lacked the experience to scale a business. Many of the companies went through more than two hiring mistakes for key positions, and a few had to make four or five hires for CFO, HR, or CIO positions.

6. Even if assembling a management team went well, many CEOs were surprised at the difficulty of getting that team to work together effectively.

Some companies hired psychologists or executive coaches to help the management team learn how to communicate and relate to each other constructively. Again, the human dynamics of growth were frequently the biggest management challenge, underscoring the unpredictability of business growth.

7. Managing the pace of growth presented a major challenge for many companies. For some, growth happened too fast, forcing companies to put on the brakes to allow the people, processes, and controls to catch up. Some, in fact, came close to losing the business because they grew too fast. The stress on the companies generated by too-rapid growth brought deeper understanding of growth's complexity. Growth impacted the culture, structure, people, processes, and controls, and CEOs were forced to think about, plan for, and manage those impacts.

8. As these private companies grew, the roles of CEOs changed, often dramatically. CEOs who initially did everything had to shift to managing everything, to managing managers, and then to coaching managers and leading culture and strategy. Growth required the CEO, as Dave Lindsey (see Chapter 5, Defender Direct Case) once stated, "to continuously redefine his/her relationship to the business." CEOs struggled to remove themselves from daily putting out fires to devoting time to think strategically about how to deal with the big issues facing the business. They needed "firehouse" time. One CEO told me the only way he got time to think was to leave for an hour some days and take a drive in the country. Another CEO told me he took a day a week and went elsewhere to think about the five most important challenges the company was facing.

9. Most CEOs learned that growth required them to upgrade their people. This caused stress because such changes adversely affected loyal employees who had helped build the business. Many CEOs stated that they had to undertake these difficult upgrades more than once. Given the risks of making mistakes in hires described above, the added stress of disrupting loyal employees and changing team dynamics was wearing on CEOs, who yearned for team stability. Many CEOs said the challenges of hiring and managing a leadership team was the hardest part of the job.

10. Growth was not an easy process and the various tensions usually resulted in a zig-zag pattern of growth. Managing company growth created tensions between professional accountability and having a family environment; between managing the rate of growth versus delivering quality; between being cautious about turning business away and also worrying that

too much business would overwhelm people and processes. As one CEO stated, "Managing a growing business is like sailing—you know where you are and you know where you want to go and you have to be able to execute a whole lot of tacking to get there."

11. Many CEOs stressed that they had to get honest with themselves and at some point question why they should continue to grow and whether growth would change them and their company so much that the business would no longer be fun. Some stated that companies needed to grow for the right reasons and at some point simply generating more money is not a good enough reason.

I found it interesting that private company CEOs, without prompting, talked about the pace of growth, the need to manage growth, and the risk that too much growth could destroy their company. Those private company CEOs told me that they were less concerned about competitors than they were about self-inflicted wounds.

12. The CEOs of private companies with outside institutional capital (private equity) at their inception had a different view of growth. They pushed growth as fast as they could and focused more on revenue growth than profits. In some cases, these private equity–supported companies outgrew their capabilities but their CEOs were less concerned because of the financial safety net supplied by the company's institutional shareholder. Interestingly, in spite of this rush to grow, my research showed those companies took longer to reach certain revenue levels than non-institutionally funded companies.

13. Some of the CEOs were cognizant of the fact that at a certain revenue level they were likely going to engage bigger, well-capitalized competition. That competition would expose them to significant risk and may require taking on an institutional partner or selling. Both alternatives meant big changes for the company, the CEOs, and the employees. In some cases, the CEO's goal was to keep his or her revenue level below that inflection point.

Even though my sample size was small, nonetheless, the private company CEOs had a nuanced view of growth, its risks, and its challenges. To illustrate some of the risks of growth from their perspective, here are some more anonymous direct quotes:

"You don't want to bring on all the business that you can—growth can easily swallow you."

"Understand that growth puts you in a different competitive space."

"Delegation is the most difficult thing to learn."

"Most people can't develop skills as fast as the business can grow."

"It takes one set of skills to manage a company and an entirely different set of skills to grow a company."

"Ultimately you have to delegate everything not in your unique skill set."

"If you are making mistakes you are making progress."

"The management challenge is balancing when to let up on the gas pedal to let the people and processes catch up."

"I tried to bring in expertise too early."

"The dilemma that you go through as you try to grow the organization is that everyone has to grow their individual capacity to lead."

"You can't strangle a small company and choke it with too much process."

"In a high-growth business it is easy to get spread too thin and try to be too many things to too many people."

"We do not have an inalienable right to grow or to profits or customers."

"Don't grow just for the money."

"I don't think delegation is a linear process."

"The hardest thing to do really has been for me as the CEO is the tough decisions about people—deciding who can scale and who can't as we grow."

"We hired too fast and made a lot of mistakes."

"When we got to $100 million we began to encounter issues we never saw before."

"The way to grow is to fail and fix the failures."

Arguably, what comes through from these CEOs is that growth is difficult. And it is unlikely that one can predictably manage growth on a smooth and continuous basis. Further, growth has its risks. By growing too fast, a company can outstrip its capabilities, people, processes, or controls. Growth is a process to be proactively managed on a daily basis. It is important to note that the private companies I interviewed were nearly all success stories and that unsuccessful companies may have different lessons to teach. Clearly, those failures to manage the risks of growth would be an interesting study of "grow and die."

In the fall of 2007, while reading *BusinessWeek* magazine, I came across an article that caught my attention: "Room & Board Plays Impossible to Get—Private Equity Sees Growth for the Retailer but Founder John Gabbert Prefers His Own Pace."[2] The reporter, Jena McGregor, wrote; "By all conventional standards, Room & Board should be bigger than it is."[3] Given my interest in corporate growth, I was intrigued by the story, which illuminated a contrarian view to the Growth Mental Model. I wrote to John Gabbert and asked if I could do a case study on Room & Board because I thought business students needed to hear his views. He graciously agreed and the Room & Board story follows. Room & Board is a good example of a company that has prospered while managing its growth. It is a Smart Growth company.

Room & Board Case

Room & Board is a privately owned home-furnishings retailer, offering products that combine classic, simple design with exceptional quality.[4] At the time of my interview, approximately $250 million of revenue a year was generated through Room & Board's fully integrated and multichannel sales approach, consisting of its eight national retail stores, an annual catalog, and its Web site.

Based in Minneapolis, Minnesota, Room & Board's story is one of contrarian success; it is a company that eschewed the standard retail-industry business model, disavowed debt and equity-growth financing, and embraced a unique multiple-stakeholder model that valued quality and relationships ahead of the bottom line while producing stellar financial results. That the company has achieved consistency and harmony between its values and actions also has added to its uniqueness. Its culture supports an energized, positive growth environment for its employees that fosters high employee engagement and, in turn, high customer engagement.

Room & Board is wholly owned by John Gabbert, who created it more than twenty-five years ago. Now Gabbert, having reached the age of sixty, has been confronting his biggest challenge: how to institutionalize the unusual business model, culture, and employee environment he has built. His primary objective has been to preserve and protect his "relationship" business model, which has been the heart and soul of Room & Board's success.

History

Gabbert grew up working in a family retail business that sold traditional home furnishings and at the age of twenty-four succeeded his father as the CEO. Family dynamics proved challenging, so when he was thirty-three he left the family furniture business to pursue his own business, initially basing his furniture company on IKEA's business model. He also diversified into other businesses but, by the late 1980s, feeling overextended and unfulfilled, he decided to focus all his energy on building a business with people he liked and on a model that represented quality. All this drew him into the design aspect of the furniture business.

To Gabbert, quality relationships are just as important as quality home furnishings. This belief helped shape Room & Board into a business focused on creating long-lasting relationships with customers, vendors, and employees, who are all fully integrated into the model of selling quality furnishings. At Room & Board, quality is also about providing value, which is inherent in its products, which last and whose style and design are timeless—furniture that customers can count on enjoying for many years. But Room & Board goes further by believing that a customer's home should be a favorite place where a customer should be able to create a meaningful special environment. This customization has been made attractive by offering customers a multitude of special-order products, ranging from fabric choices on throw pillows to customer-designed solid-wood storage pieces.

Supply Chain

The retail-furniture industry is generally controlled by large manufacturers that dictate style, product availability, and price, and that make many products overseas with cheaper labor than is found in the United States. Room & Board decided early on that it did not want to play that game, so the company created its own supply chain of approximately forty different vendors, nearly all privately owned family businesses, many having grown alongside Room & Board over the years.

More than 85% of the company's products are made in the United States in places like Newton, North Carolina; Martinsville, Virginia; Minneapolis, Minnesota; Grand Forks, North Dakota; Shell Lake, Wisconsin; and Albany, Oregon, by craftsmen and artisans using high quality hardwoods, granite, and steel. Most of these products are made exclusively for Room &

Board. More than 50% of the products are manufactured by twelve of its key vendors. Room & Board meets with its vendors frequently to plan growth, discuss needs, and share financials to ensure that everyone is making a fair living while creating high-quality, well-designed products.

Over the years, these vendor relationships have evolved into true partnerships, which has allowed Room & Board to set an annual goal of having 85% of its products in stock at all times, contributing to quick deliveries. Special-order products are programmed ahead of normal production with the aim of delivering the product as fast as possible to the customer.

This model allows Room & Board more control of its destiny; it has control over product quality, inventory availability, and the risk of supply-chain disruptions. This unique model carries its own risk, however, as almost all of Room & Board's suppliers are private, family businesses that share the company's challenge of growing at a rate that sustains their economic health.

Culture

Room & Board has rejected common attributes of private-company culture: hierarchy, command and control from the top, information on a need-to-know basis, and, in the retail industry, high turnover resulting in customer-service challenges. Its culture is based on the principles of trust, respect, relationships, transparency, entrepreneurial ownership of one's job and career, and the importance of a balanced life. Room & Board eschews rules, lengthy policy manuals, and elitism. Rather, it believes individuals thrive in an environment where they are empowered to make decisions, and everyone's view is listened to and respected.

These core beliefs are outlined in its Guiding Principles, partially based on the following expectation: "At Room & Board we hope you find meaning in your work. There is both tremendous productivity for the company and personal fulfillment for each staff member when someone finds their life's work. It's a wonderful circle of success."

Room & Board has tried to achieve this "circle of success" by creating an environment of collaboration and engagement. This engagement is evidenced by deep relationships with customers, fellow employees, and suppliers. Respect for different views, openness to feedback, and responsibility for one's actions all drive the staff's behavior.

What has worked for Room & Board as it has tried to achieve balance was defined by Gandhi: "Harmony exists when what you feel, what you think, and what you do are consistent." Many businesses talk a good game, but Room & Board actually tries to "walk the talk." In this company environment, there is a heightened sensitivity regarding the impact of actions across functions and an awareness of the real message being communicated.

Room & Board believes that success is rooted in shared accountability; therefore, there are no rules for personal leave or sick pay. All 670 employees are shown the company's annual strategy priorities and a complete detailed financial package every month, so everyone can understand the goals and the business. All financial and operating numbers are transparent to encourage responsibility for owning and, in turn, affecting Room & Board's success. In discussing the company's normal eight-hour day, Gabbert stated: "I learned a long time ago that most people only have so many productive hours a day—it is the number of productive hours that count, not the number of hours at work. We strive to have an environment that results in energy and productivity. That is why we have a full physical-fitness facility with classes going on during the workday, a masseuse, as well as a great kitchen for employees to prepare healthy lunches."

Room & Board also operates on the principle that people who have a balanced life, with a life outside work, are happier and deal well with customers and with each other. Gabbert, understanding that what sets his company apart is having engaged employees who try to make every customer experience special, said: "I never wanted to be the biggest. I never thought about size. I just wanted to be the best and to spend my time at work with good people doing something more meaningful than just making money or keeping score."

Employees

The retail industry is generally known for its high employee turnover, hiring part-time employees to keep employee benefits low and instituting commission-based compensation to lower fixed costs. But Room & Board is proof that a very profitable, quality business can be built by not following any of those common retail practices.

Instead, Room & Board has very low employee turnover, mostly full-time employees, and full benefits for part-time employees, and it pays its retail sales staff on a salary basis rather than on individual sales. The rejection of a commission-based structure, together with its integrated and multichannel purchasing options, allows Room & Board customers to shop and purchase in the manner that makes the most sense to them. "We want customers to rely on us for the best advice and to trust that we have their best interests in mind—sales commissions run against that type of trust," said Gabbert.

At the time of the study, Room & Board stores more than five years old had average employee tenure of over five years, which is very high for the retail industry. Delivery and warehouse personnel in delivery centers open for more than four years had an average tenure of five years. Employee tenure was 5.7 years for the central office, and total employee tenure for the company averaged nearly five years.

Room & Board also takes a different approach to measuring employee satisfaction: by tracking how many employees refer family and friends for jobs and how many employees participate in the company's 401(k) program. Room & Board believes that these measures truly contribute to long-term employee engagement. Following the philosophy that employees need good physical, mental, and financial health, Room & Board has an extensive physical-fitness facility and a healthy-lunch program, and offers its employees personal financial-planning services and 401(k) investment advice from an outside financial consulting firm at no cost. In addition, all employees can buy Room & Board products at a substantial discount.

Key Expectations for Employees and Leaders

Room & Board's Guiding Principles are the foundation for the company's expectations and also serve as a tool to help employees understand their connection to the business. The document, which speaks primarily to respect, individual accountability, and engaging the business, includes the following statements:

- Respect is foundational to our work environment. Everyone is expected to build relationships based upon mutual respect and collaboration.
- Use good judgment when making decisions and apply principles, not rules, to each situation. The more you seek to understand how your role is related to our business objectives and tied to the broader success of the company, the more rewarding, enjoyable, and challenging the effort.

Just as all employees are expected to understand and embrace the core beliefs outlined in the Guiding Principles, leaders are expected to adhere to their own additional roadmap. Room & Board sets forth a number of leadership objectives for its central office, store, and delivery/distribution leadership team, including the following:

- You take ownership for your business—you're independent and therefore do not wait to be told what to do.
- You lead less with rules and rely more on principles.
- You value building relationships; collaboration is much more important to you than competition.
- You appreciate and desire longevity within your role. You do not seek to move from location to location or from department to department to get ahead; your growth occurs from richer experiences within your current role.

Delivery Centers

Another point of differentiation from other retailers is Room & Board's philosophy regarding deliveries. Many furniture chains outsource their deliveries. Room & Board does not, operating its own delivery centers staffed by full-time Room & Board professionals. These teams deliver all the local products. For national deliveries, Room & Board has an exclusive relationship with a Minneapolis company. To ensure ongoing collaboration, a few employees from the national shipping company's office work out of Room & Board's central location.

In addition, the company has dedicated delivery teams for just Room & Board products. It is not unusual for customers to assume that these delivery professionals are Room & Board employees, not just because of their Room & Board uniforms but also because they adhere to the same principles that all Room & Board employees follow; namely, that the customer experience during every step of the process is hassle-free and treated as an opportunity to create long-lasting relationships. The individuals who have the last interaction with customers are viewed as brand ambassadors and are expected to act as such.

Room & Board's goal of providing a great customer experience at every step of the buying-and-receiving process requires delivery personnel to deliver and set up the product and leave the customer happy. Delivery times are scheduled to allow time for customer interaction, discussions, and the proper placement of the new purchases. If there is a problem, delivery personnel are empowered to solve it on the spot because delivery personnel are trained to "leave the customer in a good place." The focus on interaction with the customer, from the beginning of the experience to the end, drives customer satisfaction, in terms of loyalty and referrals, to a rate of more than 95%.

Real Estate

To avoid the high rent typical in retail malls, Room & Board's founder owns most of its locations, freestanding sites with ample parking and easy access for customers. The company often chooses to renovate an existing location, blending its store in with a particular environment rather than building a new one. This practice serves as inspiration to customers who deal with similar challenges when designing and furnishing their own spaces. Moreover, it prevents Room & Board from adopting a cookie-cutter image for its stores and fosters the company's philosophy of unique design. The central-office facility is furnished with Room & Board products, so even employees who are not in customer-facing roles understand what the company sells, its quality, and its lasting design.

Pricing Model

Room & Board's pricing model is simple: no sales, no volume discounts, and no discounts for interior designers. Everyone pays the same price. As John Gabbert put it: "Nothing makes me madder than to buy something and then see it go on sale. I feel taken advantage of. That is why we have no sales, and we guarantee all prices for a year after purchase for each calendar year. If we sell a product within a year of your purchase for less than you paid, we will refund the difference."

Conclusion

Room & Board has achieved the enviable market position of managing its growth and avoiding the capital-market pressures produced by debt financing and equity partners or by being a public company. It has built a loyal and highly engaged workforce dedicated to its way of doing things and has managed to be a model of productivity and engagement without sacrificing quality. The company has not strived for the lowest operational costs, but instead has embraced a vertically integrated business model and earned good net margins.

The beauty of the Room & Board success story is how it has created a consistent, seamless, self-reinforcing system that cuts across culture, structure, execution philosophy, employee hiring, and benefits. The result is a company with a high-performance environment that manufactures 85% of its products in the United States, pays well, sells quality products, and makes good profits.

Room & Board has adhered to a multiple-stakeholder philosophy of capitalism, much like the European model and less like the sole-stakeholder model more common in the United States. It has believed it will do well if its customers, employees, and suppliers do well. To create shareholder value has not been Room & Board's sole purpose. Room & Board has achieved all of the above along with stellar financial results as set forth in Tables 8.1 and 8.2.

TABLE 8.1 Room & Board Financial Results

YEAR	SALES (IN MILLIONS)	NEW-STORE OPENINGS
1995	$33	
1996	$45	
1997	$53	Oakbrook, IL
1998	$67	
1999	$82	
2000	$98	
2001	$92	
2002	$95	South Coast, CA
2003	$110	
2004	$132	New York, NY; downtown Chicago store moves to Rush and Ohio location
2005	$173	San Francisco, CA
2006	$208	
2007	$229	

Source: Room & Board.

TABLE 8.2 Room & Board Financial Results

KEY METRICS	GOALS
Sales growth	10% annually
Net profit	8% pretax
Customer satisfaction	>96%
Product in warehouse at time of sale	>85%
Vendor lead time	<7 weeks

CHANNELS OF DISTRIBUTION, APPROXIMATE BREAKDOWN	
Store sales	70%
Phone sales	12%
Web sales	18%

MARKETS	($ IN MILLIONS)
Colorado	$18
Minneapolis	$24
Chicago	$44
San Francisco	$33
Southern California	$23
New York City	$46
National sales	$42

MAIN PRODUCT LINES	
Sofas and chairs	36%
Bedroom	17%
Dining room	12%

Source: Room & Board.

John Gabbert has built a successful company while rejecting the grow or die axiom by being very sensitive to the impact growth can have on his fundamental business principles.

Notes

1. Research conducted by Professor Edward D. Hess, Darden Graduate School of Business, funded by the Batten Institute, and the University of Virginia Darden

Foundation. All quotes from this study are anonymous in order to protect the research participants unless otherwise noted.

2. Jena McGregor, "Room & Board Plays Impossible to Get," *BusinessWeek*, October 1, 2007, 80.

3. Ibid.

4. Edward D. Hess, "Room & Board" (Case Study UVA-S-0150, University of Virginia Darden School Foundation, Charlottesville, 2008). This case has been updated for material events. All quotes are directly from the case.

CHAPTER 9

....

It Is Time for Smart Growth

THERE ARE MANY good reasons for businesses to choose to expand into new markets, to open more outlets, to diversify their product lines—that is, to grow. However, some business leaders push growth agendas under the mistaken belief that the alternative to growth is an inevitable decline. Every business does not have to grow—but it does have to improve to stay competitive.

The major thesis of this book is that businesses, Wall Street, the SEC, investors, and all stakeholders in business should adopt a more realistic, balanced, and nuanced view of how, when, and under what circumstances businesses should choose to grow. I wrote this book to attack the commonly held beliefs that

1. all businesses must continuously grow or they will die;
2. growth is always good; and
3. public company growth should occur smoothly and continuously and such growth should be measurable quarterly.

These beliefs thoroughly permeate the business environment in the United States, influencing the teaching in business programs in universities, the ways business leaders make decisions about their companies' growth, and the ways investors evaluate businesses. Unfortunately, these beliefs are not based on science or business reality. They should be discarded.

Study after study debunks the belief that businesses, even high-quality businesses, can consistently produce the smooth and continuous growth called for under the Growth Mental Model. And, paradoxically, attempts to meet the unrealistic demands of the Growth Mental Model often undermine the core strengths of otherwise healthy companies. Likewise, the belief that businesses must "grow or die" has no foundation.

Challenging these beliefs about growth is not enough; these mistaken ideas about growth must be replaced with a new growth concept, Smart Growth, which is grounded in research from multiple scientific disciplines coupled with business best practices.

The best way to mitigate the power of the Growth Mental Model is through earnings transparency and reducing executive compensation when companies play the short-term Earnings Game. Only then will businesses, generally, be able to have the latitude to look at the bigger picture, develop long-term strategies, foster innovation, and take the time to build internal growth systems. In Chapter 7, I call for the SEC and boards of directors to require disclosure of how public companies produce every penny of earnings in order to create earnings transparency. Under current SEC rules, businesses are required to report quarterly and annual earnings. These rules, although enacted to provide investors with information about a company's economic health, leave plenty of room for the Earnings Game to flourish. To dismantle the Earnings Game, the SEC should provide investors with the information needed to determine what percentage of a company's earnings are Authentic Earnings; that is, earnings produced by selling more products and services in arms-length transactions to customers and from operating more efficiently and productively. The Earnings Game prospers because of current SEC reporting requirements.

However, there is nothing that prohibits companies from providing additional information now as to how much of their earnings are Authentic Earnings and how much result from the Earnings Game. Boards of directors need not wait for the SEC to act. They can take action not only to disclose Authentic Earnings but, also, to unhitch executive compensation programs from the Earnings Game and, instead, to reward Authentic Earnings.

As discussed in Chapters 2–6, Wall Street's fixation on smooth and continuous growth is misplaced. Such growth is rare—the exception not the rule. The expectation generated by the Growth Mental Model that quarterly earnings reports are accurate measures of a company's economic health and an indication of future performance is unrealistic. The Earnings Game generates unwise corporate behavior and erodes the long-term economic strength and competitiveness of our country. Equally troubling, the Earnings Game may create an earnings bubble and illusory stock values.

Further, the business axiom "grow or die" needs to be retired. It is not based in science or business reality. Every business does not have to grow; it only has to continually improve to meet customer needs and differentiate itself from the competition. A grow or die mentality just as easily can produce a grow and die result if a business grows too fast and outstrips its managerial or financial capabilities; or its controls and processes; or dilutes too much of its culture or customer value proposition; or enters a different competitive space where it cannot effectively compete.

What should replace the grow or die axiom? It should be replaced by "improve to stay competitive." This is not as pithy as grow or die, to be sure, but it is more consistent with research findings and business reality.

Additionally, it is best to jettison the view that growth means getting bigger and replace it with the view that growth means getting better: delivering better products, competing better, having better business processes, executing better, and providing a better customer value proposition. Both McDonald's and Starbucks have learned that the right strategy may be not to get bigger but to get better. Likewise, Tiffany has survived profitably and as a great brand by living the corporate strategy of "growth without compromise."

Smart Growth

Smart Growth rejects the Growth Mental Model, the Earnings Game, and the beliefs that growth is always good; that every business must grow or die; and that being bigger is always better. Smart Growth is not anti-growth. To the contrary, Smart Growth brings intellectual rigor, decision processes, a growth/innovation process model, risk management, research results, and business realities to bear upon the concept of growth. Smart Growth strives for Authentic Earnings with the endgame being an enduring business that creates value for its customers, employees, owners, and the communities in which it operates.

Smart Growth accepts the reality that growth is a complex change process dependent on human behavior, which makes consistent growth difficult. Growth, fundamentally, is dependent on people. A key ingredient for consistent high performance, based on my research and research at Harvard, Stanford, and the University of Michigan business schools, is high employee engagement.[1] Creating high employee engagement is a primary objective of the Enabling Internal Growth System discussed in Chapter 4.

The value of high employee engagement in the development of strong, high-performance companies is evidenced in the Best Buy, Sysco, UPS, and Room & Board cases and other organizations noted in Chapter 4.

The Enabling Internal Growth System is also the building block for a continuous growth/innovation process illustrated by the Darden Growth/ Innovation Model, which also is discussed in Chapter 4. The goal of Smart Growth is to dislodge assumptions about growth and, instead, ground growth on rigorous decision making. By that I mean rigorous debating whether, why, and how a business should grow; determining whether it is ready to grow; and assessing the risks of growth. Smart Growth provides a Growth Decision Process and a Growth Risks Audit designed to bring rigor and risk management into the growth process, as discussed in Chapter 7.

Smart Growth's goal is to build more enduring businesses resulting in more value creation for all stakeholders and more systemic economic stability and security. Our economy is now impacted too much by those who profit from short-term advantages and short-term anomalies. We have built a transaction-based financial system that supports too many professionals whose livelihood depends on fees or short-term gains, volatility, and high velocity. This, in many cases, creates disproportionate gains for the top 1% of income earners and disproportionate losses at the lower income levels, resulting directly or indirectly from job losses. This short-term view and short-term greed does not advance our economic national security; our social, family, and community stability; or our long-term competitiveness.

If short-term interests and the Earnings Game continue to dominate Wall Street, then maybe we need innovation and new game-changing business models in our capital markets. *I think it is in our national interests to systematically promote and enable the building of enduring Smart Growth companies.* I question whether our current system does that. Maybe there needs to be a new capital market formed for Smart Growth companies that are trying to build enduring companies to benefit multiple stakeholders. That market would be funded by long-term investors and not short-term traders or short-term renters of securities. It would require minimum holding periods or penalize short-term holds. So, there could be two separate public stock markets: one for short-term holders and one for long-term holders, and companies could choose the market on which to list their stock, or a private trading exchange could be created for companies that aspire to be Smart Growth companies. Another idea is to extend the holding period for long-term capital gains for taxable entities to more than two years in order to promote long-term ownership and separate the "renters" of stock from the real owners of stock. Likewise, short-term holds by non-taxable entities would be penalized. In addition, executive compensation must be aligned with building enduring companies.

Why is this issue important? It is important because business is the primary vehicle through which most people try to achieve the economic ability to make a better life for themselves and their families. Our system is out of balance now because it is dominated by short-term interests.

Our economic system is also being hurt by its unrealistic assumptions and views about growth, which motivates bad corporate behaviors; enables the meaningless, wasteful, wealth-transferring Earnings Game; and results in too much unnecessary business volatility and destruction. Smart Growth attempts to change our beliefs about growth and ground them in research, business realities, and human dynamics in order to create more enduring businesses.

Next is a look at two companies that have long-term views: Costco and UPS. Note that in both cases, these companies have had leadership with the courage to resist Wall Street Rules.

Costco Wholesale Corp. Example

Costco Wholesale Corp. is the fifth-largest retailer in the United States and eighth-largest in the world.[2] It operates 553 warehouses in the United States, Canada, United Kingdom, Taiwan, Korea, Japan, and Mexico. For its fiscal year ending August 31, 2008, it generated over $72 billion of revenue, employed 142,000 full- and part-time employees, and had over 54.5 million members who pay an annual membership fee with an 87% renewal rate.

Costco's business model is built upon the principles of rapid inventory turnover, cost reduction by not advertising, low employee turnover, low employee theft, and price markups limited to either 14% or 15% over costs. Costco's exception to its low-cost mentality is employee pay and benefits. The average employee pay is $18 per hour and Costco pays for almost all health care insurance of all employees.

Costco defends its employee expenses as good business because it results in lower turnover, more engaged employees, and less theft. In fact, Costco's employee turnover is around 6% for employees with more than a year of service, substantially below retail industry averages.

Costco's stated goal is to be the best retail employer with respect to wages. As one can imagine, Costco is criticized by Wall Street analysts for its wage and markup policies: "One analyst, Bill Dreher of Deutsche Bank, complained last year that at Costco 'it is better to be an employee or a customer than a shareholder.'"[3]

Costco's CEO, Jim Sinegal, responds to comments like these regularly:

> You have to recognize . . . and I don't mean this in an acrimonious sense—that the people in that business (Wall Street) are trying to make money between now and next Thursday. We're trying to build a company that's going to be here 50 to 60 years from now. We owe that to the communities where we do business. We owe that to our employees that count on us for security. We have 140,000 employees and their families: that's a significant number of people who count on us. We owe it to our suppliers. Think about the people who produce products for us—you could probably multiply our family of employees by three or four times. And we owe it to our customers to continue to offer good prices.[4]

Sinegal is stating that he is managing the brand and the business model for the long term not for the short term. He clearly understands his business model, his customer value proposition, and what Costco represents to its customers and is relentless in protecting it and working to avoid even small changes that could dilute it. He responds to similar criticism on his strict gross profit margins of no more than 14% or 15% by stating that "increasing markups to say 16 or 18 percent might [cause Costco to] slip down a dangerous slope and lose discipline in minimizing costs and prices."[5]

Sinegal also justifies his employee wages policy by asserting that many Costco customers are more loyal *because* Costco's low prices do not come at the expense of the workers. Sinegal sets a tough standard for the CEOs of his competitors to follow by taking only $350,000 a year in salary plus $80,000 a year in a cash bonus, preferring to take the rest of his compensation in stock and option awards ($4.5 million in fiscal 2008). Sinegal rejects the Growth Mental Model and Wall Street Rules. "I think the biggest single thing that causes difficulty in the business world is the short-term view. We become obsessed with it. But it forces bad decisions."[6]

Sinegal's views are refreshing. He is not only cognizant of the risks of growth but also relentless in refusing to compromise the Costco model that works. And, he stands up to frequent Wall Street analysts' criticisms by re-fusing to risk the business model for short-term gains.

Sinegal is inspirational because he has confronted the Growth Mental Model and Wall Street Rules directly, publicly, and has had the courage to protect Costco's business model. He understands that growth in earnings at the expense of wages or margins can negatively impact Costco. He under-stands the essence of what he has built. He understands the alignment and interrelationship of his policies—his internal system—and the fact that tinkering with one aspect may create a slippery slope. Most important, he has the courage to say to Wall Street, "No! I will not play your game; it is different from our game."

United Parcel Service Case

United Parcel Service of America, Inc., is a worldwide package delivery company with a long history of success.[7] In 1998, UPS redefined its business from package delivery to Synchronized Commerce in an attempt to be-come its customers' full-service logistics solution provider. This change in strategy attempted to drive organic growth but as we shall see has produced only lackluster results ten years later.

Brief History

Prior to the introduction of the Synchronized Commerce Strategy in 1998, UPS had grown spectacularly from its humble beginning in 1907, when nineteen-year-old Jim Casey borrowed $100 to start a messenger and home-delivery service for Seattle department stores. By 2008, UPS had become a global public company, with a market cap of nearly $50 billion, more than 425,000 employees, $51 billion in revenue, and operations in more than 200 countries. A recognized leader among package delivery companies, its growth had been above industry averages and historically had occurred through geographical expansion.

However, in 1998, UPS changed its business model to Synchronized Commerce and adopted a new growth strategy it called the Four Quadrant model. UPS hoped to expand its market space from $90 billion to $3.2 tril-lion by transforming itself into a logistics-solutions company. But ten years after those changes, UPS generated only 12% of its revenue from its new synchronized commerce business.

Growth History

The growth of UPS over the past 100 years can be viewed as an iterative geographical expansion. UPS began as an intra-city business in Seattle in 1907 and, by 1919, had expanded to Oakland, California. Over the next fifty-eight years, UPS established stores across the United States, opening its first one in New York City in 1930. UPS extended its service through its new locations, just like any expanding retailer, and, in the process, became an inter-city package deliverer.

The company's geographical expansion went international in 1975 when UPS opened a store in Ontario, Canada. European expansion began in 1976, with a new store in Dusseldorf, Germany. UPS then expanded throughout the world: the Asia-Pacific region in 1988 and Latin America in 1989. By 1995, the company had entered China, its last untapped market.

Initially, and for forty-six years, UPS operated as an intra-city delivery business, transporting packages from large department stores to customers' homes. Then, in 1953, the company expanded its scope, providing residential deliveries for other types of businesses and later for business deliveries. This change in scope followed changes in the American lifestyle and shopping patterns that emerged with the creation of suburbs, regional malls, and an interstate highway system. UPS was forced to go in a new direction.

UPS responded to the changes in demographics, transportation, and customer needs by transforming itself, first, into a national delivery company and, ultimately, in the 1990s, into a global delivery company. The company broadened its customer base further by delivering more than 50% of the packages that customers bought over the Internet. By 2007, UPS's customer base included all types and sizes of businesses, from Dell to the individual entrepreneur selling products on the Internet.

By 2008, UPS's worldwide revenues of $51 billion were derived primarily from package and document deliveries. From 2002 to 2007, the company expanded the scope of its services under its Synchronized Commerce model to provide freight forwarding, customs clearance, inventory management, pick and pack, export financing, and customer returns and repairs.

UPS Operations

Headquartered in Atlanta, Georgia, UPS has more than 425,000 employees worldwide, of whom more than 260,000 work under union agreements. UPS is vertically integrated. For example, it operates the world's ninth-largest airline, which employs more than 2,900 pilots and maintains a fleet of 603 jets. Flying more than 1,900 flight segments to more than 800 airports around the world, UPS airplanes move more than 4 million packages and documents daily. The company delivers more than 15.5 million packages a day and is the Internet's largest fulfillment source. And it delivers those 15.5 million packages on time 99% of the time—and defect-free. UPS also operates one of the largest motorized fleets in the United States, with more than 99,000 vehicles.

In its role as a large technology and telecommunications company, UPS operates the largest DB2 database in the world, with 412 terabytes of dynamic memory. Its mainframe capacity allows for the transmission of more than 22 million instructions per second. UPS has more than 4,700 employees in its technology unit. In addition, the company operates the world's largest phone system. Its mobile radio network transmits more than 3 million packets of tracking data each day. One example of the vastness of the scale of its communications is that UPS receives more than 145 million hits per business day on its Web site, with 252 million hits on peak days.

The enormous size of the company is further illustrated by its Worldport technology and package hub, based in Louisville, Kentucky. This automated airport and package-sorting center comprises 5 million square feet, the equivalent of eighty football fields, and processes some 1.2 million packages a night during a four-hour period.

Employees

The company's 87,000 drivers hold esteemed positions in the company. The average tenure of a driver has been sixteen years, and driver turnover has been less than 2% a year. Union drivers earn up to $70,000 a year. Senior drivers receive nine weeks' paid annual leave, and UPS pays 100% of their health insurance premiums.

With more than one-third of its employees from minority groups, UPS has a diverse workforce. More than 25% of the company's U.S. managers are also members of minority groups. Women represent 27% of its U.S.

management team and 21% of its overall workforce. More than 70% of its full-time managers have been promoted from within. The company's promote-from-within policy and employee-centric culture are further illustrated by the fact that more than 50% of its full-time drivers started as part-timers.

At less than 6%, annual employee turnover at UPS is low. Long tenures and low turnover permeate the company, from its front-line employees to its district managers to its twelve-person executive team. The average tenure for district managers has been fourteen years.

The senior management team has averaged twenty-nine years of service. Ten of the twelve executives, including one woman and one African American, have spent their entire working lives at UPS. Interestingly, 75% of its vice presidents started at UPS in non-management positions. Kurt Kuehn, a member of the senior management team and CFO, stated, "Most senior managers like me began at UPS as part-timers in college or as package sorters or assistants. We loved it, and we stayed." In 1999, UPS became a public company, in the largest IPO in the history of the New York Stock Exchange. By 2007, about half of UPS stock was owned by its current and former employees and their families.

Customer Reach

UPS is big and global. It makes more than 15 million deliveries daily to nearly 8 million customers. Its customer-contact points include 4,600 UPS stores in the United States, 1,300 global Mail Boxes Etc. stores, 1,000 UPS customer centers, 13,000 UPS authorized outlets, and 38,000 UPS drop boxes.

Measurements

UPS has focused on efficiency and productivity measurements, and in 2007, it spent more than $10 billion integrating its processes and technology to make the company a real-time 24/7, 365-day operation. Behind every driver are the sophisticated technology and operations-support team that tracks the exact location of any package or document, anywhere, anytime. On a daily basis, UPS organizes every part of its logistics chain for maximum efficiency, down to the order in which packages are loaded on vans. Using technology, UPS creates routes daily that eliminate left-hand turns, saving driving time, millions of gallons of fuel, and fuel costs annually.

In September 2003, UPS unveiled a new technology system designed to improve customer service and provide greater internal efficiency. This new system was expected to reduce mileage by more than 100 million miles and save the company almost 14 million gallons of fuel annually. In addition, the new system featured advanced tools allowing UPS to analyze and edit dispatch plans in order to optimize delivery routes and times. "We have a saying at UPS," said Kurt Kuehn. "In God we trust; everything else we measure."

Another important ingredient in the UPS recipe for success is its engineering process and measurement mentality. UPS measures everything: CO_2 emissions, the time it takes to wash a windshield, the pace a driver needs to walk to a customer's house, the most efficient way to start a package van's ignition, the optimal way to load a package van, and the optimal daily delivery routes.

In 1921, founder Jim Casey hired industrial engineers to do efficiency, time, and motion studies. Casey started UPS on a path of process engineering that, over the years, has developed into a powerful operations-research division. The division spent its first eighty-seven years internally focused on measuring everything that could be measured, such as studying, modeling, and simulating the movements of people, conveyor belts, and packages.

As a result, UPS has developed 340 methods for drivers to follow to increase their efficiency and ensure their safety. This measurement mentality has taught everyone to pay attention to the details and the little things that can threaten safety and impede on-time delivery. Another example of the passion for measurement is the way UPS measures its managers. The company uses a balanced scorecard and has published sixteen UPS key performance indicators for the economic, social, and environmental areas. UPS measures water consumption, ground-network fuel efficiency, and global aircraft emissions. The purpose of this measure-everything mentality was expressed by Jim Holsen, vice president of Engineering, who said, "We're never satisfied with the way things are, if they can be improved."

This measurement compulsiveness does not mean that UPS is a micromanaged, rigid, robotic workplace where every action is dictated by best practices. UPS has overcome that tendency through its performance culture of paying its people well, holding everyone—from the package sorter to the CEO—to the same high standards, and being a predominantly employee-owned company. In 1942, strong controls were offset by local autonomy from the district-manager level when drivers were given the power and authority to do what was needed to serve customers. As Jim Casey said, "Each local manager is in charge of his district. We want him to look upon it exactly as if it were his own business. We want him to solve his problems in his own way."

Culture: The Essence of UPS

To understand how UPS has continued to grow its business over a 100-year period while avoiding the common death spiral of corporate hubris and insularity, it is important to understand the UPS culture and the UPS operations-research mentality. Both are so integrated and intertwined that they are a seamless whole. And both have been continually perpetuated at UPS through stories, processes, measurement systems, human-resource policies, and leadership.

Jim Casey built UPS over a fifty-year period with a distinct and well-defined culture that embraced the values of integrity, quality, dignity, respect, stewardship, partnership, equality, and humility. To understand UPS is to understand Casey, a man who went to work at the age of nine because his father was ill, and who founded UPS at nineteen. Casey was a self-made success who rose above his humble background but never forgot his roots, treating every individual and employee with dignity and respect.

Casey often wrote and spoke about the type of company UPS should be and the values it needed to foster. He left his imprint on UPS through the values that are taught to every new employee. UPS executives believe it is their duty to make sure those values, those ways of doing business, and those ways of taking care of employees continue. They do not want the UPS culture to change or fail on their watch.

The richness of the UPS culture is evidenced by the *Employee Policy Manual*, which every employee receives, and the compendium of Casey's speeches in the company's book, *Legacy of Leadership*. These speeches prove that Casey wanted to build a business where employees take pride in working for a company that conducts business as an outstanding corporate citizen.

The UPS culture is multifaceted and consists of the following:

- A performance culture with "partneurial" mutuality of accountability, regardless of position;

- A constant challenge-and-be-critical-and-be-better culture described as constructive dissatisfaction; and
- An employee-centric ownership culture with executives as stewards of the business.

Mutual Accountability

Kurt Kuehn described the UPS culture as follows: "A culture of mutual accountability. Everyone is accountable to everyone else for performance—doing what's right and doing it well." And he added, "With our measurement system, we try to take personalities and politics out of judging performance."

At UPS, the CEO is as accountable to his employees as they are to him. And in response to this, the CEO has a special telephone installed in his office so that any UPS employee can call him directly at any time.

This mutual accountability is partneurial because employees are viewed as partners. In fact, most are owners of the business. This mutual accountability breeds a more egalitarian culture that discourages and devalues arrogance, hubris, or self-aggrandizement. For example, all of the top twelve executives at UPS have offices on the fourth floor instead of the top floor of the headquarters building. All the executives have offices of the same size, and almost all share senior administrative assistants. These executives are not provided with limos or drivers. UPS does not own a corporate jet. Executives fly commercial and follow the same travel policies as other employees. There is no executive dining room. It is rare to see Italian suits, French cuffs, or made-to-order shirts on the fourth floor. For the most part, eleven of the twelve executives have held several different positions as they have worked their way up the corporate ladder. The UPS culture frowns on self-marketing, and the company works hard every day to continue the values and ideals put in place by Casey.

Relentless Improvement

UPS is relentless about improving and works at a problem until it is solved. By emphasizing the details—the blocking and tackling of the business—the company focuses on the processes of efficiency and productivity. This iterative learning culture was illustrated by Casey, who, when he started the business, wrote to more than 100 delivery companies across the United States to ask them how they made a profit. He reported, "We found no singular idea that was really revolutionary. It seemed to be a matter of learning as we went along, and that is about all that we have done."

The UPS culture is about the relentless pursuit of constant, incremental improvement. It is about how the company could be faster, smarter, and more efficient. This has led to the rewarding and honoring of constructive dissatisfaction. Dissent, inquiry, questioning, challenging, and critiquing are all valued and encouraged because they help UPS improve. The company takes the long-term approach. For instance, it has taken the international-operations division twenty-eight years to become profitable. UPS, like the "little engine that could," works at a problem or a process incrementally and iteratively until it is improved.

Stewardship

The third strong aspect of the UPS culture is the partneurial, employee-centric ownership and leader-stewardship that helps everyone in the company achieve their potential. According to Casey, "One measure of your success will be the degree to which you build up others who work with you. While building up others, you will build up yourself." Casey continued: "Good management is not just organization. It is an attitude inspired by the will to do right. Good management is taking a sincere interest in the welfare of the people you work with. It is the ability to make people feel that you and they are the company—not merely employees." On the subject of future leaders, Casey said:

> Who will those leaders be? They will be people who now, today, are forging ahead—not speculating or with fanfare but modestly and quietly. They are the plain, simple people who are doing their best in their present jobs with us; whatever those jobs may happen to be. Such people will not fail us when called on for bigger things. It is for them, our successors, to remember that all the glamour, romance, and success we have in our business at any stage of its existence must be the product of years of benefiting from the work of many devoted people. And there can be no glamour, no romance, and no truly great success unless it is shared by all.

The employee-centric culture of UPS is further evidenced by the following:

- Promotion-from-within policies and actions
- Employee stock-ownership plans
- Diversity programs
- Employee education programs
- Local employees working in international operations
- Employee internal free-agent program allowing any UPS employee to move anywhere in the company and advance

Casey believed in, and acted on, the policy that it is the employees and not the executives who make a company successful. UPS believes it has an obligation to share its success fairly with those who make it happen.

The three aspects of the UPS culture—mutual accountability, constructive dissatisfaction, and employee-centric policies and ownership—are the foundation of the UPS way of doing business. Integrated into these cultural values and policies are operations research and a measurement mentality.

Cultural Fit in Hiring

UPS hires people who fit into its culture and its iterative improvement and measurement workplace. The people UPS avoids hiring are those who want a fast track to the top. Instead, UPS has looked for candidates who want to be part of a team that is the best at what it does and who love the blocking and tackling of team business. The payoff for a job well done is the opportunity for a career with professional development.

New Business Model and Strategy

When UPS ran out of geographical areas in which to grow, at least four things could have happened. First, it could have hit the growth wall and plateaued. Second, it could have tried to sell new, complementary services to its existing customer base. Third, it could have made a major diversification move through an acquisition. And fourth, it could have focused on being better not bigger. In 1998, the company picked the second option when it announced it would provide Synchronized Commerce solutions for its customer base. To effectuate this strategy, UPS made approximately thirty acquisitions to add capabilities. Synchronized Commerce expanded UPS's market space, and former CEO Mike Eskew declared, "Our new mission is ambitious. It propels us from a $90-billion market into a $3.2-trillion market."

In effect, Synchronized Commerce was designed to allow UPS to sell more products and services to its existing customers. To effectuate this model, UPS acquired nearly thirty service providers with expertise in such different areas of Synchronized Commerce as freight forwarding, customer clearing, export financing, fulfillment services, and customer returns and repairs. Eskew defined Synchronized Commerce as the coordinated and efficient movement of goods, information, and financing along the supply and distribution chain.

This change was huge, as it not only challenged the UPS sales force, but also changed the focus of the company's operations-research division. Rather than focusing exclusively on improving efficiency and productivity, the focus shifted to a consulting group that sold those skills to UPS customers.

Although it is not clear that UPS understood either the magnitude or difficulty of the change they were undertaking with this new growth strategy, becoming a solutions provider required it to put in the field thousands of people who could sell like consultants, which required a substantively different skills set than its workforce had.

To provide the solutions contemplated by Synchronized Commerce for customers, it is necessary to uncover and define problems and craft different solutions for different customer needs. This is very different than selling package delivery services. Could UPS's current employee base learn and deliver that service? Would UPS need to hire thousands of consultants to call on and service its large global accounts?

And if so, how would well-educated consultants fit into the UPS culture? Clearly, such hires would dilute the UPS policy of promoting from within. Would UPS's culture reject these new consultants, and how would those people change UPS's culture? Its new growth strategy challenged so much of what was fundamental to UPS that it raised huge execution risks. Just as Starbucks growth initiatives challenged Starbucks' essence, UPS's growth initiative challenged the basic tenets of who it was. At best, UPS's Synchronized Commerce strategy has been only marginally successful after ten years of trying. It is quite possible that the strength of UPS—its strong egalitarian culture—has impeded the transition to a consulting solutions business model.

Nonetheless, UPS is still a market leader and great company in spite of the meager results from its Synchronized Commerce initiative. And UPS, as well as Best Buy, provides a good lesson: changing a company's business model to better compete and grow requires the realignment of internal systems to be consistent with and to reinforce the new model. Whether this can be accomplished is a function of how fundamental a company's culture is to the company's strengths and how much disruption of that culture will result from the new business model.

Conclusion

Costco and UPS are examples of Smart Growth companies that have built Enabling Internal Growth Systems that value the long-term creation of Authentic Earnings. It is time to reject the Growth Mental Model, the Wall Street Rules, and the Earnings Game and replace them with more realistic, empirically based growth concepts that enable and promote the building of enduring companies that continuously meet the needs of their multiple stakeholders. This could result in the creation of more long-term authentic value and more job, family, and community stability. At a minimum, directors and executives need to manage their risks of growth.

Notes
....

1. Kim S. Cameron, Jane E. Dutton, and Robert E. Quinn, eds., *Positive Organizational Scholarship* (San Francisco: Berrett-Koehler, 2003); Jane E. Dutton, *Energize Your Workplace: How to Create and Sustain High-Quality Connections at Work* (San Francisco: Jossey-Bass, 2003); James L. Heskett, W. Earl Sasser, Jr., and Leonard A. Schlesinger, *The Value Profit Chain: Treat Employees Like Customers and Customers Like Employees* (New York: Free Press, 2003); James L. Heskett, W. Earl Sasser, Jr., and Leonard A. Schlesinger, *The Service Profit Chain* (New York: Free Press, 1997); Edward D. Hess, *The Road to Organic Growth* (New York: McGraw-Hill, 2007); Edward D. Hess and Kim S. Cameron, eds., *Leading with Values: Positivity, Virtue and High Performance* (Cambridge: Cambridge University Press, 2006); Edward D. Hess, "Organic Growth—Lessons from Market Leaders" (Working Paper, 2007); Charles A. O'Reilly III and Jeffrey Pfeffer, *Hidden Value: How Great Companies Achieve Extraordinary Results with Ordinary People* (Boston: Harvard Business School Press, 2000).

2. Jeff Brotman and Jim Sinegal, Letter to Costco Shareholders, December 12, 2008; Jeff Chu and Kate Rockwood, "CEO Interview: Costco's Jim Sinegal," *FastCompany*, October 13, 2008, www.fastcompany.com/node/1042487/print; Costco Company Profile, 2008 Annual Report, http://phx.corporate-ir.net/phoenix.zhtml?c=83830&p=irol-homeprofile; Steven Greenhouse, "How Costco Became the Anti-Wal-Mart," *New York Times*, July 17, 2005, www.nytimes.com/2005/07/17/business/yourmoney/17costco.html?_r=1&pagewanted=print; Evan Carmichael, Jim Sinegal Quotes, www.evancarmichael.com/Famous-Entrepreneurs/1107/Jim-Sinegal_Quotes.html; Greg Lamm, "2008 Executive of the Year," *Puget Sound Business Journal*, March 19, 2008, www.enterpriseseattle.org/index.php?option=com_content&task=view&id=210&itemid=104; Dyan Machan, "CEO Interview: Costco's James Sinegal," *SmartMoney*, March 27, 2008, www.smartmoney.com/investing/stocks/ceo-interview-costcos-james-sinegal-22782/; O'Reilly and Pfeffer, *Hidden Value*.
3. Greenhouse, "How Costco Became the Anti-Wal-Mart."
4. Chu and Rockwood, "CEO Interview."
5. Greenhouse, "How Costco Became the Anti-Wal-Mart."
6. Carmichael, Jim Sinegal Quotes.
7. Edward D. Hess, "United Parcel Service of America, Inc." (Case Study UVA-S-0143, University of Virginia Darden School Foundation, Charlottesville, 2007). This case has been updated for material events. All quotes are directly from the case.

Appendix

Bibliography

Adamy, Janet. "At Starbucks, Low-Key Vet Plots Course." *Wall Street Journal,* March 18, 2008. www.djreprints.com/link/DJRFactiva.html?FACTIVA=wjco 20080318000060.

Adamy, Janet. "Schultz's Second Act Jolts Starbucks—Already Intense, He Faces New Pressure: Peltz Owns a Stake." *Wall Street Journal,* May 19, 2008. www .djreprints.com/link/DJRFactiva.html?FACTIVA=wjco20080519000131.

Adamy, Janet. "Starbucks Reveals Locations of Stores to Be Closed: Announces Job Cut." *Wall Street Journal,* July 18, 2008, B2.

Adamy, Janet. "Corporate News: Starbucks Keeps Sandwiches, Tweaks Recipe." *Wall Street Journal,* July 26, 2008. www.djreprints.com/link/DJRFactiva.html? FACTIVA=wjco20080726000097.

Adamy, Janet. "Starbucks Makes 1,000 New Job Cuts." *Wall Street Journal,* July 30, 2008. http://global.factiva.com/aa/default.aspx?pp=Print&hc=Publication.

Adamy, Janet. "At Starbucks, a Tall Order for New Cuts, Store Closures." *Wall Street Journal,* January 29, 2009, B1.

Adamy, Janet. "Starbucks Plays Common Joe." *Wall Street Journal,* February 9, 2009. http://online.wsj.com/article/SB12341384876076157.html.

"America's Oldest Companies." *Nation's Business* 64, 7 (July 1976): 36.

Arbaugh, J. B. (Ben), and S. Michael Camp. "Management Growth Transitions: Theoretical Perspectives and Research Directions." In *The Blackwell Handbook of Entrepreneurship,* ed. Donald L. Sexton and Hans Landström, 308–328. Oxford: Blackwell Publishers, 2000.

Arendt, Jeffrey D. "Adaptive Intrinsic Growth Rates: An Integration Across Taxa." *Quarterly Review of Biology* 72, 2 (1997): 149–177.

Arnott, Stephen A., Susumu Chiba, and David O. Conover. "Evolution of Intrinsic Growth Rate: Metabolic Costs Drive Trade-Offs Between Growth and Swimming Performance in *Menidia Menidia*." *Evolution* 60, 6 (2006): 1269–1278.

Attarian, John. "The Steady-State Economy: What It Is, Why We Need It." Negative Population Growth, 2004. http://www.npg.org/forum_series?steadystate.html.

Auerswald, Philip, Stuart Kauffman, José Lobo, and Karl Shell. "The Production Recipes Approach to Modeling Technological Innovation: An Application to Learning by Doing." *Journal of Economic Dynamics and Control* 24, 3 (2000): 389–450.

Ayala, Francisco J. "Darwin's Greatest Discovery: Design Without Designer." *Proceedings of the National Academy of Science* 104 (2007): 8567–8573.

Baaij, Marc, Mark Greeven, and Jan Van Dalen. "Persistent Superior Economic Performance, Sustainable Competitive Advantage, and Schumpeterian Innovation: Leading Established Computer Firms, 1954–2000." *European Management Journal* 22, 5 (2004): 517–531.

Baghai, Mehrdad, Stephen C. Coley, David White, Charles Conn, and Robert J. McLean. "Staircases to Growth." *McKinsey Quarterly* 4 (1996): 38–61.

Bailey, Jeff. "JetBlue Cancels More Flights in Storm's Wake." *New York Times*, February 18, 2007. www.nytimes.com/2007/02/18/business/18jetblue.html.

Bailey, Jeff. "JetBlue's C.E.O. Is 'Mortified' After Fliers Are Stranded." *New York Times*, February 19, 2007. www.nytimes.com/2007/02/19/business/19jetblue.html.

Bailey, Ronald. "Post-Scarcity Prophet: Economist Paul Romer on Growth, Technological Change, and an Unlimited Human Future—Interview." *Reason Magazine*, December 2001. www.reason.com/news/show/28243.html.

Ball, Ray, and Philip Brown. "An Empirical Evaluation of Accounting Income Numbers." *Journal of Accounting Research* 6, 2 (1968): 159–178.

Bartiromo, Maria. "Bob Nardelli Explains Himself." *BusinessWeek,* July 24, 2006.

Behar, Howard, and Janet Goldstein. *It's Not About the Coffee: Leadership Principles from a Life at Starbucks.* New York: Penguin, 2007.

Beinhocker, Eric D. *The Origin of Wealth: The Radical Remaking of Economics and What It Means for Business and Society.* Boston: Business School Press, 2006.

Birchall, Jonathan. "Starbucks to Close 600 US Stores." *Financial Times*, July 1, 2008. www.ft.com.cms/s/0/086fd976-47b2-11dd-93ca-000077b07658.html.

Birchall, Jonathan. "Starbucks to Cut 6,700 Jobs Amid Falling Sales." *Financial Times*, January 28, 2009. www.ft.com.cms/s/0/2d72f8fc-ed84-11dd-bd60-0000779fd2ac.html.

Bogle, John C. *Enough: True Measures of Money, Business and Life.* Hoboken, NJ: John Wiley & Sons, 2009.

Bogler, Daniel, and Adrian Michaels. "Attempting to Shift the Stretch-Goal Posts." *Financial Times,* June 9, 2000, 32.

Bogler, Daniel, and Adrian Michaels. "How a Stumble Became a Headlong Fall Over the Cliff." *Financial Times,* June 9, 2000, 18.

Boyle, Matthew. "Risky Loans: Harley Hits the Slick; Its Finance Arm Pumped Up Sales with Hog Wild Lending That Could Harm Its Pristine Credit Rating." *Business Week*, October 27, 2008, 54.

"Brand Management." *Economist*, March 1, 2007. www.economist.com/business/displaystory.cfm?story_id=E1_RSSGPSN.

Breen, Bill. "Living in Dell Time." *Fast Company*, December 19, 2007.

Brooker, Katrina, and Julie Schlosser. "The Un-CEO. A. G. Lafley Doesn't Over-promise. He Doesn't Believe in the Vision Thing. All He's Done Is Turn Around P&G in 27 Months." *Fortune*, September 16, 2002. http://money.cnn.com/magazines/fortune/fortune_archive/2002/09/16/328576/index.htm.

Brotman, Jeff, and Jim Sinegal. Letter to Costco Shareholders. December 12, 2008.

Brown, Paul B. "More than One Way to Help a Business Grow." *New York Times*, November 13, 2007. www.nytimes.com/2007/11/13/business/smallbusiness/13toolkit.html.

Brown, Shona L., and Kathleen M. Eisenhardt. "The Art of Continuous Change: Linking Complexity Theory and Time-Paced Evolution in Relentlessly Shifting Organizations." *Administrative Science Quarterly* 42 (1997): 1–34.

Brown, Shona, L., and Kathleen M. Eisenhardt. *Competing on the Edge: Strategy as Structured Chaos*. Boston: Harvard Business School Press, 1998.

Bruner, Robert F. *Deals from Hell: M&A Lessons That Rise Above the Ashes*. Hoboken, NJ: John Wiley & Sons, 2005.

Bryan, Lowell L., and John Kay. "Dialogue: Can a Company Ever Be Too Big?" *McKinsey Quarterly* 4 (1999): 102–111.

Buckley, Neil. "P&G Chief Puts Smiles Back on Investors' Faces." *Financial Times*, May 6, 2002.

Buffett, Warren. 2003 Shareholder Letter. Berkshire Hathaway, www.berkshirehathaway.com/letters/2003ltr.pdf.

Burgelman, Robert A., and Andrew S. Grove. "Let Chaos Reign, Then Rein in Chaos—Repeatedly: Managing Strategic Dynamics for Corporate Longevity." *Strategic Management Journal* 28 (2007): 965–979.

Burlingham, Bo. *Small Giants: Companies that Choose to Be Great Instead of Big*. New York: Penguin, 2005.

"The Business of Survival." *Economist*, December 18, 2004, 104–105.

Byrne, Harlan S. "A Return Visit to Earlier Stories—A Little Leeway: Procter & Gamble CEO John Pepper Is Being Patient in Pharmaceuticals." *Barron's*, January 1, 1996, 12.

Cabral, Luis. "Sunk Costs, Firm Size and Firm Growth." *The Journal of Industrial Economics* 43, 2 (1995): 161–172.

Cameron, Kim S., Jane E. Dutton, and Robert E. Quinn, eds. *Positive Organizational Scholarship*. San Francisco: Berrett-Koehler, 2003.

Carmichael, Evan. Jim Sinegal Quotes, www.evancarmichael.com/Famous-Entre preneurs/1107/Jim-Sinegal_Quotes.html.

Cathy, S. Truett. *Eat Mor Chikin: Inspire More People.* Decatur, GA: Looking Glass Books, 2002.

CBS2. "JetBlue Attempts to Calm Passenger Furor." CBS2.com. February 15, 2007. http://cbs2.com/national/jetblue.tarmac.JFK.2.279800.html.

Chan, Konan, Louis K. C. Chan, Narasimhan Jegadeesh, and Josef Lakonishok. "Earnings Quality and Stock Returns." *Journal of Business* 79, 3 (2006): 1041–1082.

Chan, Louis K. C., Jason Karceski, and Josef Lakonishok. "The Level and Persistence of Growth Rates." *Journal of Finance* 58, 2 (2003): 643–684.

Charan, Ram, and Noel M. Tichy. *Every Business Is a Growth Business: How Your Company Can Prosper Year After Year.* New York: Three Rivers Press, 1998.

Cheng, Mei, K. R. Subramanyam, and Yuan Zhang. "Earnings Guidance and Managerial Myopia." November 2005. http://ssrn.com/sol3/papers.cfm?abstract_id=816304.

Christensen, Clayton M. *The Innovator's Dilemma: When New Technologies Cause Great Firms to Fail.* Boston: Harvard Business School Press, 1997.

Christensen, Clayton M., Stephen P. Kaufman, and Willy C. Shih. "Innovation Killers." *Harvard Business Review* 86, 1 (2008): 98–105.

Chu, Jeff, and Kate Rockwood. "CEO Interview: Costco's Jim Sinegal." *FastCompany,* October 13, 2008. www.fastcompany.com/node/1042487.

Clippinger, John Henry III, ed. *The Biology of Business: Decoding the Natural Laws of Enterprise.* San Francisco: Jossey-Bass, 1999.

Coca-Cola Company. Annual Report. 2008. www.thecoca-colacompany.com/investors/form_10K_2008.html.

Cohen, Daniel A., Aiyesha Dey, and Thomas Z. Lys. "Real and Accrual-Based Earnings Management in the Pre- and Post-Sarbanes Oxley Periods." AAA 2006 Financial Accounting and Reporting Section (FARS), June 2007. http://ssm.com/abstract=813088.

Collier, T. J. "Grow Fast or Die." *San Diego Metropolitan Magazine,* November 1998.

Collingwood, Harris. "The Earnings Game: Everyone Plays, Nobody Wins." *Harvard Business Review* 79, 6 (2001), 65–74.

Collins, David J., and Cynthia A. Montgomery. "Creating Corporate Advantage." *Harvard Business Review* 76, 4 (1998): 70–83.

Collins, James C. *Good to Great.* New York: Harper Business, 2001.

Collins, James C., and Jerry I. Porras. *Built to Last: Successful Habits of Visionary Companies.* New York: HarperCollins, 1994.

Colvin, Geoffrey, and Katie Benner. "GE Under Siege." *Fortune,* October 15, 2008.

"Comeback Kings?" *Economist,* January 8, 2009. www.economist.com/business/displaystory.cfm?story_id=12896749.

"Companies & Finance—the Americas—the What, Not the Where, to Drive P&G." *Financial Times,* September 3, 1998, 18.

Costco Company Profile. 2008 Annual Report. http://phx.corporate-ir.net/phoenix
.zhtml?c=83830&p=irol-homeprofile.

Coutu, Diane L. "Sense and Reliability—A Conversation with Celebrated Psychologist Karl E. Weick." *Harvard Business Review* 81, 4 (2003): 84–90.

Cox, Larry W., Michael D. Ensley, and S. Michael Camp. 2003. "The 'Resource Balance Proposition': Balancing Resource Allocations and Firm Growth." In *Issues in Entrepreneurship: Contracts, Corporate Characteristics and Country Differences*, ed. Gary D. Libecap, 47–68. New York: JAI, 2003.

D'Aveni, Richard A. *Hypercompetition*. New York: Free Press, 1994.

D'Aveni, Richard, and L. G. Thomas. "The Rise of Hypercompetition from 1950 to 2002: Evidence of Increasing Structural Destabilization and Temporary Competitive Advantage." Working Paper, Tuck School of Business, Dartmouth College. October 11, 2004.

D'Aveni, Richard A., with Robert Gunther. *Hypercompetitive Rivalries: Competing in Highly Dynamic Environments*. New York: Free Press, 1994.

Darby, Michael R., and Lynne G. Zucker. "Growing By Leaps and Inches; Creative Destruction, Real Cost Reduction, and Inching Up." *Economic Inquiry* 41, 1 (2003): 1–19.

Darden School of Business, Batten Institute. "Darden's Batten Institute Announces That Decade-Long Study of Corporate Earnings Points the Way to Outperforming Stocks. Prof. Ed Hess' 'OGI' Identifies 27 Organic Growth All-Stars Whose Stock Bested S&P 500 by Factor of Ten over Ten-Year Period." Press Release, March 14, 2008.

Davenport, Thomas H. "Whatever Happened to Complexity Theory?" *Trends and Ideas*, Fall 2003, 3–4.

De Geus, Arie. *The Living Company: Habits for Survival in a Turbulent Business Environment*. Boston: Harvard Business School Press, 2002.

Dechow, Patricia M. "Accounting Earnings and Cash Flows as Measures of Firm Performance: The Role of Accounting Accruals." *Journal of Accounting and Economics* 18, 1 (1994): 3–42.

Donohue, Thomas J. "Enhancing America's Long-Term Competitiveness: Ending Wall Street's Quarterly Earnings Game." Keynote address, Wall Street Analyst Forum, New York, November 30, 2005. www.uschamber.com/press/speeches/2005/051130tjd_wallstreet.htm.

Drazin, Robert, and Robert K. Kazanjian. "Research Notes and Communications: A Reanalysis of Miller and Friesen's Life Cycle Data." *Strategic Management Journal* 11 (1990): 319–325.

Drucker, Peter F. *Innovation and Entrepreneurship*. New York: HarperCollins. 1985.

Dumaine, Brian. "P&G Rewrites the Marketing Rules." *Fortune*, November 6, 1989, 34.

Dutton, Jane E. *Energize Your Workplace: How to Create and Sustain High-Quality Connections at Work*. San Francisco: Jossey-Bass, 2003.

Dyer, Davis, Frederick Dalzell, and Rowena Olegario. *Rising Tide: Lesson From 165 Years of Brand Building at Procter & Gamble.* Boston: Harvard Business School Press, 2004.

Edgecliffe-Johnson, Andrew. "P&G Cuts 15,000 Jobs in Attempt to Pep Up Sales—Group to Focus on Reviving Innovation." *Financial Times,* June 10, 1999.

Edgecliffe-Johnson, Andrew. "P&G Cautions Over Recovery Before 2001." *Financial Times,* August 2, 2000.

Eisenhardt, Kathleen M., and Claudia Bird Schoonhoven. "Organizational Growth: Linking Founding Team Strategy, Environment, and Growth Among U.S. Semiconductor Ventures." *Administrative Science Quarterly* 35, 3 (1990): 504–529.

Ellison, Sarah, Ann Zimmerman, and Charles Forelle. "Sales Team—P&G's Gillette Edge: The Playbook It Honed at Wal-Mart; Consumer-Products Giant Helps Huge Retailer Make Specialty Items Mainstream; Coffee Beans for Beginners." *Wall Street Journal,* January 31, 2005, A1.

England, Richard W. "Natural Capital and the Theory of Economic Growth." *Ecological Economics* 34 (2000): 425–431.

Evans, George W., Seppo Honkapohja, and Paul M. Romer. "Growth Cycles." 5659 NBER Working Paper, 1996, 1–51.

Evans, Jonathan St. B.T. "Theories of Human Reasoning: The Fragmented State of the Art." *Sage* 1, 1 (1991): 83–105.

"Face Value: A Post-Modern Proctoid." *Economist,* April 12, 2006. www.economist.com/businessfinance/displayStory.cfm?story_id=6795882.

Fama, Eugene F. "Agency Problems and the Theory of the Firm." *Journal of Political Economy* 88, 2 (1980): 288–307.

Fama, Eugene F., and Kenneth R. French. "The Equity Premium." *Journal of Finance* 57, 2 (2002): 637–659.

Finkelstein, Sydney. *Why Smart Executives Fail and What You Can Learn from Their Mistakes.* New York: Portfolio, 2003.

Foster, Richard N., and Sarah Kaplan. *Creative Destruction: From "Built to Last" to "Built to Perform."* London: Prentice Hall, 2001.

Foust, Dean. "Things Go Better With . . . Juice; Coke's New CEO Will Have to Move Quickly to Catch Up in Noncarbonated Drinks." *BusinessWeek,* May 17, 2004, 81.

Frank, Mary Margaret, and Sonja Olhoft Rego. "Do Managers Use the Valuation Allowance Account to Manage Earnings Around Certain Earnings Targets?" *JATA* 28, 1 (2006): 43–65.

Freeman, R. Edward, Jeffrey S. Harrison, and Andrew C. Wicks. *Managing for Stakeholders.* New Haven, CT: Yale University Press, 2007.

Fuller, Joseph, and Michael C. Jensen. "Just Say No to Wall Street: Putting a Stop to the Earnings Game." *Journal of Applied Corporate Finance* 14, 4 (2002): 41–46.

Garber, Amy. "New MCD Chief: Strategy to Stay the Same." *Nation's Restaurant News,* December 13, 2004, 1–2.

Garber, Amy. "The Golden Anniversary of the Golden Arches." *Nation's Restaurant News*, April 4, 2005, 37.

George, Bill. *Authentic Leadership: Rediscovering the Secrets to Creating Lasting Value*. San Francisco: Jossey-Bass, 2003.

Geroski, Paul A. "Understanding the Implications of Empirical Work on Corporate Growth Rates." *Managerial and Decision Economics* 26, 2 (2005): 129–138.

Geroski, Paul A., S. Lazarova, G. Urga, and C. F. Walters. "Are Differences in Firm Size Transitory or Permanent?" *Journal of Applied Econometrics* 18, 1 (2003): 47–59.

Geroski, Paul A., Stephen J. Machin, and Christopher F. Walters. "Corporate Growth and Profitability." *Journal of Industrial Economics* 45, 2 (1997): 171–189.

Gómez, José M. "Bigger Is Not Always Better: Conflicting Selective Pressures on Seed Size in *Quercus Ilex*." *Evolution* 58, 1 (2004): 71–80.

Gotthard, Karl. "Increased Risk of Predation as a Cost of High Growth Rate: An Experimental Test in a Butterfly." *Journal of Animal Ecology* 69, 5 (2000): 896–902.

Graham, John R., Campbell R. Harvey, and Shivaram Rajgopal. "The Economic Implications of Corporate Financial Reporting." *Journal of Accounting and Economics* 40 (2005): 3–73.

Graham, John R., Campbell R. Harvey, and Shivaram Rajgopal. "Value Destruction and Financial Reporting Decisions." *Financial Analysts Journal* 62, 6 (2006): 27–39.

Grant, Jeremy, Louisa Hearn, and Ian Bickerton. "Deal Forces New Realities on Competition." *Financial Times,* January 28, 2005. http://us.ft.com/ftgateway/superpage.ft?news_id=ft001282005006900840&page=1.

Greenhouse, Steven. "A New-Found Pep at P&G." *New York Times,* February 3, 1985, 3.

Greenhouse, Steven. "How Costco Became the Anti-Wal-Mart." *New York Times,* July 17, 2005. www.nytimes.com/2005/07/17/business/yourmoney/17costco.html?_r=1&pagewanted=print.

Greenwald, Bruce, and Judd Kahn. "All Strategy Is Local." *Harvard Business Review* 83, 9 (2005): 1–10.

Greenwald, Bruce, and Judd Kahn. *Competition Demystified: A Radically Simplified Approach to Business Strategy*. New York: Penguin Group, 2008.

Greiner, Larry E. "Evolution and Revolution as Organizations Grow." *Harvard Business Review* 76, 3 (1998): 55–64.

Greve, Henrich R. "A Behavioral Theory of Firm Growth: Sequential Attention to Size and Performance Goals." *Academy of Management Journal* 51, 3 (2008): 476–494.

"Growth Pains Take Their Toll on P&G." *Financial Times,* August 5, 1998, 27.

Hamel, Gary, and C. K. Prahalad. *Competing for the Future: Breakthrough Strategies for Seizing Control of Your Industry and Creating the Markets of Tomorrow*. Boston: Harvard Business School Press, 1994.

Hamel, Gary, with Bill Breen. *The Future of Management*. Boston: Harvard Business School Press, 2007.

Hamner, Susanna. "Harley, You're Not Getting Any Younger." *New York Times,* March 22, 2009.

Hargadon, Andrew. *How Breakthroughs Happen: The Surprising Truth About How Companies Innovate.* Boston: Harvard Business School Press, 2003.

Harley-Davidson Inc. 2008 Annual Report, Part 1. www.harley-davidson.com/wcm/Content/Pages/Investor_Relations/2008_annual_report_launch.jsp?locale=en_US.

Hays, Constance L. *The Real Thing: Truth and Power at the Coca-Cola Company.* New York: Random House, 2004.

Healy, Paul M., and James M. Wahlen. "A Review of the Earnings Management Literature and Its Implications for Standard Setting." *Accounting Horizons* 13, 4 (1999): 365–383.

Heskett, James L., W. Earl Sasser, Jr., and Leonard A. Schlesinger. *The Service Profit Chain.* New York: Free Press, 1997.

Heskett, James L., W. Earl Sasser, Jr., and Leonard A. Schlesinger. *The Value Profit Chain: Treat Employees Like Customers and Customers Like Employees.* New York: Free Press, 2003.

Hess, Edward D. "Why Successful Companies Often Fail." *The Catalyst,* February 2003.

Hess, Edward D. "Rapid Growth: Be Careful What You Ask For." *The Catalyst,* July 2003.

Hess, Edward D. "What Is the Meaning of Business?" *The Catalyst,* October 2003.

Hess, Edward D. "When Should Your Business Stop Growing?" *The Catalyst,* March 2004.

Hess, Edward D. "Best Buy Co., Inc." Case Study UVA-S-0142. University of Virginia Darden School Foundation, Charlottesville, 2007. This case has been updated for material events.

Hess, Edward D. "The Coca-Cola Company." Case Study UVA-S-0145. University of Virginia Darden School Foundation, Charlottesville, 2007. This case has been updated for material events.

Hess, Edward D. "The Home Depot, Inc." Case Study UVA-S-0144. University of Virginia Darden School Foundation, Charlottesville, 2007. This case has been updated for material events.

Hess, Edward D. "Organic Growth—Lessons from Market Leaders." Working Paper. 2007.

Hess, Edward D. *The Road to Organic Growth.* New York: McGraw-Hill, 2007.

Hess, Edward D. "Sysco Corporation." Case Study UVA-S-0140. University of Virginia Darden School Foundation, Charlottesville, 2007. This case has been updated for material events.

Hess, Edward D. "Tiffany & Company." Case Study UVA-S-0141, University of Virginia Darden School Foundation, Charlottesville, 2007. This case has been updated for material events.

Hess, Edward D. "United Parcel Service of America, Inc." Case Study UVA-S-0143. University of Virginia Darden School Foundation, Charlottesville, 2007. This case has been updated for material events.

Hess, Edward D. "Darden Private Growth Research Project." 2008.

Hess, Edward D. "McDonald's Corporation." Case Study UVA-S-0147. University of Virginia Darden School Foundation, Charlottesville, 2008. This case has been updated for material events.

Hess, Edward D. "Organic Growth Index 'OGI' 1996–2006." 2008.

Hess, Edward D. "Room & Board." Case Study UVA-S-0150. University of Virginia Darden School Foundation, Charlottesville, 2008.

Hess, Edward D. "Defender Direct." Case Study UVA-ENT-0115. University of Virginia Darden School Foundation, Charlottesville, 2009.

Hess, Edward D., and Kim S. Cameron, eds. *Leading with Values: Positivity, Virtue and High Performance.* Cambridge: Cambridge University Press, 2006.

Hess, Edward D., and Robert K. Kazanjian, eds. *The Search for Organic Growth.* Cambridge: Cambridge University Press, 2006.

Hess, Edward D., and Jeanne Liedtka. "Darden Growth/Innovation Model." 2008.

"Howard Schultz's Starbucks Memo." *Financial Times,* February 23, 2007. http://us .ft.com/ftgateway/superpage.ft?news_id=ft00223200718394558568&page=2.

Hsieh, Peggy, Timothy Koller, and S. R. Rajan. "The Misguided Practice of Earnings Guidance." *McKinsey on Finance* 19 (2006): 1–5.

Hume, Scott, "Jack Greenberg's New Populism." *Restaurants & Institutions* (July 1, 1999): 60–66.

Hymowitz, Carol, and Gabriella Stern. "Taking Flak: At Procter & Gamble, Brands Face Pressure and So Do Executives—Amid Harsh Public Criticism by CEO, Some Bail Out; Artzt Calls It Training—Cutting Prices, Cutting Jobs." *Wall Street Journal,* May 10, 1993, A1.

Isidore, Chris. "JetBlue Founder: Storm Cost CEO Job." CNNMoney.com. June 26, 2007. http://money.cnn.com/2007/06/26/news/companies/neeleman/index .html.

JetBlue. "JetBlue Airways Pre-Cancels 23 Percent of Its Scheduled Flights for Feb. 17 and Feb. 18, 2007." Press Release, February 17, 2007. http://investor.jetblue.com/ phoenix.zhtml?c=131045&p=irol-newsArticle&ID=964503&hig.

JetBlue. "JetBlue Extends Operational Recovery Through Monday, Feb. 19." Press Release, February 17, 2007. http://investor.jetblue.com/phoenix.zhtml?c=131045& p=irol-newsArticle&ID=964506&hig.

JetBlue. "JetBlue Names Russell Chew Chief Operating Officer." Press Release, March 7, 2007. http://investor.jetblue.com/phoenix.zhtml?c=131045&p=irol-news Article&ID=971589&hig.

JetBlue. "Alex Battaglia Named Vice President of JetBlue's JFK Operations." Press Release, March 20, 2007. http://investor.jetblue.com/phoenix.zhtml?c=131045&p= irol-newsArticle&ID=975729&highlight=.

JetBlue. "JetBlue Airways Names Dave Barger President and Chief Executive Officer. Founder David Neeleman Will Continue to Serve as Chairman of the Board." Press Release, May 10, 2007. http://investor.jetblue.com/phoenix.zhtml?c=131045& p=irol-newsArticle&ID=998672&highlight=.

"JetBlue Apologizes After Passengers Stranded." MSNBC.com, February 16, 2007. www.msnbc.msn.co/id/17166299/print/1/displaymode/1098/.

Johnson-Laird, Phil, and Ruth Byrne. "The Mental Model Theory of Thinking and Reasoning." Mental Models, May 2000. www.tcd.ie/psychology/other/ruth_byrne/mental_models/theory.html.

Joyce, William, and Nitin Nohria. *What Really Works: The 4+2 Formula for Sustained Business Success.* New York: HarperCollins, 2003.

Kahneman, Daniel. "Maps of Bounded Rationality: Psychology for Behavioral Economics." *American Economic Review* 93, 5 (2003): 1449–1475.

Kahneman, Daniel, and Alan B. Krueger. "Developments in the Measurement of Subjective Well-Being." *Journal of Economic Perspectives* 20, 1 (2006): 3–24.

Kaplan, Steven N., and Bernadette A. Minton. "How Has CEO Turnover Changed? Increasingly Performance Sensitive Boards and Increasingly Uneasy CEOs." NBER Working Paper Series 12465, 2006, 1–32.

Karkach, Arseniy S. "Trajectories and Models of Individual Growth." *Demographic Research* 15, 12 (2006): 347–400.

Kauffman, Stuart A. "Technology and Evolution: Escaping the Red Queen Effect." *McKinsey Quarterly* 1 (1995): 118–129.

Kauffman, Stuart A. "The Evolution of Future Wealth." *Scientific American* 295, 5 (2006): 44.

Kauffman, Stuart, José Lobo, and William G. Macready. "Optimal Search on a Technology Landscape." *Journal of Economic Behavior & Organization* 43, 2 (2000): 141–166.

Kazanjian, Robert K., and Robert Drazin. "An Empirical Test of a Stage of Growth Progression Model." *Management Science* 35, 12 (1989): 1489–1503.

Kelleher, James B. "Analysis—Harley Hits a Rough Patch as Key Execs Jump Off." Reuters, January 13, 2009. www.reuters.com/article/reutersEdge/idUSTRE50 C6G20090113.

Kim, E. Han, Adair Morse, and Luigi Zingales. "What Has Mattered to Economics Since 1970." *Journal of Economic Perspectives* 20, 4 (2006): 189–202.

Krehmeyer, Dean, Matthew Orsagh, CFA, and Kurt N. Schacht, CFA. "Breaking the Short-Term Cycle: Discussion and Recommendations on How Corporate Leaders, Asset Managers, Investors, and Analysts Can Refocus on Long-Term Value." CFA Centre for Financial Market Integrity, Business Roundtable Institute for Corporate Ethics, July 2006.

Kroc, Ray. *Grinding It Out: The Making of McDonald's.* New York: St. Martin's Press, 1987.

Krull, Steven. "Corporate Guidance and Earnings Announcements: Are Companies Gaming the System to Beat the Analyst Mean When Announcing Earnings?" Hofstra University. www.hofstra.edu/pdf/biz_mlc_krull3.pdf.

Kutschera, Ulrich, and Karl J. Niklas. "The Modern Theory of Biological Evolution: An Expanded Synthesis." *Naturwissenschaften* 91 (2004): 255–276.

Kwee, Zenlin, Frans A. J. Van Den Bosch, and H. W. Volberda. "Coevolutionary Competence in the Realm of Corporate Longevity: How Long-Lived Firms Strategically Renew Themselves." ERIM Report Series, ERS-2007-076-STR. http://papers.ssrn.com/sol3/papers.cfm?abstract_id=1069322.

Lamm, Greg. "2008 Executive of the Year." *Puget Sound Business Journal,* March 19, 2008. www.enterpriseseattle.org/index.php?option=com_content&task=view&id=210&itemid=104.

Land, George. *Grow or Die: The Unifying Principle of Business Transformation.* New York: Random House, 1973.

Laverty, Kevin J. "Economic 'Short-Termism': The Debate, the Unresolved Issues, and the Implications for Management Practice and Research." *Academy of Management Review* 21, 3 (1996): 825–860.

Leung, Shirley. "McDonald's Posts 11% Drop in Net; Fewer Restaurants to Be Opened." *Wall Street Journal,* October 23, 2002, B3.

Levitt, Arthur. "The Numbers Game." Speech delivered at NYU Center for Law and Business, New York, September 28, 1998. www.sec.gov/news/speech/speecharchive/1998/spch220.txt.

Levitt, Arthur, with Paula Dwyer. *Take On the Street: What Wall Street and Corporate America Don't Want You to Know.* New York: Pantheon Books, 2002.

Levy, David L. "Applications and Limitations of Complexity Theory in Organization Theory and Strategy." In *The Handbook of Strategic Management.* New York: M. Dekker, 2000.

Lewin, Arie Y., and Henk W. Volberda. "Prolegomena on Coevolution: A Framework for Research on Strategy and New Organizational Forms." *Organization Science* 10, 5 (1999): 519–534.

Lewin, Roger. *Complexity: Life at the Edge of Chaos.* Chicago: University of Chicago Press, 1999.

"LEX Column—Procter & Gamble." *Financial Times,* June 10, 1999, 22.

Liedtka, Jeanne M., and Edward D. Hess. 2008. "Designing Learning Launches." Technical Note, University of Virginia, Darden Business Publishing UVA-BP-0529.

Liedtka, Jeanne M., Robert Rosen, and Robert Wiltbank. *The Catalyst: How You Can Become an Extraordinary Growth Leader.* New York: Crown Business, 2009.

Lipton, Mark. *Guiding Growth: How Vision Keeps Companies on Course.* Boston: Harvard Business School Press, 2003.

Lubin, Joann S. "A Few Share the Wealth." *Wall Street Journal,* December 12, 2005, 31.

Machan, Dyan. "CEO Interview: Costco's James Sinegal." *SmartMoney*, March 27, 2008. www.smartmoney.com/investing/stocks/ceo-interview-costcos-james-sinegal-22782/.

MacIntosh, Julie, and Jonathan Birchall. "P&G Looks to Pull Out of Pharmaceuticals." *Financial Times*, February 5, 2009. www.ft.com/cms/s/0/e8b5692c-f31c-11dd-abe6-0000779fd2ac.html.

Marcus, Bernie, and Arthur Blank, with Bob Andelman. *Built from Scratch: How a Couple of Regular Guys Grew the Home Depot from Nothing to $30 Billion*. New York: Times Books, 1999.

"A Marriage Made in Heaven—and in the Bathroom." *Economist*, January 28, 2005. www.economist.com/agenda/displaystory.cfm?story_id=3619402.

Mauboussin, Michael J. *More Than You Know: Finding Financial Wisdom in Unconventional Places*. New York: Columbia University Press, 2006.

McCraw, Thomas K. *Prophet of Innovation: Joseph Schumpeter and Creative Destruction*. Cambridge, MA: Harvard University Press, 2007.

McDonald's Corporation. *McDonald's Corporation's Current Report*. November 3, 2003. U.S. Securities and Exchange Commission's EDGAR database. www .sec.gov/Archives/edgar/data/63908/000104746903035700/a2121466z8-k.htm (accessed August 30, 2009).

McDonald's Corporation. "Report on the Corporate Responsibility Committee of the Board of Directors of McDonald's Corporation: Regarding the Adequacy and Effectiveness of McDonald's Policies, Plans and Strategies to Support Balanced Lifestyles." www.aboutmcdonalds.com/mcd/investors/corporate_gover nance/board_report_on_strategies_to_support_balanced_active_lifestyles. html?DCSext.destination=http://www.aboutmcdonalds.com/mcd/investors/ corporate_governance/board_report_on_strategies_to_support_balanced_ active_lifestyles.html (accessed August 30, 2009).

McGregor, Jena. "Room & Board Plays Impossible to Get." *BusinessWeek*, October 1, 2007.

Meek, Gary K., Ramesh P. Rao, and Christopher J. Skousen. "Evidence on Factors Affecting the Relationship Between CEO Stock Option Compensation and Earnings Management." *Review of Accounting and Finance* 6, 3 (2007): 304–323.

Miller, Claire Cain. "Starbucks to Close 300 Stores and Open Fewer New Ones." *New York Times*, January 29, 2009.

Miller, Danny. *The Icarus Paradox: How Exceptional Companies Bring About Their Own Downfall*. New York: Harper Business, 1990.

Miller, Danny, and Peter H. Friesen. "Archetypes of Organizational Transition." *Administrative Science Quarterly* 25 (1980): 268–279.

Miller, Danny, and Peter H. Friesen. "Momentum and Revolution in Organizational Adaptation." *The Academy of Management Journal* 23, 4 (1980): 591–614.

Miller, Danny, and Peter H. Friesen. "A Longitudinal Study of the Corporate Life Cycle." *Management Science* 30, 10 (1984): 1161–1183.

Miller, Jeffrey S. "Effects of Preannouncements on Analyst and Stock Price Reactions to Earnings News." *Review of Quantitative Finance and Accounting* 24, 3 (2005): 251–275.

Mintzberg, Henry, Bruce Ahlstrand, and Joseph Lampel. *Strategy Safari: A Guided Tour Through the Wilds of Strategic Management.* New York: Free Press, 1998.

Mitleton-Kelly, Eve. "Ten Principles of Complexity & Enabling Infrastructures." In *Complex Systems and Evolutionary Perspectives of Organisations: The Application of Complexity Theory to Organisations.* ed. Eve Mitleton-Kelly. New York: Elsevier Science, 2003.

Morgenson, Gretchen. "Was There a Loan It Didn't Like?" *New York Times,* November 2, 2008.

Morris, Betsy. "Coke: The Real Story How Did Coca-Cola's Management Go from First-Rate to Farcical in Six Short Years? Tommy the Barber Knows." *Fortune,* May 31, 2004, 84–92.

Munch, Stephan B., and David O. Conover. "Nonlinear Growth Cost in *Menidia Menidia*: Theory and Empirical Evidence." *Evolution* 58, 3 (2004): 661–664.

Myers, James N., Linda A. Myers, and Douglas J. Skinner. "Earnings Momentum and Earnings Managment." *Journal of Accounting, Auditing & Finance* 22, 2 (2007): 249–284. http://ssrn.com/abstract=968453.

Nardelli, Bob, Patricia Sellers, and Julie Schlosser. "It's His Home Depot Now After Nearly Four Years at the Helm, Ex-GE Guy Bob Nardelli Tells Us How He's Finally Getting Results." *Fortune,* September 20, 2004.

Neeleman, David. "An Apology from David Neeleman." Letter to Customers. JetBlue. www.jetblue.com/about/ourcompany/apology/index.html.

Nelson, Emily. "Rallying the Troops at P&G—New CEO Lafley Aims to End Upheaval by Revamping Program of Globalization." *Wall Street Journal,* August 31, 2000, B1.

Nelson, Richard. "How New Is New Growth Theory?" *Challenge* 40, 5 (1997): 29–58.

Newbert, Scott L. "Value, Rareness, Competitive Advantage, and Performance: A Conceptual-Level Empirical Investigation of the Resource-Based View of the Firm." *Strategic Management Journal* 29, 7 (2008): 745–768.

Nocera, Joe. "Curing What Ails Starbucks." *New York Times,* January 12, 2008.

Olson, Matthew S., and Derek van Bever. *Stall Points: Most Companies Stop Growing—Yours Doesn't Have To.* New Haven, CT: Yale University Press, 2008.

O'Neil, Valerie. "Starbucks Announces Strategic Initiatives to Increase Shareholder Value; Chairman Howard Schultz Returns as CEO." Press Release, January 7, 2008. www.starbucks.com/aboutus/pressdesc.asp?=816.

O'Reilly III, Charles A., and Jeffrey Pfeffer. *Hidden Value: How Great Companies Achieve Extraordinary Results with Ordinary People.* Boston: Harvard Business School Press, 2000.

O'Toole, James O. *Leading Change: The Argument for Values-Based Leadership.* New York: Ballentine Books, 1996.

Overby, Stephanie. "What JetBlue's CIO Learned About Customer Satisfaction." *CIO*, April 5, 2007. www.cio.com/article/102500/What_JetBlue_s_CIO_Learned_About_Customer_Satisfaction.

Paley, Amit R., "Credit-Rating Firms Grilled Over Conflicts." *Washington Post*, October 23, 2008, A1.

Pearlstein, Steven. "Leap of Illogic on Wall Street Leaves GE Flat-Footed." *Washington Post*, May 21, 2008. http://washingtonpost.com/wp-dyn/content/article/2008/05/20/AR2008052001806_pf.html.

Pearson, Andrall E. "Tough-Minded Ways to Get Innovative." *Innovative Enterprise*, August 2002.

Penrose, Edith. "The Theory of the Growth of the Firm." In *The International Encyclopedia of Business and Management*, ed. Malcolm Warner. Oxford: Oxford University Press, 1996, 2440–2448.

Pfeffer, Jeffrey, and Robert I. Sutton. *Hard Facts, Dangerous Half-Truths, and Total Nonsense: Profiting from Evidence-Based Management*. Boston: Harvard Business School Press, 2006.

Porter, Michael E. *Competitive Strategy: Techniques for Analyzing Industries and Competitors*. New York: Free Press, 1980.

Porter, Michael E. *Competitive Advantage: Creating and Sustaining Superior Performance*. New York: Free Press, 1985.

"P&G Prepares for Thorough Shake-Up." *Financial Times,* June 7, 1999, 30.

"P&G to Get Ahead by Marketing." *Financial Times,* June 5, 1997, 29.

Procter & Gamble Company. Annual Report 2000–2008. www.pg.com/investor/annualreports.shtml.

Procter & Gamble Company. 2008 Annual Report. The Procter & Gamble Company—Financial and Strategic Analysis Review. Reference Code: GMDCPG32329GSA.

"Procter & Gamble—Jager's Gamble." *Economist,* October 30, 1999. www.economist.com/business/displaystory.cfm?story_id=E1_PNGTNV.

"Procter & Gamble Succumbs to Wall Street Blues." *Financial Times,* September 10, 1998, 40.

"Procter & Gamble: Will She, Won't She?" *Economist,* August 9, 2007. www.economist.com/business/displaystory.cfm?story_id=9619074.

"Procter and Gamble—After Artzt." *Financial Times,* March 21, 1995, 21.

"Procter's Gamble." *Economist,* June 10, 1999. www.economist.com/business/displaystory.cfm?story_id=E1_PNNVDJ.

Quinn, Robert E., and Kim Cameron. "Organizational Life Cycles and Shifting Criteria of Effectiveness: Some Preliminary Evidence." *Management Science* 29, 1 (1983): 33–51.

Rappaport, Alfred. "The Economics of Short-Term Performance Obsession." *Financial Analysts Journal* 61, 3 (2005): 65–79.

Rees, William E. "Globalization, Trade and Migration; Undermining Sustainability." *Ecological Economics* 59, 2 (2006): 220–225.

Regine, Birute, and Roger Lewin. "Management Practice Based on Complexity Science." Harvest Associates. www.harvest-associates.com/pubs/manage.html.

Reynolds, Paul D., Nancy M. Carter, William B. Gartner, and Patricia G. Greene. "The Prevalence of Nascent Entrepreneurs in the United States: Evidence from the Panel Study of Entrepreneurial Dynamics." *Small Business Economics* 23, 4 (2004): 263–284.

"The Rise of the Superbrands—Consumer Goods." *Economist*, February 3, 2005. www.economist.com/displaystory.cfm?story_id=3623265.

Ritter, Jay R., and Ivo Welch. "A Review of IPO Activity, Pricing, and Allocations." *The Journal of Finance* 75, 4 (2002): 1795–1828.

Romer, Paul M. "Increasing Returns and Long-Run Growth." *Journal of Political Economy* 94, 51 (1986): 1002–1037.

Romer, Paul M. "The Origins of Endogenous Growth." *Journal of Economic Perspectives* 8, 1 (1994): 3–22.

Romer, Paul M. "Why, Indeed, in America? Theory, History, and the Origins of Modern Economic Growth." *American Economic Review* 86, 2 (1996): 202–206.

Romer, Paul M. "Growth Policy." Policy Brief, Stanford Institute for Economic Policy Research, October 2001.

Roychowdhury, Sugata. "Earnings Management Through Real Activities Manipulation." *Journal of Accounting and Economics* 42, 3 (2006): 335–370.

Rugman, Alan M., and Alain Verbeke. "Edith Penrose's Contribution to the Resource-Based View of Strategic Management." *Strategic Management Journal* 23, 8 (2002): 769–780.

Sammut-Bonnici, Tanya, and Robin Wensley. "Darwinism, Probability and Complexity: Market-Based Organizational Transformation and Change Explained Through the Theories of Evolution." *International Journal of Management Reviews* 4, 3 (2002): 291–315.

Samuelson, Judith. "The Aspen Principles: A Better Way Forward." *Directors & Boards*, Summer 2008.

Saporito, Bill, and Ani Hadjian. "Behind the Tumult at P&G." *Fortune*, March 7, 1994. http://money.cnn.com/magazines/fortune/fortune_archive/1994/03/07/79047/index.htm.

Schilit, Howard. *Financial Shenanigans: How to Detect Accounting Gimmicks and Fraud in Financial Reports*. 2nd ed. New York: McGraw-Hill, 2002.

Schiller, Zachary. "Marketing the Marketing Revolution at Procter & Gamble—Its 50-Year-Old Way of Selling Competing Products Gives Way to a New Concept: The Category." *BusinessWeek*, July 25, 1988, 72.

Schiller, Zachary. "Top of the News P&G's Worldly New Boss Wants a More Worldly Company—Edwin Artzt's Procter Will Be Savvier, Pushier, and a Lot More Global." *BusinessWeek*, October 30, 1989, 40.

Schiller, Zachary. "The Corporation—No More Mr. Nice Guy at P&G—Not by a Long Shot." *BusinessWeek*, February 3, 1992, 54.

Schiller, Zachary. "Procter & Gamble Heads for the Medicine Cabinet." *Business-Week,* August 7, 1995, 28.

Schroeder, Alice. *The Snowball: Warren Buffett and the Business of Life.* New York: Bantam Dell, 2008.

Schultz, Howard. "The Commoditization of the Starbucks Experience: Howard Schultz's Starbucks Memo." *Financial Times,* February 23, 2007. http://us.ft.com/ ftgateway/superpage.ft?news_id=ft0022320071839455856&page=2.

Schultz, Howard. "Howard Schultz Transformation Agenda Communication #1." Press Release, January 7, 2008. Starbucks Press Room. www.starbucks.com/ aboutus/pressdesc.asp?id=814.

Schultz, Howard. "Howard Schultz Transformation Agenda Communication #3." Press Release, January 30, 2008. Starbucks Press Room. www.starbucks.com/ aboutus/pressdesc.asp?id=822.

Schultz, Howard. "Howard Schultz Transformation Agenda Communication #6." Press Release, February 11, 2008. Starbucks Press Room. www.starbucks.com/ aboutus/pressdesc.asp?id=830.

Schultz, Howard. "A Message from Howard—Building a Stronger Company for the Future." Press Release, July 29, 2008. Starbucks Press Room. www.starbucks .com/aboutus/pressdesc.asp?id=884.

Schultz, Howard. "A Message from Howard—Fiscal Year 2009—A New Beginning." Press Release, September 26, 2008. Starbucks Press Room. www.starbucks .com/aboutus/presc.asp?id=900.

Schultz, Howard. "A Message from Howard—Difficult Decisions in a Time of Uncertainty." Press Release, January 28, 2009. Starbucks Press Room. www .starbucks.com/aboutus/pressdesc.asp?id=982.

Schultz, Howard, and Dori Jones Yang. *Pour Your Heart into It: How Starbucks Built a Company One Cup at a Time.* New York: Hyperion, 1997.

Schumpeter, Joseph A. *Capitalism, Socialism and Democracy.* New York: Harper-Collins, 2008.

Sellers, Patricia. "McDonald's Starts Over." *Fortune,* June 22, 1998.

Sellers, Patricia, "Coke's CEO Doug Daft Has to Clean Up the Big Spill." *Fortune,* March 6, 2000, 58–59.

Sellers, Patricia. "Exit the Builder, Enter the Repairman: Home Depot's Arthur Blank Is Out. New CEO Bob Nardelli Is In." *Fortune,* March 19, 2001.

Senge, Peter. *The Fifth Discipline.* New York: Doubleday, 1990.

Shane, Scott A. *The Illusions of Entrepreneurship.* New Haven, CT: Yale University Press, 2008.

Sherman, Andrew J., and Milledge A. Hart. *Mergers and Acquisitions from A to Z.* New York: AMACOM, 2006.

Sibly, R., P. Calow, and N. Nichols. "Are Patterns of Growth Adaptive?" *Journal of Theoretical Biology* 112, 3 (1985): 553–574.

Skarzynski, Peter, and Rowan Gibson. *Innovation to the Core: A Blueprint for Transforming the Way Your Company Innovates.* Boston: Harvard Business Press, 2008.

Slywotzky, Adrian J., and Richard Wise. "The Growth Crisis and How to Escape It." *Harvard Business Review* 80, 7 (2002): 72–83.

Slywotzky, Adrian, and Richard Wise with Karl Weber. *How to Grow When Markets Don't.* New York: Warner Books, 2003.

Smit, Sven, Caroline M. Thompson, and S. Patrick Viguerie. "The Do-or-Die Struggle for Growth." *McKinsey Quarterly* 3 (2005): 35–45.

Smith, Robert. "JetBlue Offers Passengers Rights, Compensation." NPR, February 20, 2007. www.npr.org/templates/story/story.php?storyId=7501286.

Solomon, Jolie B., and John Bussey. "Cultural Change: Pressed by Its Rivals, Procter & Gamble Co. Is Altering Its Ways—Firm Trims Its Work Force, Sets Up Project Teams; Some in Union Are Irked—One-Page Memo Loses Clout." *Wall Street Journal,* May 20, 1985, J.

Solow, Robert M. "A Contribution to the Theory of Economic Growth." *Quarterly Journal of Economics* 70, 1 (1956): 65–94.

Solow, Robert M. "Growth Theory and After." *American Economic Review* 78, 3 (1988): 307–317.

Solow, Robert M. "Perspectives on Growth Theory." *Journal of Economic Perspectives* 8, 1 (1994): 45–54.

Solow, Robert M. "The Neoclassical Theory of Growth and Distribution." *BNL Quarterly Review* 215 (2000): 349–381.

Solow, Robert M. "The Last 50 Years in Growth Theory and the Next 10." *Oxford Review of Economic Policy* 23, 1 (2007): 3–14.

Souder, David. "Which Firms Invest for the Long Term? Longitudinal Evidence from Cable TV Operators." Academy of Management Proceedings, 2008.

Starbucks. Annual Report 2000–2008. www.investor.starbucks.com.

Starbucks. "Starbucks Poises Organization for Continued Global Growth." Press Release, July 17, 2007. Starbucks Press Room. www.starbucks.com/aboutus/pressdesc.asp?id=782.

Starbucks. "Starbucks Continues to Align Organization for Sustained Global Growth." Press Release, February 25, 2008. Starbucks Press Room. www.starbucks.com/aboutus/pressdesc.asp?id=834.

Starbucks. "Starbucks Unveils New Strategic Initiatives to Transform and Innovate the Customer Experience." Press Release, March 19, 2008. Starbucks Press Room. www.starbucks.com/aboutus/pressdesc.asp?id=850.

Starbucks. "Starbucks Increases Number of U.S. Company-Operated Store Closures as Part of Transformation Strategy." Press Release, July 1, 2008. Starbucks Press Room. www.starbucks.com/aboutus/pressdesc.asp?id=877.

"Starbucks: Grounds Zero." *Economist,* July 3, 2008. www.economist.com/business/displaystory.cfm?story_id=11670630.

"Starbucks Runs into Trouble." *Economist,* January 8, 2008. www.economist.com/business/displaystory.cfm?story_id=10490218.

"Starbucks v. McDonald's." *Economist,* January 10, 2008. www.economist.com/business/displaystory.cfm?story_id=10498747.

"Staying Pure." *Economist,* February 23, 2006. www.economist.com/business/displaystory.cfm?story_id=E1_VVQVVJD.

Stewart, Thomas A. "Growth as a Process." *Harvard Business Review* 84, 6 (2006): 60.

Stone, Brad. "The Empire of Excess: Lax Real Estate Decisions Hurt Starbucks." *New York Times,* July 4, 2008. www.nytimes.com/2008/07/04/business/04starbucks.html.

Surowiecki, James. "All Together Now?" *The New Yorker,* June 9, 2008. www.newyorker.com/talk/financial/2008/06/09/080609ta_talk_surowiecki?printable=true.

Swasy, Alecia. "Slow and Steady: In a Fast-Paced World, Procter & Gamble Sets Its Store in Old Values—Rules, Habit, Hierarchy Seem to Work for Soap Giant Despite Hot Competition—No More Monopolies, Though." *Wall Street Journal,* September 21, 1989, J.

"Taking It on the Chin." *Economist,* April 16, 1998. www.economist.com/business/displaystory.cfm?story_id=E1_TGDVNS.

"A Talent for Longevity: Corporate Durability: What Makes a Company Last?" *Economist,* April 14, 2001, 59–60.

Tan, Hwee-Cheng, and Karim Jamal. "Effect of Accounting Discretion on Ability of Managers to Smooth Earnings." *Journal of Accounting and Public Policy* 25, 5 (2006): 554–573.

Tomasko, Robert M. *Bigger Isn't Always Better.* New York: AMACOM, 2005.

Tomkins, Richard. "International Company News—P&G Chief Artzt to Step Down in July." *Financial Times,* March 15, 1995, 32.

Tomkins, Richard. "Heirs Apparently as Different as Chalk and Cheese." *Financial Times,* March 21, 1995, 21.

Tomkins, Richard. "Pepper Preparing to Step Down from Top Job at P&G." *Financial Times,* September 10, 1998, 31.

Tomkins, Richard. "P&G Clouds the US Corporate Mirror." *Financial Times,* June 10, 1999, 28.

Treacy, Michael, *Double-Digit Growth.* New York: Penguin, 2003

United States District Court, Eastern District of Wisconsin, Milwaukee Division. "In Re: Harley-Davidson, Inc. Securities Litigation." Civil Action No. 05-C-0579-CNC.

Useem, Jerry. "The Big . . . Get Bigger." *Fortune,* April 15, 2007. http://money.cnn.com/magazines/fortune/fortune_archive/2007/04/30/8405390/index.htm.

van Putten, Alexander B., and Ian C. MacMillan. *Unlocking Opportunities for Growth: How to Profit from Uncertainty While Limiting Your Risk.* Upper Saddle River, NJ: Wharton School Publishing, 2009.

Wagner, Jeffrey. "On the Economics of Sustainability." *Ecological Economics* 57, 4 (2006):   659–664.   www.sciencedirect.com/science?_ob=ArticleURL&_udi= B6VDY-4GSJR6Y-1&_user=709071&_rdoc=1&_fmt=&_orig=search&_sort=d& view=c&_acct=C000039638&_version=1&_urlVersion=0&_userid=709071& md5=d9d6a28e3e4014ba208ae5eaef7dd68a.

Weick, Karl E., and Kathleen M. Sutcliffe. *Managing the Unexpected: Assuring High Performance in an Age of Complexity.* San Francisco: Jossey-Bass, 2007.

Werhane, Patricia H. "Mental Models, Moral Imagination and System Thinking in the Age of Globalization." *Journal of Business Ethics* 78, 3 (2008): 463–474.

Wernerfelt, Birger. "A Resource-Based View of the Firm." *Strategic Management Journal* 5, 2 (1984): 171–180.

White, Michael C., Daniel B. Marin, Deborah V. Brazeal, and William H. Friedman. "The Evolution of Organizations: Suggestions from Complexity Theory About the Interplay Between Natural Selection and Adaptation." New York: Plenum Publishing Corporation, 1997.

Wiggins, Jenny. "The Trouble with Starbucks." *Financial Times*, December 12, 2008. www.ft.com/cms/s//aa9831ce-c266-11dd-a350-000077b07658.html.

Wiggins, Robert R., and Timothy W. Ruefli. "Sustained Competitive Advantage: Temporal Dynamics and the Incidence and Persistence of Superior Economic Performance." *Organization Science* 13, 1 (2002): 81–105.

Wiggins, Robert R., and Timothy W. Ruefli. "Schumpeter's Ghost: Is Hypercompetition Making the Best of Times Shorter?" *Strategic Management Journal* 26, 10 (2005): 887–911.

Williams, Winston. "Personality Change for P&G." *New York Times*, March 23, 1984, D.

Index

earnings: bubble of Earnings Game, 126, 182; production and public company, 14; transparency, 182. *See also* Authentic Earnings; quarterly earnings estimates

Earnings Game: Authentic Earnings *vs.*, 2–3, 124, 182; Coca-Cola Company and, 127–135; company problems, 124–125; criticism, 17–18, 182; descriptions, 14–15; disclosure, 124–125, 126, 127; dismantling, 182; earnings bubble, 126, 182; earnings management, 126, 127; example, 16–18; executive compensation and, 182; Growth Mental Model, 15, 18, 182; illusory stock values, 182; impact, 125–127; quarterly earnings estimates, 14, 18; SEC and, 182; short-term interests/ decisions, 125, 127, 137, 184; Smart Growth *vs.*, 3, 123, 183, 197; transparency, 124–125, 126; value illusion, 125; Wall Street Rules, 2–3, 14–18, 158

earnings management: Coca-Cola Company, 127; Earnings Game, 126, 127; issue, 126

ecological steady-state economics, 59

economics, biology growth theory, 97, 99, 100

economic growth theory, 6; behavioral economics, 59–60; complexity economics, 58–59; conclusion, 60–61; ecological steady-state economics, 59; Growth Mental Model and, 53–61; industrial economics, 54–56; neoclassical/new growth economics, 53–54; Penrose resource-based firm view, 56–57; Schumpeter creative destruction, 57

Eisenhardt, Kathleen, 101–102

employee: Costco Wholesale Corp., 185–186; culture of Home Depot, Inc., 153; high engagement/high performance company research, 183–184; Room & Board, 173–175

Enabling Internal Growth System, 80–81, 102, 183, 184, 197

executive compensation, 182

expansion: Coca-Cola Company, 129, 130, 132–133; Home Depot, Inc., *151, 152,* 154, *155*; Tiffany & Co. geographical, 22–23

Farrah, Pat, 150–151

Fuller, Joseph, 17

Gabbert, John, 170, 171, 173, 174, 176, 178

General Electric (GE), 126; Home Depot, Inc. and, 154, 155

Geroski, Paul, 54–55

Goizuetta, Robert, 127, 128, 129–131

Greenberg, Jack, 65–66

Greiner, Larry, 93

"grow or die": biology growth theory and "grow and die" *vs.*, 98, 100; business belief, 181, 182, 183; dangers of, 183; Growth Mental Model, 12–13; "improve to remain competitive" *vs.*, 183; Smart Growth *vs.*, 123, 137; as unscientific/unrealistic axiom, 183

growth, 8; bad, 4–5, 9, 19, 137; beliefs and economic system harm, 185; beliefs and Smart Growth, 185; challenges in Darden private growth company research, 163–164; as change, 124, 138, 140, 164, 166, 183; conditions of bad, 137; dependency on people, 183; good, 4, 9, 19, 137; questions, 5; reality/targets of Coca-Cola Company, 135; resiliency story of McDonald's, 61–70; Starbucks